KATHERINE SWYNFORD

The progenie page from Chaucer's works. *(Hulton Archive/Getty Images)*

KATHERINE SWYNFORD

The History of a Medieval Mistress

JEANNETTE LUCRAFT

SUTTON PUBLISHING

First published in the United Kingdom in 2006 by
Sutton Publishing Limited · Phoenix Mill
Thrupp · Stroud · Gloucestershire · GL5 2BU

British Library Cataloguing in Publication Data
A catalogue record for this book is available from the British
Library.

ISBN 0-7509-3261-9

Typeset in 11/14.5pt Sabon.
Typesetting and origination by
Sutton Publishing Limited.
Printed and bound in England by
J.H. Haynes & Co. Ltd, Sparkford.

To Daddy

Contents

List of Illustrations

Frontispiece: The progenie page from Chaucer's works

Between pages 102 and 103

Acknowledgements

I am grateful to the staff of the History Department at Huddersfield University, particularly Dr Tim Thornton, Dr Katherine Lewis and Dr Pat Cullum. I would also like to thank Dr Nicholas Bennett of Lincoln Cathedral for answering my queries on Katherine's tomb.

Thanks and love must also go to my parents for all their support and encouragement, and to my wonderful husband, Mike, for his endless patience and unshakeable belief in me.

Abbreviations

CCR	*Calendar of Close Rolls*
CFR	*Calendar of Fine Rolls*
CPR	*Calendar of Patent Rolls*
DNB	*Dictionary of National Biography*, ed. Sidney Lee (London: Smith, Elder and Co., 1885–98)
JGR 1372–6	*John of Gaunt's Register 1372–1376*, ed. Sydney Armitage-Smith (London, 1911)
JGR 1379–83	*John of Gaunt's Register 1379–1383*, ed. Sydney Armitage-Smith (London, 1937)

Introduction

The prioress twisted around to look at her charge, and thought that Katherine would do Sheppey credit. The girl had grown beautiful. That fact the convent perhaps could not lay claim to, except that they had obviously fed her well; but her gentle manners, her daintiness in eating – these would please the Queen as much as Katherine's education might startle her. Katherine could spin, embroider and brew simples, of course; she could sing plain chant with the nuns, and indeed had a pure golden voice so natural and rich that the novice-mistress frequently had to remind her to intone low through her nose, as was seemly. But more than that, Katherine could read both French and English because 'Sir' Osbert, the nuns' priest, had taken the pains to teach her, averring that she was twice as quick to learn as any of the novices. He had also taught her a little astrology and the use of the abacus . . .[1]

This is the Katherine Swynford known to millions through Anya Seton's novel, the medieval heroine waiting for her knight in shining armour, strengthened by some surprisingly modern female attributes of independence and self-reliance. But how close is the novel's depiction to the real Katherine Swynford? Was she this heroine, skilful and intelligent, yet remaining very much the medieval feminine ideal, gentle, courteous and beautiful?

Goodman claims that 'Katherine Swynford is one of the most famous, enigmatic and controversial of medieval women'.[2] Enigmatic she certainly is. Goodman's is the only work of any length that seeks to uncover the real Katherine, and then his work is limited to a pamphlet of about 6,000 words. Any other work on her is brief to say the least. Famous – yes, almost entirely because of Seton's novel. First published in the 1950s, it still remains amazingly popular, still in print and appearing a respectable ninety-fifth in the BBC's 'Big Read' initiative. Controversial – well, she was fodder for the medieval equivalent of the tabloid press, and the position of royal mistress is still one that courts controversy. Television channels, newspapers and Internet sites the world over discussed the recent marriage of Prince Charles and his long-term mistress Camilla Parker-Bowles, conducting opinion polls on the public perception of this 'scarlet' woman who so blatantly continued her relationship with the man she clearly loves in complete disregard for the fact that the public preferred his wife.

Indeed, there are remarkable parallels to be drawn between Katherine's relationship with John of Gaunt and that of Charles and Camilla. Both are enduring relationships that, while not exactly conducted in secret, were not publicly recognised as 'official'. Both couples were seen by some as flaunting their affairs in an undignified manner. The popularity of John, Duke of Lancaster, and Charles, Prince of Wales, has waxed and waned repeatedly, and the presence of Katherine and Camilla has affected the public perception of the two men. Charles's first wife, Diana, was the archetypal blue-eyed blonde beauty much loved by the British public; so too was Gaunt's first wife, Blanche. Both Charles and Diana, and John and Blanche, were viewed as golden couples; the popularity of both men was possibly at the highest during these marriages.

But, as much as the public wanted these relationships to be love matches, it is clear that in both cases the love match was with the mistress. Diana was eminently suitable to be a future queen, young, virginal, beautiful, from the right background – and it is perhaps not too cold-hearted to say that it was this suitability for position that was the leading attraction for Charles. Likewise with John and Blanche. Blanche too was young, undoubtedly a virgin, beautiful, from the right background, English in the extreme – and she just happened to bring a very attractive dowry in the form of the Lancastrian heritage. Whatever emotional feeling Gaunt had towards Blanche, the power that she brought him, a third son with little hope of securing power through the inheritance of the throne, was surely the leading attraction.

The parallel continues in the fact that both Diana and Blanche died tragically young. After the death of these women, the 'illicit' relationships became increasingly public, until both men felt able to marry their mistresses. Gaunt had reached the end of his political career, and therefore the scandal of the marriage could not harm him in any real sense. Charles, however, has his main career, that of king, still ahead of him. His decision to marry has more potential to harm than Gaunt's marriage. Perhaps Gaunt showed more prudence in waiting, despite his obviously deep love for Katherine. And Katherine obviously understood that, for Gaunt, duty had to come first.

So Goodman's claim is correct: Katherine is enigmatic, famous and controversial. But what else can be said about her? The aim of this book is to reveal more of the real Katherine Swynford. There are obstacles in the way, notably a lack of evidence for her life. Her will is frustratingly, and curiously, unavailable. The bequests made by Katherine's contemporaries and peers fill the usual sources for medieval wills. A process of probate was undertaken, yet, mysteriously, Katherine's will was never recorded. No personal letters or diaries remain for us to use to establish her personality. Her thoughts and feelings are not available. Her record as documented in the past is connected to her famous and powerful lover. In the vast documentary collection of the Lancastrian empire under John of Gaunt, glimpses of Katherine can be seen, as they can in the records of her Beaufort children with Gaunt, and the records of Gaunt's son Henry IV. It is in this sense that any trace of Katherine is found in academic, historical publications. She is the appendage of other notables. Little credit is given to the idea that she was a real individual with her own life, and with the ability to control that life. In this book my hope is that the reader will indeed see Katherine as an individual, maybe one that is not too far removed from the romantic figure of Seton's novel. Seton portrays Katherine as a strong character who desires to control her own destiny. I disagree with what that desired destiny was, but believe that this strong character with control of her life is more than just a fictional characterisation – that it is one that has actual factual root.

Of course, like so many others, my introduction to Katherine was through Seton. As a teenager I read the novel many times, dreaming of this medieval world of knights and their ladies, much as the youthful Katherine is also found dreaming.

> Her eyes flew back to the royal table. Philippa, used to this sight, did not understand how like a summer dream it was, how impossible to believe that one was actually beholding them in their golds and scarlets, their ermines and coronets, their gauzy veils and jewels; the Plantagenets, a dozen or more of them, laughing, talking, eating, just like all the lesser folk along the side of the Hall.[3]

And as a teenager I fell in love with the story of Katherine and Gaunt. So is it therefore inevitable that I will find the real Katherine to be a positive, strong character? This is the danger of historical biography. Inevitably, one chooses a subject because of personal interest and motivations. Could then this personal interest, and subsequent desire to find that a person had particular qualities, lead to a distortion of the evidence to uphold a theory that really has no ground in fact?

> In studying the lives of other people it is impossible to think of them objectively, as objects, or to pretend that they can be understood without imagination, participation, moral concern and therefore bias.[4]

> In far too many ways the women whom medieval historians have to study are the imaginative constructions of men: the theoretical women of medical, philosophic, legal, and religious literature; the women seen as the property of masters, fathers, husbands; the women fantasised by poets, romances, preachers, hagiographers. And yet, historians, men and women alike, have no choice but to do that same sort of work: imagine the women of the past.[5]

But my process of imagining Katherine Swynford does not just cover the romantic issues of her relationship with Gaunt, or her character in the role of lover or mother. I am interested in her as a medieval woman and with what she can tell us about medieval society. Investigating Katherine leads to a multitude of questions. For instance, were mistresses an accepted part of royal or noble life? Did affairs such as Katherine and Gaunt's offend the moral status quo at court or in the wider country? Was Katherine unique in her role? How do descriptions of her compare to those of other women in the royal household who occupied similar positions and had similar, perhaps dubious, reputations? How were her bastard children treated? What status and education did Katherine have to be accepted within the royal court prior to her involvement with Gaunt? What level of education could she have achieved? Perhaps the most interesting question is this: to what extent could a medieval woman control the way she was presented to, and perceived by, the wider world? In the twenty-first century we have such a strong sense of individualism, of personal identity, and of how this can be manipulated and spun to our own ends. Is this purely a modern phenomenon? Is it anachronistic to suggest that it was a phenomenon available to women in fourteenth-century English noble society? Could Katherine have controlled her identity, manipulated her public appearance to counter the controversy of her relationship? I believe she could. My imagining of Katherine goes far beyond the qualities that entranced Gaunt for a quarter of a century, beyond that of her as a mistress.

So this book goes beyond a biography of one individual to investigate what the life of that individual can reveal about a society. I believe that the reading of primary sources such as the chronicles of Thomas Walsingham or Henry Knighton tells us not just something of the individual that they write about but also something of the writers themselves and their audience. As a teacher I am always conscious of the fact that history is not the events or people of the past. History is what has been recorded about the past, both at the moment of happening and after the passing of time. Investigating why certain issues were recorded, and by whom, and when, is as interesting and as revealing as the issue itself. The process of the historical writer is to attempt to engage with the past and the people of the past so as to build a more complete picture. I believe this process is made easier, and more accurate, if the reasons why recordings were made are uncovered. It is very easy to read Walsingham's text on Katherine and state that that depiction must be what she was – and many have done so. But why did Walsingham state 'facts' that many others did not? What purpose did he have for writing what he did? Who were his audience and what would they have wished for and expected to read? Did he write about others in a similar way to Katherine? Who were these people? What was their link to Katherine? Walsingham and his peers were not writing personal letters or diaries. They wrote with the intention and knowledge that they were writing history. Their work needs to be approached with this in mind. To me, this is how history is done. History is not a modern phenomenon of writing about past facts to declare to others 'this is what happened'. It is a way of reading and interpreting what others have written to establish why they thought as they did, and what these thoughts tell us about the people and societies of that time. It is in this way that I have approached my 'biography' of Katherine Swynford.

I start my quest by outlining the details of Katherine's family and background as they are known, the biography of her as it emerges from the factual records of births, deaths, marriages, employment, land-owning and so on, to provide the narrative of Katherine's life. Then I investigate how Katherine has travelled through history to us today, how she has been viewed and written about in the intervening centuries.

These centuries of comment reflect what was written in her own time, the contemporary records of the chroniclers who recorded details of Katherine and other women in similar positions to her. There is much to explore in the terminology and form used by these medieval journalists in the descriptions of Katherine and her relationship with, and influence on, Gaunt.

This contemporary picture of her is then placed against the context of life in the medieval royal court. Much is known of the provision of education, the type of entertainment, the lifestyle of this arena, and within this knowledge can be found answers to some of the questions we have about Katherine's life. I finish with an attempt to see Katherine as she wished to be seen – a difficult task without her will or other personal papers but one enlightened by her coat of arms. Saintly manifestations in the form of emblems and badges were of great importance and significance to medieval people and carried many meanings beyond that of mere religious devotion. Through these means, through the passage of this book, I hope a clear view of Katherine Swynford will become apparent.

CHAPTER 1

Katherine's Life and Family

Katherine's father, Gilles or Paon Roet, native of Roeulx near Mons in Hainaut, travelled to England in the entourage of Philippa, member of the ruling family of Hainault and future bride of Edward III.[1] Paon was possibly the son of Jean de Ruet (d. 1305), who was in turn son of Huon de Ruet, giving Katherine a Hainauter, rather than English, heritage.[2] The year of Jean de Ruet's death necessitates a birth date for Paon of, at the latest, the early years of the fourteenth century, making Paon middle-aged when he became a father to Katherine.

It would appear that Paon was not yet a knight when he made his journey to England with the future English queen, but on his arrival he impressed Edward III sufficiently in the art of chivalrous warfare to be appointed King of Arms for Guienne, possibly gaining this rank as early as 1334.[3] Paon remained within the households of the King and Queen during his time in England, obviously a trusted member of their retinue, and is mentioned by Froissart in connection with Philippa's famous plea for the burgesses of Calais in 1347:

> Then she rose and had the six burgesses set on their feet and took away the ropes from their necks and led them with her to her hostel and had them clothed and set at dinner and made comfortable that day. And in the morning, she gave each six nobles and had them let out of the army by Monsieur Sanse d'Aubrecicourt and Monsieur Paon de Roet, as far as they could and until it seemed to the two knights that they would be out of danger; and at parting the knights commended them to God and returned to the army, and the burgesses went to St Omer.[4]

1

By 1350 Paon had left the services of the English court and returned to his native land of Hainaut. The reason for this is unknown. He appears in the *Cartulaire des Comtes de Haynault* several times between 1350 and 1352 as an official of Margaret, Empress of Bavaria, Countess of Hainaut and sister to Queen Philippa. The official scribes record his name as Gilles de Roet, Ruet or Rueth 'dit' Paon, Paonnet or Paunet. In 1351 he is designated as both 'maistre vallet del hotel medame' and 'maistre chevalier de no hostel'.[5]

It is possible that Paon had a familial connection to the rulers of Hainaut. The younger brother of the last lord of Roeulx, descended from the counts of Hainaut, was Fastré de Ruet. This gentleman accompanied Sir John Beaumont in 1326 to assist the English against the Scots. Both Fastré and his brother Eustace died in the 1330s. It has been speculated that Paon was of a collateral line of this family, but whether this is so, or Paon was merely named after the town of his birth, remains unknown.[6] It is nice though to believe that Katherine came from such a background, and the strong connection between the Roet family and the English throne does suggest that Katherine's forebears had some noble breeding. What is known is that Paon's last appearance in the records of Hainaut was in August 1352, and his death can be inferred to have followed soon after.[7] A description of his monument in the old St Paul's Cathedral can be found in Weaver's *Funeral Monuments*, but this tomb dated from a time much removed from his death, as the inscription read: 'Here lies Paganus Roet, Guyenne King of Arms, father of Catherine Duchess of Lancaster . . .'.[8]

Nothing is known of the woman or women whom Paon married, although it is possible to speculate that, given his time in the court of the English King and Queen, his wife or wives were of English origin. Nor is much known about his children. Evidence suggests that Paon had at least four children, all of whom had connections with either the English or the Hainaut court. Of these children it would appear that Elisabeth, or Isabelle as she also appears in the records, was Paon's first child. She entered the nunnery of Sainte Wandru at Mons in 1349, the prebend being vacant because of the death of Beatrix de

Wallaincourt. The record of this event in the *Cartulaire des Comtes de Haynault* recounts how Countess Margaret granted the prebend of the Chapter of Sainte Waudru to Elisabeth, daughter of Paon Roet.[9] Elisabeth's entrance into the monastic life in this year would suggest a birth date for her of *c.* 1335.[10] The records of the convent show that she was still in residence there in May 1367, but she died the following year. An entry in the convent charters for 13 July 1368 records 'letters for which Albert, duke of Bavaria accords Jeanne d'Ecaussines, daughter of Gilles, the prebend of the chapter of Sainte-Waudru, vacant on the death of Isabelle de Roet'.[11]

It is possible that Paon also had a son. The *Black Prince's Register* records the activities of a Walter Roet, yeoman of the Prince of Wales. The Prince paid this yeoman 40*s* on 10 May 1355. Further accounts for both 1354 and 1355 show that the Prince had ordered letters to be sent to Stephen Maulyns, the provost of the church of Mons, with regard to £40 owed to the prince under a bond. These letters requested that Maulyns pay the £40 in equal share to two of his retainers, Sir Eustace d'Aubrecicourt and a Walter de Roe or Rude.[12] Presumably this Walter was the same yeoman previously mentioned. It would also seem likely that Sir Eustace d'Aubrecicourt was the Monsieur Sanse d'Aubrecicourt who, along with Paon Roet, escorted the burgesses of Calais to safety. A speculative birth date for Walter would be the late 1330s.

Much more is known of Paon's other children, Philippa and Katherine. Evidence for Philippa's life has led historians to place her birth date as *c.* 1345–7. In 1357 'damoiselle' Philippa Pan was in the household of Countess Elizabeth of Ulster, wife of Edward III's third son, Lionel.[13] The meaning of the name 'Pan' and why Philippa was called this is unclear. There have been many interpretations of it and how it determines the identity and familial connections of this figure, even suggestions that this designation discounts Philippa from being Katherine's sister. 'Pan' was a shortened from of *panetaria* and could, therefore, signify that Philippa was mistress of the pantry. But this seems most unlikely bearing in mind the age that could be assumed of such an official and also because of the gifts made to Philippa Pan.[14] However, Paon de Roet's name was occasionally recorded in the form of Panneto and therefore Philippa Pan could be a shortening of 'Philippa, daughter of Panneto'.[15] This would seem a more likely scenario than that of a 10–12-year-old girl being mistress of the pantry. Furthermore, it is possible that Philippa's role in the household was that of rokestere to Philippa of Eltham, daughter of the Countess of Ulster and Prince Lionel. A rokestere was a member of the small retinue provided to royal children at birth, and the position was normally held by a young girl, whose main task was cradle rocking.[16]

At some stage Philippa transferred to the household of the English Queen, possibly on the death of Elizabeth of Ulster in 1362; a grant to her in 1366 describes her as 'domicelle' of the Chamber of the Queen. At a similar time Philippa married the English poet Geoffrey Chaucer, who had also been a member of Elizabeth of Ulster's household. On the marriage of John of Gaunt to Constance of Castile, Philippa entered the household of Constance, the new Duchess of Lancaster. In the late 1370s she was resident in Lincolnshire, probably at the home of her sister Katherine, collecting her annuities within this county. Philippa was admitted to the fraternity of Lincoln Cathedral in 1386 but died shortly after. On 18 June 1387 annuities were paid to both her and her husband, but by 7 November the same year Chaucer was collecting his alone.[17]

Katherine Swynford is the most famous of Paon's four children. The birth of Katherine is conventionally dated to *c.* 1350, making her the youngest known child of Paon. Her place of birth is unknown but was most likely somewhere in England, probably London, given the connections between her father and the royal court. There is a strong possibility, however, that Katherine was born earlier than 1348, making her the older sister to Philippa, and her birthplace was almost definitely England. In Thomas Speght's seventeenth-century work on Chaucer, Philippa is recorded as 'altera filiarum', which can be translated to mean either 'the other daughter' or 'the second of two daughters'.[18] I believe that from this and other evidence, most notably the date by which Katherine was married to her first husband and the age at which she had her youngest child, Katherine was probably older than Philippa, with a birth date of *c.* 1345, while Philippa was born *c.* 1347.

It is from the writings of Froissart that the details of Katherine's early life are known. The chronicler tells us that she grew up within the English court, joining the household of Blanche of Lancaster after the marriage of the wealthy heiress to John of Gaunt in 1359.[19] It is possible that Paon Roet, Katherine's father, on his departure from England early in the 1350s, entrusted the care of his daughters to Queen Philippa.[20] The English Queen was known for her willingness to care for the children of those in her service. Almost all the letters of Philippa that are extant were written on behalf of others.[21] If Paon was a favourite in the King's retinue, then it would seem highly likely that the Queen's good and kind nature would have led her to place his daughters in suitable positions. Within the royal court Katherine would have had a favoured upbringing, surrounded by the luxurious lifestyles of English noble society. While she may not have been privy to all these luxuries herself, this lifestyle would undoubtedly have had an influence on her. The Lancastrian household was especially known for sharing its privileges with those of lower ranks, particularly in the education of children. Katherine would have learnt to read, sew, play and appreciate music and dance, and undergone religious instruction alongside the children of lords and dukes. Desirable manners and social skills would also have been learnt alongside these children.

The earliest entry that confirms Katherine's activities is found in the public records for the year 1365. In this year she is mentioned in the records of Bishop Buckingham of Lincoln as Katherine Swynford, 'ancille', or servant, of the Duchess of Lancaster. This entry holds twofold interest. First, it provides early evidence of Katherine's piety. Her appearance in the records marks the granting of permission by Buckingham for Katherine to hear mass in a private ceremony.[22] It was more usual at this time for people to go to the local church to hear mass. This grant followed an increasing fashion among the gentry for mass to be celebrated privately within a household chapel. Secondly, the reference to her as Swynford indicates that at this time she was already married to Hugh Swynford, retainer of the Duke of Lancaster. This match was most likely made during the years 1363–5.

For Katherine to be married by 1365 strongly suggests that the conventional birth date for her of 1350 is too late. This date would have made her 15 at the oldest when she married. It is something of a misconception that medieval people married young. On the Continent, there are records of medieval couples who were married in their teens. This can be explained by their notion of the extended family. Recently married couples were expected to live with, and to be partly supported by, their parents. In England, however, couples were much more independent and set up home on their own. To do so they had to have financial means and so were generally in their early twenties before marrying. The only exceptions were those of the highest ranks who married for political motives and gains. Here there were marriages among younger people, but Katherine and her first husband do not fall into this social rank. Moreover, Katherine was governess of the Duke and Duchess of Lancaster's children by 1366–70. Surely a girl under 20 years of age would not have been given this responsible position? Furthermore, the youngest of Katherine's own children was born in 1379. Given Katherine's proven fecundity, it seems odd that she had no further children if she was only 29 in 1379. If she was 34, however, having no further children does not seem quite so unusual.

After her marriage to Hugh, Katherine will presumably have spent some time living at the manors of her husband in Lincolnshire. The descriptions of the Colby and Kettlethorpe manors in the *Calendar of Inquisitions Post Mortem* on Hugh's inheritance in 1362 suggest that the living here would have been noticeably plainer than Katherine had become accustomed to at court. Furthermore, from the same entry, these would appear to have been Hugh's only landholdings. The land at Colby is described as 'hard, stony and uncultivated because of its barrenness', and, of the manor itself, 'the dovecot and windmill are said to be in ruins'. Kettlethorpe fares little better, with the meadows described as being 'overflowed by the waters of the Trent in ordinary years'.[23] The high probability of flooding at Kettlethorpe during the second half of the fourteenth century was due to its location near the confluence of the Fossdyke and the River Trent. During the 1300s there were regular complaints about the silting-up of the Fossdyke, including one in 1365, in which year Katherine can be presumed to have been in residence at Kettlethorpe:

Commission to Philip de Lymburg, William de Skipwyth, Adam de Lymbergh, Illard de Usflet, Robert de Moston and Walter de Poynton, on complaint by the citizens of Lincoln for themselves and the merchants of York, Nottingham and Kyngeston upon Hull as well as for other merchants elsewhere, by petition in the next Parliament, that a dyke called 'Fosdyke' from the water of Trente to the city of Lincoln by which ships and boats with merchandise and victuals used to pass to and from Lincoln is so obstructed by some of those parts having lands, meadows and pastures on both sides of it who in summertime drive their cattle over it to their feedings, as well as by an usual growth of grass and the rising of the sand in it that there is now no passage by it, to survey the dyke, to find by inquisition in the county of Lincoln the names of those who are bound to cleane and repair the same, to compel these by amercements and other means to do this and to hear and determine the whole matter.[24]

Katherine's request to Bishop Buckingham for permission to have private mass could indeed have been linked to the isolation she experienced, cut off in this remote and flooded part of Lincolnshire. However, curiously, there is no evidence that Katherine attempted to clear the dyke to prevent further flooding. In 1375 she was one of the landowners named as responsible for maintaining the dyke by a commission reporting into the condition of the waterway, but there are no records to suggest that any action was taken in response to the commission's findings.[25] This is odd, given how badly her land, and therefore her income, were affected by this flooding.

Colby and Kettlethorpe were recent acquisitions of the Swynford family. Colby was in the hands of Katherine's father-in-law Thomas

Swynford only by 1345 and Kettlethorpe as late as 1356. In the early 1340s Thomas was a member of the commission of the peace for Bedfordshire, in 1345 he was sheriff of Buckingham and in 1345–7 was escheator for Bedfordshire and Buckinghamshire. After his acquisition of Kettlethorpe Thomas was a member of various commissions of the peace in Lincolnshire, implying that he made his new manor his home.[26]

Little is known of Katherine's marriage to Hugh Swynford. Whether the marriage was formed through mutual love and respect or whether it was simply deemed a suitable match for these two members of the household and retinue of the Duke and Duchess of Lancaster is unknown. Anya Seton in her novel depicts Katherine as marrying against her will, a simple girl fresh from a convent upbringing who dreams of marrying a handsome knight but instead is forced into marrying someone she loathes. Hugh is described as ugly and lacking in personality but with a vast love for Katherine. Katherine, seeing that her sister, the Duchess of Lancaster and the Queen all agree to the marriage, feels unable to say no. But would this have been the reality? It is easy to believe that the fictional Katherine, naive and anxious to please, could easily have had her hand forced. But the real Katherine, used to the ways of court, educated within noble society – surely this young woman would have had a choice over her marriage partner? She was retained to the Duke and Duchess of Lancaster and therefore subject to their wishes. If they had wanted her to marry Hugh, she might have felt obliged to agree, whatever her personal view on the matter. But the Lancasters were known for caring for their retinue, and Katherine was someone held in such regard that only a few years after her marriage she was made governess to the ducal children. It seems strange, therefore, that Katherine was forced into an unwanted marriage. Hugh Swynford also seems a strange choice for the Duke and Duchess to have picked as the husband of their future governess. The description of his land suggests that his income was dependent on his Lancastrian grants; the yield from his landholdings was surely slight. The fact that his father had recently acquired the lands also suggests that Hugh's family and background were not of high estate. The most likely scenario therefore seems to be that Katherine wished to marry Hugh. She may already have developed feelings for Gaunt, but no doubt she believed him beyond her reach. Hugh, on the other hand, was within reach, was a knight and a landholder, however meagre, and was presumably someone for whom she had feelings. Indeed, Hugh may have been someone with whom she had a pre-marriage dalliance, and it could have been the discovery that she was pregnant that made Katherine agree to marry him.

Hugh and Katherine had at least two children during their marriage. The date of their son, Thomas's, birth is stated as 21 September 1368 in his proof of age and in the inquisition after his father's death.[27] It is not clear from the available records whether his sister, Blanche, was older or younger than Thomas. Indeed, it is possible to argue in favour of both scenarios. Goodman believes that Blanche was older, born *c.* 1366 and named for the Duchess of Lancaster. It is known that Gaunt was godparent to Katherine's daughter, and it is therefore highly probable that, if this child was indeed born before the death of the Duchess, Gaunt's wife stood godmother to Blanche. However, Given-Wilson argues to the contrary and believes that Blanche was the younger of the two Swynford children, born *c.* 1370. If this was the case, then it would seem likely that the child was still named for the Duchess but this time in honour of her memory.[28]

There is no clear evidence as to which theory is correct, and they are both plausible arguments. For Gaunt to stand godfather to the child of one of his retainers was indeed an honour and would suggest that Katherine had already reached the high rank of governess to the Duke's daughters. Therefore, to argue that Thomas was the eldest would seem most circumspect. Yet it is possible that Blanche Swynford was part of the ducal household by 1369, in which case she would indisputably be older than Thomas.[29] Either way, for Katherine to be appointed to the position of governess was a high honour in itself. Whether Gaunt's role as godparent came before or after the granting of this position, it is obvious that either Hugh or Katherine had gained favour in the eyes of the Duke sometime during the 1360s for the couple to receive such high honours from Gaunt.

As with the date of the birth of her daughter, it is unclear precisely when Katherine became governess to Philippa and Elizabeth of Lancaster. It is most likely to have been in the period 1366–70. Marie Bruce has argued that the Duchess of Lancaster herself was responsible for the appointment of Katherine, but there is unfortunately no evidence from the Duchess's household to suggest this.[30] Both Lewis Radford and Keith Dockray state that, on the death of Blanche in 1368–9, Katherine took charge of the ducal household. This suggests that she was already governess by this time, but, again, this is no more than supposition.[31] As will be seen in a later chapter, Katherine did possess the necessary skills to run a noble household successfully, and excelled in the role of organiser. If Katherine did take on such a role after the death of Blanche, this surely would support the theory that it was Blanche herself who had been responsible for Katherine's rise in the Lancastrian household. For Katherine to be chosen as someone capable of running the household after Blanche's death, she must have had important responsibilities during Blanche's lifetime, indicating the high esteem with which Blanche viewed Katherine. But the documents available for this period do not provide any exact evidence surrounding Katherine's appointment and role in the ducal household, and the details seemed destined to remain a mystery.

Two years after the death of the Duchess Katherine was a widow. Hugh died on 13 November 1371 while fighting in Aquitaine under Gaunt's command, leaving Katherine with the estates that they had held in jointure during his life.[32] This provision of jointure for Katherine will have allowed her a deal of financial independence, although it is debatable how much financial security would have been afforded her from the manors of Colby and Kettlethorpe. However, along with the salary she will have received for her role as governess, it would seem likely that, financially at least, Katherine was reasonably secure.

Indeed, these finances were revised in Katherine's favour from the spring of 1372. At this time the regularity of her appearances in the records of John of Gaunt as receiver of grants and gifts increases. Historians have traditionally dated the commencement of the liaison between the Duke and Katherine to this time because of the nature of these grants and gifts. Sydney Armitage-Smith comments that before 1372 'the Duke's gifts and grants to Katherine are no greater than might have been made to any other member of his household; immediately after they begin to become significant'.[33]

Evidence from other sources confirms this date of spring 1372 as the start of the couple's relationship. Gaunt was not in England from July 1370 to November 1371 because of the war in Aquitaine, negating any argument for an earlier commencement of the affair. The couple themselves stated in their request to the Pope in 1396 for confirmation of their marriage that the liaison did not begin until after the deaths of both Blanche and Hugh.[34] It is highly unlikely that the couple would have lied in a document of such significance; the condemnation that would have faced them, in both life and death, would surely have led them to refrain from such an action. It would, therefore, appear that Gaunt acquired a mistress at the same time as he acquired his second wife, Constance, heir to the throne of Castile and of pivotal importance to Gaunt's political ambitions. It is difficult to ascertain when Constance became aware of Katherine's presence, or indeed to ascertain her feelings towards her husband's illicit liaison. Katherine was the messenger assigned to tell Edward III of the birth of the daughter of Constance and Gaunt, and was paid 20 marks for this errand, but Constance was at Hertford when she gave birth. Katherine was clearly in London with Gaunt. This daughter of the Castilian queen was also named Katherine, perhaps suggesting an interesting aspect of the relationship between wife and mistress.[35]

Katherine appears regularly in Gaunt's registers during the 1370s, described as 'nostre tres chere et bien amee'.[36] By 1375 it would appear that their affair was public knowledge. The accounts of William Ferour, Mayor of Leicester, record an expense of 16s in 1375–6 for wine – incidentally 'drunk by the bearers of the same' – sent to the lady Katherine Swynford, mistress of the Duke of Lancaster. The same accounts show that by 1377–9 Katherine was being approached as a channel of patronage. Expenses were claimed for

> a horse, price £3 6s 8d given to the lady Katherine Swynford. And for a pan of iron £2 0s 6d given to the said Katherine for expediting the business touching the tenement of Stretton, and for other business for which a certain lord besought the aforesaid Katherine with good effect for the said business and besought so successfully that the aforesaid town was pardoned the lending of silver to the king in the year.[37]

In the autumn of 1379 Gaunt was staying at Katherine's Kettlethorpe manor, evidenced by entries in his registers dated 15–16 November. However, just twenty months later, in the aftermath of the Peasants' Revolt, the chronicles report that the couple had parted.[38] Katherine's appearance in the registers certainly changes at this time. On 6 March 1381 Katherine was presented with what Goodman has described as 'a highly personal and cosily domestic gift': 'and to Herman, goldsmith, for a silver chafing pan with three feet and a handle for Dame Kateryne de Swynneford, £40'.[39] But just six months later it would appear that Katherine was being paid off. At this time she was granted the generous sum of 200 marks a year for life for her good service as governess. Furthermore, John of Gaunt's register includes a 'quit claim', a lengthy and legally couched document, for February 1382, which released Katherine, the former governess of Philippa and Elizabeth, and any of her future heirs from having any claim on Gaunt or his heirs, or for Gaunt and his heirs to have any claim on Katherine.[40] These entries would suggest that the chronicles were correct and that the couple did indeed part during the latter half of 1381. But evidence from the 1380s contradicts this: it would appear that Katherine was very much part of the Lancaster family unit. In 1383 Katherine spent some of her income from Gaunt on improving her Kettlethorpe manor, enclosing 300 acres of her manor lands and woods as parkland, an action that remained in force until 1810. This may indicate that for some periods during the 1380s Katherine was on her own manor, but, as with the 1370s, this did not necessitate a break from Gaunt. Katherine can be seen to have been very much in contact with the Duke, returning some of her income to Gaunt as a loan. In 1386–7 Gaunt ordered the part payment of 500 marks, lent to him by Katherine 'in his great necessity'.[41]

During the lifetime of Constance, and in particular during the period 1386–9, when Gaunt was in Castile furthering his claims to the Castilian Crown, Katherine can be found as a member of the household of Mary de Bohun, wife of Gaunt's son Henry of Bolingbroke, the future Henry IV. Gaunt obviously wished his mistress to live in the comfort to which she had become accustomed, and where better to place one's mistress when politics have to take priority than the household of one's son. Here, safety and well-being would surely be provided for her. The chamber and wardrobe accounts of Mary for the year 1387 provide evidence of Katherine's presence, with details recorded of Christmas gifts for Katherine of white and silk brocade and furs of pure minever.[42] It is extremely likely that during Katherine's time in this household she would have been in contact with Gaunt. Katherine also made regular appearances at court. From 1387 robes were issued to her annually for the feast of St George.[43] There may have been an initial break in relations in the early 1380s, with Katherine retiring to live at her Kettlethorpe manor, but the evidence is clear: by the mid-1380s the lovers were again in close contact.

However, life during this decade was not all smooth sailing for Katherine. In 1384 her house at Grantham in the county of Lincolnshire was broken into, her goods stolen and her servants assaulted.[44] But this county held strong ties for Katherine. She lived in the city of Lincoln for some time, renting the chancery of Lincoln Cathedral in the Minster Yard in 1386–7 and 1391–2.[45] Again, the Lancasters did not forget her during her stays here. The Duchy of Lancaster Records for 14 May 1391–14 May 1392 show 'one diamond in a gold ring to dnē K. Swynford' and 'four baldekyn of white damask given to the countess of Derby and dnē Kath' Swynford (78/4*d* per piece)'. Presumably these were New

Year gifts from either Henry of Bolingbroke or Gaunt himself. In addition, Gaunt's household attendance roll for either March or November 1391 includes the entry 'Dame Katherine Swynford, 12*d* per day.' Also listed in attendance with her are 'Monsieur de Derby, 4*d* per day' and her four Beaufort children with Gaunt, each with 6*d* per day.[46]

Gaunt's second wife and key to his, ultimately failed, political dreams died on 25 March 1394. The last few years of Constance's life were spent at Leicester Castle, while her husband lived openly in London with his mistress.[47] Nearly two years after her death, on 14 January 1396, John of Gaunt and Katherine married in Lincoln Cathedral. Twenty-four years after she had first become intimately involved with Gaunt, Katherine was Duchess of Lancaster and for a time first lady of England. The new duchess played a leading role in this same year in the ceremonies that surrounded the marriage of Richard II and his young French bride Isabella, entertaining the new queen in both London and Calais.[48]

Shortly after her marriage to Gaunt, Katherine became a member of the Coventry Guild of the Holy Trinity, St Mary, St John the Baptist and St Katherine.[49] Katherine's piety was also expressed through her continued links to Lincoln and its cathedral church. The *Calendar of Patent Rolls* for 17 September 1398 records the following entry:

> Licence for the king's uncle John, duke of Lancaster, to found a chantry of two chaplains in the cathedral church of Lincoln, and to grant to them the advowson of Somercotes St Peter's co. Lincoln, in perpetuity, and for them to appropriate the same in mortmain, to celebrate divine service in the said cathedral church for the good estate of the duke and Katherine his wife.[50]

The couple also donated to the cathedral many gifts adorned with their insignia.[51]

After only three years of marriage Katherine was again a widow, and, on Gaunt's death, returned to Lincolnshire once more. In 1400–1 Katherine was tenant of The Priory, Minster Yard, Lincoln, and in 1403 was living in a house belonging to the Dean and Chapter of Lincoln Cathedral, usually occupied by one of the canons. Presumably these two properties were the same.[52]

It has been suggested that Katherine may have remarried after the death of Gaunt. In Blomefield's work on the county of Norfolk he notes how Katherine held the town of Aylesham for life as part of her bequest from Gaunt. However, Blomefield records another account in which, during the same period, the town of Aylesham was held by 'Katherine, wife of John Leeches'.[53] Rye states that this third marriage by Katherine was possible, as 'the family of Leche or Leaches was a good one and armigerous, and held under the duchy of Lancaster'.[54] Unfortunately, Blomefield does not provide the reference for this information, and I have not yet found any evidence that can be checked. However, the fact that Katherine was resident in Lincoln from the time of Gaunt's death to her own, coupled with the wording on her tomb, which clearly indicates that she held the title of Duchess of Lancaster to her death, would surely mean that this account is in error.

Furthermore, Katherine's close connections with royalty remained in place after the death of Gaunt. Remarkably, she was able to forge close connections with both Richard II and Henry IV, showing great political skill on Katherine's part. Richard and Henry were so strongly at odds with one another – Richard exiling Henry on the death of Gaunt, Henry capturing and imprisoning Richard on his return, taking the throne as his – that for Katherine to be liked and well treated by both says a lot for her strength of character. While it is unlikely that any third marriage by Katherine took place so soon after Gaunt's death as to have been during the reign of Richard, surely Henry would have made some attempts to reclaim the Lancastrian lands that Katherine held if a third marriage had occurred after his accession to the throne? Gaunt left a substantial bequest of money and jewels to his 'most dear wife Katherine'.[55] This included intimate items such as 'all the buckles, rings, diamonds, rubies, and other things that would be found in a little box of cypress wood to which he himself had the key', but more significantly included a life interest in all the lands that he had granted to Katherine. After the seizure of the Lancastrian estates by Richard II upon the death of Gaunt, Katherine was able to secure her lands from the king, and, after the accession to the throne of Henry IV, Gaunt's former grants to Katherine of £200 a year on the issues of Duchy land in Huntingdon and 700 marks per annum on those in Lincolnshire were confirmed. It was not until Katherine's death that these assignments were transferred to Henry's queen, Joan of Navarre. Henry also made frequent gifts of wine to Katherine, calling her 'the king's mother'. Records also show that Katherine was in regular communication with the royal court. Money was granted to John Leventhorpe to cover expenses for a journey he undertook between London and Lincoln to speak to the Duchess of Lancaster. Leventhorpe was receiver-general, and therefore principal officer, of the Duchy of Lancaster.[56] It seems strange that, if Katherine had remarried, Henry did not recognise it through the granting of a special gift, or by reclaiming some or all of the land and annuities she held from the duchy. It is also surprising that there would appear to be no record of such an event in the chronicles of the time.

Katherine died in 1403. She was entombed in the cathedral church of Lincoln, to which she had formed so many connections during her life. Her monument was inlaid with her effigy in brass, now since defaced, and her simple epitaph, also inlaid in brass, read as follows:

Ici gist Dame Katherine, duchesse de Lancastre, jadys feme de le tres noble et tres gracious prince John duc de Lancastre, fitz a tres noble Roy Edward le tierce. Laquelle Katherine morust le x jour de May l'an de grace mil cccc tiers. De quelle alme Dieu yet et pitee. Amen.[57]

Here lies Dame Katherine, Duchess of Lancaster, third wife of the very noble and very gracious prince John Duke of Lancaster, son of the very noble King Edward III. The which Katherine died the tenth day of May the year of our grace 1403. On which our Lord have mercy. Amen.

THE SWYNFORDS

Very little evidence exists that can tell us about Katherine and Hugh's daughter Blanche Swynford. She is mentioned in Gaunt's register for January 1375, when Katherine receives the wardship of Robert Deyncourt for use as Blanche's dowry.[58] She appears again in the papal letter confirming the marriage of Gaunt and Katherine. It is from this document that it is known that Gaunt stood godfather to Blanche. The letter discloses that the petition made by Gaunt and Katherine to the Pope acknowledged the canonical bar to marriage that arose from this bond of compaternity between the couple.[59] It is possible that Gaunt's first wife Blanche of Lancaster was godmother to Blanche Swynford, and evidence would seem to suggest that Blanche was raised in the same household as the ducal daughters Philippa and Elizabeth. Wardrobe accounts from 1369 show that mourning clothes on the death of Queen Philippa were provided for Blanche Swynford 'damoiselles a les dites deux filles de lancastre'.[60] However, this could be a scribal error and these garments intended for Katherine, not Blanche.

In contrast to that of Blanche, the life of Katherine and Hugh's son Thomas is well documented as a highly trusted Lancastrian servant and friend. His birth date is recorded as 21 September 1368, and his mother's connections with Lincoln Cathedral were obviously already forged by this time, as two of the canons of the cathedral, Thomas de Sutton and John de Warsop, stood godfather to her new son.[61] In 1372, after the death of Hugh, Katherine was granted the wardship of her son's inheritance during his minority.[62] During Thomas's life his mother's lover was generous towards him. The period 1382–99 saw numerous grants to Thomas by Gaunt, the largest being a sum of £106 13s 4d. The only retainers of Gaunt's to receive higher amounts than this in the same period were John Holland, Earl of Huntingdon, stepson of Edward, Prince of Wales, and Sir Walter Blount, who was married to one of Constance of Castile's closest companions and held the position of chamberlain in Gaunt's household as well as being executor of the Duke's will. Thomas also attended Gaunt in 1386 when Henry Bolingbroke was admitted to the fraternity of Lincoln Cathedral.[63]

Gaunt's will made provision of 100 marks for Thomas 'mon tres chere bacheliere'.[64]

Thomas also received gifts from Richard II, notably a grant made in 1393 of 100 marks per annum to himself and his wife Joan Crophill.[65] However, it was Henry Bolingbroke, future King of England and legitimate son of Gaunt, with whom Thomas forged his strongest royal connection. The two men were very close in age, and it can be safely assumed that the two spent their childhood within the same court circles. When only 14 or 15 years of age Thomas was in the retinue of Henry, and the two travelled extensively together during the 1390s. The accounts for Henry's expeditions to Prussia and the Holy Land between 1390 and 1393 include numerous references to Thomas. The two were obviously in close contact in England as well as abroad, as these accounts record the expenses incurred for the bringing of two of Henry's horses from Thomas's Kettlethorpe home.[66]

The depth of the friendship of the two was most clearly demonstrated in 1399. Thomas was the warden of Richard II during his imprisonment in Pontefract Castle. Only the most highly trusted Lancastrian servant would have been granted this post. Indeed, contemporary accounts suggest that Thomas was responsible for the death of Richard. Adam Usk describes the conditions in which Richard was imprisoned, stating that the deposed king was 'tormented, bound with chains, and starved of food by Sir N. Swynford'.[67] This 'Sir N. Swynford' would almost certainly seem to have been Thomas. Records show that it was one of his valets who rode to London to inform Henry IV of the death of Richard.[68]

Henry rewarded Thomas well for his loyalty. He confirmed the annual grant of 100 marks made by Richard and added to this 'custody of the king's castle of Somerton with the fees and other profits belonging to the custody, as John Bussy, "chivaler", had of the grant of Richard II'. He also granted Thomas the rank of king's Chamber Knight.[69] The choice of a king's Chamber Knights was a very personal matter; the choice of Thomas for this role is therefore another indication of the close relationship between the two men.

The early years of the fifteenth century saw Thomas as Sheriff of Lincoln and Steward of Tickhill, and by 1404 he was Captain of Calais, engaged in negotiations with France and Flanders.[70] These negotiations demonstrate the high level of education that Thomas had received. Several letters from him in this year addressed to the French representatives and to Henry IV have survived. In these letters request is made that the French council write in Latin, not French, for ease of understanding.[71]

In 1411, eight years after the death of his mother, Thomas was struggling to secure his inheritance in Hainaut. Henry took the step of issuing a letter confirming that Thomas was the legitimate heir of these lands:

> hence it is that divers inheritances in the country of Hainaut having lately descended to our beloved and trusty knight, Sir Thomas Swynford, from the most renowned lady Katherine de Roelt, deceased, late Duchess of Lancaster, his mother, certain persons of those parts doubting that the said Thomas, son and heir of the aforementioned Katherine, was begotten in lawful matrimony, have not, by reason of such doubt, permitted the same Thomas to possess the aforesaid inheritances, or to receive the farms, rents, or issues thereof. Wherefore be it known unto you all, that the aforesaid Thomas is the son and heir of the aforesaid Katherine, begotten and born of the same Katherine in lawful wedlock, and that a certain writing of the said Thomas to these our present letters annexed, sealed with the seal of arms of the said Thomas, is his deed, and that he and his father and all his paternal ancestors have in all times past borne the said arms and used the like seal. And this we do by these presents make known unto all whom it may concern.[72]

It is possible that Thomas and his wife Joan had two sons. Thomas Beaufort, son of Katherine and Gaunt and therefore half-brother to Thomas Swynford, had an esquire, also named Thomas Swynford and presumably grandson to Katherine. And Cardinal Henry Beaufort, again son of Katherine and Gaunt, bequeathed to

'William Swynford my nephew' the sum of £400 and a number of silver vessels.[73] It is also possible that Thomas had a daughter, named Katherine after his mother. She is recorded as marrying Sir William Drury of Rougham.[74] Thomas may also have been married twice. J. Elder records his wife as being Elisabeth Beauchamp of Powicke.[75] Thomas died in 1433.[76]

THE CHAUCERS

Philippa Roet, younger sister to Katherine and born *c.* 1347, was married to the English poet Geoffrey Chaucer by 1366.[77] The life of Chaucer is well documented, with a wealth of contemporary records available.[78] During his life he held a number of public positions ranging from esquire and soldier to diplomat, justice of the peace and controller of customs. The date and place of his birth are not known, but evidence suggests a birth date for him somewhere in the early 1340s, making him around seven years older than his wife. It is possible that he was a student at the almonry school of St Paul's Cathedral, one of three schools in the Vintry Ward, the area of London where Chaucer is known to have spent his childhood. He was a page in the household of the Countess of Ulster by 1357, and it was probably within this royal environment that he first met Philippa, who was also a member of the Countess's household by that date. The accounts for April 1357 record that Chaucer was granted a short cloak, a pair of red and black breeches and a pair of shoes.[79]

It is presumed that Geoffrey and Philippa had two daughters and two sons. Of the daughters little is known beyond single accounts in the records, but from these accounts their Lancastrian connections are obvious. Agnes Chaucer was an attendant at the coronation of Henry IV, while her sister Elizabeth became a nun at Barking Abbey in 1381, her admission expenses paid by John of Gaunt as part of a larger gift to the abbey of £51 8s 2d.[80] The dower-like nature of this gift has led some Chaucerians to speculate that Elizabeth was in actual fact the daughter of Philippa and Gaunt. Williams surmises that annuities granted to Philippa in 1366 and to Geoffrey nine months later were tantamount to an admission of such by the Duke, as, to Williams, they were obviously granted as provision for the child.[81] However, as the initial grant to Philippa was made on the eve of the Duke's departure to Spain, it is possible that the intention was for both Philippa and Geoffrey to receive the annuity at this time, but a scribal error led to only Philippa being granted the award. The second grant would therefore be a correction of the original. Certainly the period of nine months cannot have been the time from Philippa announcing to Gaunt that she was carrying his child to the time of the birth; it is inconceivable that Philippa would have known on conception that she was pregnant. Moreover, Gaunt was known for his generosity to those in his retinue and Philippa received gifts that were in line with those he granted to others in his household. Furthermore, the payment to Barking Abbey could easily have been made at the request of Katherine as a favour to her sister, as Barking was one of the most prestigious English convents and therefore a desirable home for Elizabeth, although at the time the abbey was suffering somewhat because of a flood that had devastated a large part of the abbey's possessions.

It has been suggested that Katherine desired that Elizabeth be moved to Barking from her original convent of St Helen's in Bishopgate to be with her cousin Margaret Swynford. Margaret had been admitted to Barking three years previously in 1377.[82] However, this is the only known reference to Margaret Swynford, and her relationship, if any, to Katherine is unclear. It is possible that she was the third child of Hugh and Katherine, but equally she could have been from another branch of the Swynford family. Until such time as more information on Margaret is uncovered, her relationship to Katherine can only be a matter of conjecture.

Chaucer himself made reference to one of his children, dedicating his work *A Treatise on the Astrolabe* to 'lyte Lowys my sone'. Lewis Chaucer appears just once in the official records of the time, listed on a retinue roll compiled at Carmarthen Castle in 1403. Also present on this list is his elder brother, Thomas Chaucer. Again, Chaucerians have suggested that Thomas was the child of Philippa and Gaunt and not Chaucer's son. Krauss argues that this situation would 'make understandable Gaunt's single display of generosity toward Geoffrey and his life-long interest in Philippa and Thomas. It would solve all mysteries connected with Thomas's rather unusual usage in the matter of arms and with the failure of the heraldic decorations on his tomb to indicate his paternity.' Indeed, he goes so far as to suggest that it was common knowledge that Chaucer was not Thomas's father.[83] However, I have not seen any contemporary record that indicates that the fatherhood of Thomas was in doubt. Furthermore, the question of the arms on Thomas Chaucer's tomb is easily explained.

There are twenty arms displayed in all on Thomas's tomb in Ewelme Church, Oxfordshire. His own arms are displayed as *Gules, 3 wheels, Or*, the arms of the Roet family.[84] Here is Krass's 'failure of the heraldic decorations . . . to indicate his paternity'. Thomas chose to display his maternal arms over those of Chaucer. However, when the context of the other nineteen arms on his tomb is investigated, his reason for doing this seems obvious – that is, it was fuelled by ambition. It would appear that in death Thomas wished to be associated with the rich and the great.[85] The arms included on his tomb belong to the powerful families of the Beauforts, the Nevilles and the Burghershes.[86] Would not the Roet arms, linked to these families through his mother and aunt, be more appropriate ones to display than those of Chaucer? It would certainly seem that Thomas was more concerned about demonstrating his political connections than his familial links, as the arms of Thomas Swynford are noticeably absent. Furthermore, heraldic law would have allowed Thomas to display his mother's arms if she was a Roet heiress with no surviving male heir between her and her father's estate.[87] This situation is one that is believed to have been true for Philippa. It is highly possible that on her death the use of the Roet arms passed to Thomas. The Roet arms are displayed elsewhere in the church. They form one of a set of four arms displayed above a window and also appear in the front face of the step to the raised floor on which the altar stands. But was it indeed Thomas who requested that his tomb be decorated in such a way and that these arms be displayed for him? Ewelme Church was built by Thomas's daughter, Alice, and her husband shortly after their marriage in 1431–2. Thomas died in 1434. Perhaps the tomb decoration was dictated by Alice during the building of the church. The tomb itself represents Thomas in brass, with a unicorn, the Chaucer family badge, at his feet. Most interesting of all is the suggestion that the twenty shields on the tomb are of a later date, added in the time of John, Duke of Suffolk (d. 1491).[88] It may be that it was later descendants of Thomas who wanted to proclaim their Roet connections, possibly with the rise of the Lancastrians in the form of Henry Tudor to the throne.

Thomas's links with powerful families are certainly apparent during his life. During the 1380s and 1390s he was in the retain of Gaunt, receiving numerous annuities from the Duke in connection with this contract. In 1402 he was 'the king's sergeant his chief butler' and held this position intermittently until his death, along with the position of forester to the Earl of March. His career also included the posts of Sheriff of Oxfordshire and Berkshire, and Constable of Wallingford. He married Maud Burghersh, and their daughter, Alice, married William de Pole, Duke of Suffolk. Philippa's son was a member of the landed gentry, with landholdings in Oxfordshire, Hampshire and Buckinghamshire.[89] Presumably he also held land in Hainaut, as the Roet inheritance split between Katherine and Philippa on the death of Paon would have transferred to Thomas on the death of his mother. Details of these landholdings are as yet unknown.

THE BEAUFORTS

Katherine was mother to four illegitimate children as a result of her affair with the Duke of Lancaster. It is widely held that this affair started in the spring of 1372 and from this the birth dates of their children have been presumed as John 1373, Henry 1375, Thomas 1377 and Joan 1379.[90] I have come across only one focused attempt to argue for alternative dates. The Chaucerian Albert Stanburrough Cook speculates that John Beaufort was born in the mid-1360s and Henry around 1368, inferring that the liaison between Gaunt and Katherine started considerably earlier than has previously been acknowledged, and while, more importantly, both parties were still married to their first spouses. Cook bases his theory on the careers of the eldest Beauforts, suggesting, for example, that John must have been older than 17 years when he took part in the jousts at St Inglevere in 1390–1, and that Henry had to be 30 years of age in 1398 when he became Bishop of Lincoln. However, neither of these suppositions is accurate. Cook also suggests that the troubles faced by Thomas Swynford in relation to his Hainaut inheritance were based on the knowledge that an older sibling of his was of illegitimate birth, and therefore cast doubt on his own status of birth.[91] But this would have required a lie on the part of the Duke and Katherine in their petition to the Pope to recognise their marriage.

Gaunt recognised his children from the first, which also suggests that Katherine was already a widow by the time of the births, as there was no apparent confusion over the paternity of the children. The duke granted them the name of Beaufort and reflected their Lancastrian heritage in the choice of their Christian names.[92] It has been widely supposed that the Beaufort name was granted because the children, or at least the eldest, were born in the castle of Beaufort in Anjou, but, as Armitage-Smith acknowledged,

> Katherine never saw Beaufort, and her children were certainly not born there. The explanation of the choice of this name for the Duke's illegitimate family must be found in the fact that among the many territorial titles which came by descent to John of Gaunt it was found convenient to choose one which would not prejudice the rights of his legitimate heir.

The castle and lordship of Beaufort was in Anjou and had therefore been lost to the French in 1369, and, as a consequence, was available to grant to a bastard lineage without prejudice.[93] The actual birthplace of the Beauforts is unknown.

The Beauforts were favoured by Richard II after 1389, reflecting the close alliance between the King and John of Gaunt following the

Duke's return from Castile.[94] This show of royal favour undoubtedly made it easier for Gaunt to bestow honour on his children. During the 1390s the Beauforts were clearly included in the Lancastrian and Richardian worlds. Lists of Gaunt's household from the early 1390s show the Beauforts in residence with their father and half-brother, the future Henry IV.[95] John Beaufort's name is also attached to the jousting tournament at Saint-Inglevere in 1390–1, and Cook used this knowledge to support his suggestion that John's birth date must have been prior to the 1372 date acknowledged by other scholars. However, John is merely listed as wishing to compete. Froissart's full description of the jousts does not include reference to John. The fact that he did not appear actually to attend would negate Cook's speculation that John was born in the mid-1360s.[96] Indeed, it would seem that not all scholars share Cook's view that John would have been too young at 17 years old to compete in the jousts. Radford assigns John the birth date of 1373 because of the fact that he could 'tilt with success in the lists in 1390'.[97]

Harris states that 'it is a mark both of John's military ability and of the political accord between Gaunt and the king that Richard made him a king's knight in June 1392 with an annuity of 100 marks to add to that of £100 from his father'.[98] During the early to mid-1390s, John of Gaunt can be seen to be improving both the status and the wealth of his eldest Beaufort son. Indeed, one of his chief expenses at this time was the purchasing of land with which he could endow John Beaufort without reducing Bolingbroke's inheritance.[99] In 1394 John accompanied his father on campaign in France. Harris has suggested that this trip was in part due to a desire by Gaunt to create an appanage in Aquitaine for the Beauforts, but, if this was so, the plan never reached fruition.[100] John had to content himself with smaller demonstrations of political power at this time, notably as a channel of patronage. For example, an entry in the Patent Rolls for 28 October 1392 reads: 'Pardon, at the supplication of John Beauford, knight, to John Cros of Oveston, co. Northampton, for killing John Logowe there in self-defence on the Sunday before Midsummer in the thirteenth year.'[101]

The career of Henry Beaufort was also progressing well in the early 1390s. In 1391 he received the prebend of Sutton and Buckingham, both in the diocese of Lincoln. At this time he was studying at Oxford, after an initial period at Peterhouse College, Cambridge, in the late 1380s. While at Oxford he also received by royal grant the prebend of Thame and Ricall and the wardenship of the free chapel at Tickhill, these grants providing his income while he was studying.[102]

The Beaufort fortunes improved further after the marriage of their parents. Both Richard II and the Pope agreed to the unprecedented step of legitimating the Beauforts. At their official legitimation ceremony during the Parliament of 1397 the Beauforts undertook the role of 'mantle-children', placed under the care-cloth with their parents to indicate their change from bastard status.[103] After their mother had become Duchess of Lancaster, titles and gifts were bestowed on a regular basis, and the Beauforts were established as legitimate relations of the royal family. John attended Richard II at his meeting with Charles VI at Calais and was created Earl of Somerset, his place in Parliament seated between the Earl Marshall and the Earl of Warwick.[104] In 1397 his rank was increased to include the title Marquis of Dorset, possibly as a reward from Richard for the support shown by John against the appellants Gloucester, Arundel and Warwick, and he was granted the constableship of Wallingford Castle for life. In 1398 the constableship of Dover and the wardenship of the Cinque Ports were additionally assigned to him, along with the major acquisition of Admiral of the North and West. He was also granted the prestigious title of King's Lieutenant in Aquitaine. A mark of the regard Richard held for John is that the eldest Beaufort was a witness to Richard's will.[105]

In 1399, after Richard had seized the Lancastrian inheritance and exiled Henry Bolingbroke, it was by no means obvious which party John was going to support. He did not openly oppose the exiling of Henry, nor the confiscation of his lands. Indeed, Richard initially seized the lands owned by Beaufort with the rest of the Lancastrian estates, but these were returned to John. Moreover, he was one of the few peers who was prepared to support the Duke of York in his attempts to raise an army to counter Henry's return to England.[106] Perhaps this should not be surprising, given the favour he had found under Richard. But 'an ability to maintain an appearance of loyalty to divergent masters had enabled John Beaufort to survive the revolution of 1399'.[107] For, on his accession as Henry IV, the new king produced a letter that John had written to him in his exile, declaring his loyalty and goodwill.[108] It seems that John, like Katherine, had the skill and the character to be a friend to both sides.

However, John did face some humiliation and loss of dignity as punishment for his support of Richard. His title of Marquis was stripped from him, and his lieutenantship of Aquitaine was also removed. But John was made chamberlain; this position kept him at Henry's side and therefore still prominent in the new governance of the land.[109] Moreover, personal bonds between the two remained, with Henry standing godfather to John's son in 1401, granting the new child, his namesake, the generous assignment of 1,000 marks a year.[110] Furthermore, in 1403 Henry granted to John the position of King's Lieutenant of South Wales 'with full power to receive into the king's grace any Welsh rebels'. It was declared that this position was granted to John because of the king 'trusting in his loyalty and prudence'. This trust was evident elsewhere. John was appointed to attend Queen Isabel, widow of Richard, on her return to France in 1401. He also escorted Blanche, daughter of Henry, to Cologne for her wedding with the Count Palatine of the Rhine, and accompanied Joan of Navarre, Henry's second wife, from Brittany to England in 1403. In addition he was commissioned to treat with the French for redress of injuries between 1401 and 1403. He was granted the position of Captain of Calais on 1 November 1401, and held this position intermittently until his death. This confirmed the bond of trust between the half-brothers, as the garrison at Calais was the largest permanent force in the king's pay. However, it would appear that John's payment for this role was not always forthcoming from the King, as a petition from Beaufort in 1404 declared that his wages were in arrears by £11,400.[112]

John married Margaret Holland, sister and co-heir of Edmund and daughter of Thomas, Earl of Kent, some time before September 1397. On his death, Palm Sunday, 16 March 1410, he was buried in the chapel of St Thomas in Canterbury Cathedral. His widow remarried, her second husband being Thomas, Duke of Clarence. After the death of her second husband, Margaret was anxious that her spouses should have a stately memorial. A site was chosen in St Michael's Chapel at Canterbury. Woodruff and Danks report:

In order to give floorspace for a tomb of exceptional size and magnificence, the Norman apsidal chapel was taken down and rebuilt on a more extended scale, with a rectangular east end, probably at the cost of the Duchess, whose arms with those of her two husbands are sculptured on the vaulted roof of the chapel.

Shortly after the tomb had been completed, Margaret herself died and was interred alongside her husbands in the magnificent monument of Purbeck marble.[113]

John's younger brother Thomas also fared well during the reigns of Henry IV and Henry V. Under Richard, Thomas had received an annuity of 100 marks as 'retained for life to stay with the king', and in 1398 gained the castle and lordship of Castle Acre in Norfolk.[114] But his career progressed considerably after the accession of Henry. In May 1402 he was present at the appointment of an embassy to negotiate the marriage of Prince Henry (the future Henry V). In August the same year Thomas received his first military command as Captain of Ludlow.[115] By 1403 he was Admiral of the Fleet for the northern parts, receiving payment in 1404 for an expedition in this role.[116] Three years later and he was Captain of Calais, and in 1409 the position of Admiral of the Fleet was granted his for life. The year 1410 saw the culmination of his career as he received the Great Seal from Henry; indeed, Thomas was to be the only lay chancellor of the reign. However, Thomas resigned from this position in 1412, and the rest of the decade saw his energies devoted to the war with France. It is claimed that in April 1413 Thomas spoke so 'pithily and wisely' on the question of Henry's claim to France that it was on his opinion that war was proclaimed.[117] He was pious as well as wise. Records show that he undertook a pilgrimage to the shrine of St Cuthbert at Durham.[118] Information from his household rolls, collected by William Worcestre in the fifteenth century, again demonstrates his pious nature. He made provision for the poor, every day feeding thirteen poor people and granting them three pence. On Maundy Thursday he would wash the feet of the poor and give to each a sum dependent on his age. Worcestre reports that Thomas even donated his own cloak, doublet and belt so the poor would not be without. He also appears to have been strict in his requirements of behaviour, particularly among his own household.[119]

The new king, Henry V, made Thomas his Lieutenant of Aquitaine in 1414, Captain of Harfleur in 1415 and Lieutenant of Normandy in 1416. The following year, while on pilgrimage to Bridlington, Thomas heard news of a Scottish raid and siege of Roxburgh. As the King was in Normandy, he raised forces and relieved the town. His involvement with the war in France was not confined to the battlefield; in 1420 he was part of the negotiation of the Treaty of Troyes.[120]

The level of trust placed in Thomas by Henry V, and the relationship between the two men, is best demonstrated by a codicil added by the King to his will. The codicil referred to the King's young son and his upbringing as Henry VI after the death of his father. The responsibility for this upbringing was granted to Thomas, including the provision of education and the choice of the new king's personal servants.[121] McFarlane described Thomas as 'the most trusted personal friend and minister of Henry V', and this addition to his will can only support this view.[122] Goodman confirms that Thomas 'had gained an outstanding reputation as a noble with high standards of Christian conduct'. He goes on to describe his character: 'He was conspicuously charitable to the poor and wayfarers. He would not tolerate swearers, liars and talebearers in his household. He would not accept gifts and rewards.'[123]

In contrast, Thomas's sister, Joan, was a much more bullish character. She married at a young age, referred to in a grant of 20 September 1394 as Joan de Ferrers. Her first husband was Sir Robert de Ferrers of Oversley, a member of the retinue of her father, the Duke of Lancaster; he was found in the household of the Duke with Joan in the early 1390s. She appears to have been betrothed to him in 1386.[124] Joan's marriage to Robert was short; her husband died sometime before 1396, while Joan was still only 17 years of age. However, during their marriage they had two daughters together, Mary and Elizabeth.[125] Her second marriage was to the much more distinguished Ralph Neville, Earl of Westmorland and a close ally of the Lancastrian family.[126] The family of her second husband did, however, ensure that Joan's ties with the Ferrers remained. Robert, through a previous marriage, had had a daughter named Margaret, who married Ralph's second son, also named Ralph, from his first marriage.[127]

Joan and Ralph had thirteen children during their marriage. Ralph had previously been married to Margaret Stafford, and it was to his children from this first marriage that the Neville inheritance and earldom should have descended.[128] But Joan endeavoured to secure a share of the Neville wealth for her own children after she was widowed in 1425. Her husband helped her in this, as he left the greater part of his Yorkshire landholdings to Joan in jointure and named her and her son as executors of his will, while Joan's brothers Henry and Thomas were the will's supervisors.[129] It is during this time that her formidable character was displayed. She ensured that it was to her branch of the Neville family that these lands passed, although the earldom did pass to Ralph's eldest son.[130]

The lands were held in jointure by the couple through what some have seen as fraudulent means. Grants of lands assigned to Joan and Ralph by both Richard II and Henry IV, motivated no doubt in part by the royal status of Joan, were styled 'for the life of the longest liver' with an entail on the heirs of their bodies. Ross claims:

Had the attempt to provide for the Beaufort line stopped there, the children of Katharine Stafford would have had no cause of complaint. Yet, while Joan's children were growing up in the early years of the fifteenth century, a more deliberate and less justifiable scheme, designed to ensure them the enjoyment of the Nevilles' ancestral inheritance, was carried through.[131]

This scheme involved Ralph Neville conveying or enfeoffing large parts of his lands to a group of loyal friends on the basis that these lands would be re-enfeoffed back to Ralph by these trusted feoffees. Through these means the title of the lands could be held jointly by Ralph and Joan and entailed to their children. After Ralph's death, Joan continued with this programme of conveyancing to ensure that her children received the lion's share of the Neville inheritance.[132] Dobson records an interesting tale that demonstrates Joan's determination in this matter. In 1434 the Prior of Durham was a man named Wessington. An old clerk of the priory informed the Earl of Westmorland, Ralph's son with his first wife, that documentation relating to the Neville inheritance was held at the priory. The Earl requested this information from Wessington. Wessington, loyal to Joan because of her patronage of the priory, informed her of this matter and was promptly in the middle of a fight over the documents, as Joan wished to stop the Earl gaining possession of them. Joan involved her brother in the matter, to the extent that Cardinal Beaufort wrote to Wessington informing him he would face peril and danger to his soul unless the documents were given to Joan![133]

But it could be argued that the Neville landholdings were so large because of Ralph's marriage to Joan: 'in rather less than two centuries the Nevilles had thriven from simple barons to comital ranks, helped on their way by useful, though by no means unusual, marriages to heiresses.'[134] Of these marriages it was Ralph's marriage to Joan that brought the Neville family political importance:

Here, in this marriage, is the most obvious reason for Neville success in the first half of the fifteenth century. The connection with the royal house accounts at once for the prominence and

31

success of Ralph, Earl of Westmorland, and for the brilliant series of marriages of Ralph's children by Joan, which united then with the greatest families of England.[135]

As Joan was the reason for the rise in importance of the Nevilles, is it any wonder that Ralph chose a path that was entirely in the interest of his wife?

In 1437 Joan founded 'a perpetual chantry of two chaplains to celebrate divine service daily at the altar before which her mother Katherine, late Duchess of Lancaster is buried'.[136] Just three years later Joan herself was dead. Provision had been made for her to be buried in the Neville tomb in Staindrop Church, Co. Durham, and her alabaster effigy was placed there along with that of Ralph and his first wife, Margaret. But Joan chose to be buried alongside her mother, whom she describes in her will as an illustrious lady, in the cathedral church of Lincoln, her epitaph declaring her as the daughter of the Duke of Lancaster and stating the date of her death as the feast of St Brice, 13 November 1440.[137]

The most politically astute, powerful and wealthy of all of Katherine and John's children was their second child, Henry. He was described by Vergil as 'the onely man by whose high wisdome and puissant wealth king Henry [VI] might have been so supported that, all feare sett aside, he might without doubt have continued in perpetuall peace at home'.[138] The passing of time has not altered history's perception of his importance to the Lancastrian dynasty:

> his abilities and ambition won him a central role in the formulation and execution of royal policy, while the accidents of Henry V's early death and his own longevity conferred on him the unique status of elder statesman and mentor of three kings. In this sense Beaufort's life epitomised the story of Lancastrian ascendancy and decline, and his death was felt to cut the last link with the foregoing age.[139]

Henry's clerical career began during the reign of Richard II, with the study of theology and the arts at both Cambridge and Oxford in the 1390s. He was Master of Arts by 4 February 1393.[140] In 1396 he received papal provision to let the Deanery of Wells while he continued his studies. Two years later he was confirmed as the Bishop of Lincoln, described by Froissart as the richest bishopric in England. Cook has stated that to be bishop in 1398 Henry must have been born in 1368, because of the papal ruling that bishops should not be less than 30 years of age. He notes that it was possible for bishoprics to be granted at a younger age, but only with papal dispensation, of which there is no record in the case of Henry. However, Radford quotes from an account where Henry is described as an 'admodum puer' or 'mere lad' in 1398 and he states 'the expression should perhaps be taken not literally of boyhood but comparatively of a scandalously young bishop'. Moreover, Henry was not unqualified for the position of bishop at this time, having completed his studies at Oxford and taken deacon's orders the previous year.[141]

In 1399 Henry Beaufort took his place in the funeral cortège of his father, as it travelled from Northampton to St Paul's Cathedral. The cortège stopped at the abbey of St Albans, but Henry and his mother were refused admission and lodging at the abbey, as Henry, in turn, refused to give formal indemnity to the abbey, as the abbey was exempt from episcopal jurisdiction. The matter was resolved through Henry's decision to grant the indemnity, but on his visitation to the abbey soon after it was obvious that Henry had not forgiven the abbey for the snub to him and his mother; the abbot had to present Henry with a ring containing a piece from the holy cross before Henry was placated.[142]

During the reign of Henry IV, Henry's political career expanded. In 1403 he became Chancellor of England and therefore prominent in the dealings of the King. The personal bond between Henry IV and the Beauforts was displayed again in this same year as Henry was chosen by the King to officiate at his marriage to Joan of Navarre.[143] During the next eight years his diplomatic skills were developed during negotiations with the Burgandian, Flemish and French envoys. At the same time his great wealth was becoming apparent. In 1404 a payment was made to Henry in part return of 2,000 marks lent by him to the King. The amounts he loaned to the Crown increased dramatically in the following decades. In 1416 he lent the King £14,000 secured on the customs of the land, and in 1421 a further £14,000 was made available. The entry for Henry in the *DNB* makes reference to his wealth:

> As Beaufort cannot have inherited any great estates, and as the income of his see, considerable as it was, was by no means large enough to supply him with the vast sums which he lent the crown from time to time, as well as to provide him with the means of indulging his taste for magnificence, it is probable that his constant power of finding ready money was the result of a singular financial ability, combined with a high character for integrity. Knowing how to use money, and using it with boldness, careful to maintain his credit, and not afraid of making his credit serve him, Beaufort gained immense wealth.[144]

Lander, more pithily, credits Henry with the title 'arch-usurer of his day'.[145] At the date of Henry V's death the Crown owed Henry Beaufort £20,149 0s 5d. Ross argues that this great debt led to it being in Henry's interest 'to promote orderly administration and stable government as well as to maintain the Lancastrian government in power. Any change in dynasty might involve the repudiation of the former king's debt.'[146] The majority of the loans were repaid by the custom revenues being diverted directly to Henry Beaufort for a time. However, one of the loans was secured on the crown jewels, and this particular loan was not repaid. It has been suggested that Henry deliberately arranged this so that he could retain permanent control of the jewels.[147]

Henry's clerical career blossomed alongside that of his political status. In 1404 he became the Bishop of Winchester, resigning his chancellorship temporarily on translation to his new see. In 1421 his relationship with Henry V was cemented as he stood godfather to the King's new son. This relationship with Henry V perhaps grew from the King's boyhood, as it has been suggested that Beaufort was tutor to Henry.[148] In 1426 his clerical career peaked with his election as Cardinal of England, and there were rumours at the same time that the position of Pope might also one day be his.[149] The *Chronicles of London* detailed the ceremony at which Henry received his cardinal's hat:

> And as the Bishop went to masse the popys cosyn brouht the cardinallys hatte with grete reuerence, and sette it on the auter. And whanne the masse was don ther was putte vpon the bisshop a cardynall habyte off skarlette furred with puredd. And thanne ther knelyng vpon his knees before the hyh auter the popes Bullys were rede to hym; and the ffirst bulle was his charge, and the seconde bulle was that he should have and reioysen all the benefyces spirituell and temporell that he hadde had in England. And thanne the Regent of ffraunce sette the hatte on the Bisshopis hedde off Wynchestre, and bowyd and obeyed to hym and tooke hym affore him, and so went to theire Innes.[150]

Beaufort's importance during the reign of Henry V is documented in the *Gesta Henrici Quinti*. This work contains the rationale for war with France, and details speeches made by Henry Beaufort to parliament. Beaufort declared that, 'we make war so that we may have peace, because the end of war is peace'.[151] This theme runs through the *Gesta* and demonstrates how the policies of the Crown and Beaufort were in tune. Perhaps this was the reason for his success throughout the reign of three successive kings; he supported the policies of the Crown and in turn reaped political rewards. But it would seem from the accolades paid him that Beaufort always gave the kings wise counsel. Perhaps it should be said that the secret of the Lancastrian success was tied to the counsel of Beaufort. Certainly the speeches he made in parliament indicate that he felt that kings should always listen to the advice of their magnates.[152] Given-Wilson and Curteis echo the thoughts of Vergil when they state that the death of Henry in 1447 'deprived England of its wisest and most experienced administrator at a time when his guiding hand was sorely needed'.[153]

Radford argues that, during the reign of Henry IV, the Beauforts were favourites of the Crown.[154] This can be seen to have extended into the reigns of Henry V and VI. The children of John and Katherine were proven to be loyal and wise political servants to the Crown of England, perhaps driven by their sense of their own royal status. But the actual throne of England was never theirs. In their patent of legitimation Richard II declared that the Beauforts should be

> raised, promoted, elected, assume, and be admitted to all honours, dignities, pre-eminencies, estates, degrees and offices public and private whatsoever, as well perpetual as temporal, and feodal and noble, by whatsoever names they may be designated, whether they be Duchies, Principalities, Earldoms, Baronies or other fees, and whether they depend or are holden of us mediately or immediately, and to receive, retain, bear, and exercise the same as freely and lawfully as if ye were born in lawful matrimony . . .

thereby clearly stating that the Beauforts had a place in the line of succession to the throne.[155]

But Henry IV altered this document in 1407 with the addition of the clause 'except to the royal dignity'.[156] However, these words do not occur in the document confirmed by parliament during Richard's reign, and moreover Henry did not himself consult parliament about the addition and therefore this exclusion from the royal line will not have held legal merit.[157] Indeed, in the years that followed, the addition did not bar the succession of England from the Beauforts. The children of Katherine and Gaunt did not sit on the throne themselves, but their descendants certainly did. Joan Beaufort's daughter Cecily Neville was mother of the Yorkist kings Edward IV and Richard III. John Beaufort was both grandfather of Margaret Beaufort, mother of the first Tudor king, Henry VII, and father-in-law to James I of Scotland through the marriage of his daughter, another Joan, to the Scottish king, from which line descended the Stuart royal line. The unique step taken by John of Gaunt in marrying his mistress, and thereby legitimating his bastard children, led to him becoming the ancestor of kings, and to Katherine Swynford becoming the ancestress of kings. Katherine's place in history would seem to lie in the royal houses of York, Tudor and Stuart, as it was through her that they came into being. An acclaimed place in history should surely then be hers. But is this how history remembers her?

CHAPTER 2

The Historiography of Katherine Swynford

Katherine's passage through history cannot in all honesty be described as acclaimed, a sad statement for a woman whose very existence affected the face of fifteenth-century politics. Her legacy as the ancestress of kings has, in part, survived, as her name does occur with regularity in the historical texts produced in the six centuries since her death. But, far too often, it is only her name that is found. Her place would seem to be in relation to others: she is linked inevitably to Gaunt and the Beauforts, and is cited as the mother of, or lover of, other notables. Little can be found that describes her character or her actions, or that acknowledges that she had a personality.

Unfortunately, when texts are found that say more about Katherine than a mere assignment of her as mother of the Beauforts or as the lover of Gaunt, the tendency is to portray her in stereotypical terms. She appears in two contrasting forms, either as the evil temptress who diverted her lover from his political duties, or, in dichotomy, as a highly romantic character, the woman who stole the heart of a brave knight. There are reasons for this. Contemporary evidence that directly informs us about Katherine's life and character is scarce, and therefore research is problematic. Furthermore, the individual writers who espouse their views of Katherine are affected by their own moral viewpoints and political agendas; there is obvious variation in both these areas over the centuries, and, in consequence, interest in Katherine and the depictions of her are not constant through time. She was, however, an important woman and deserves a place in historical texts.

In the century after her death little was said about Katherine in the chronicles. The author of *An English Chronicle of the Reigns of*

Richard II, Henry IV, Henry V and Henry VI describes the reaction to the wedding of Gaunt and Katherine:

> And anon aftur, the duke partyd fro the kyng, and rode to Lyncolle, wher Kateryne Swynfordes abydyng was as at that tyme. And aftur the utas of xij day, the duke wedded the seyde Kateryne; the wheche wedding caused mony a monnus wonderyng, for, as hit was seyde, he haad holde heere longe before.[1]

There is no content here that relates directly to the character of Katherine. The text declares that the wedding caused gossip – 'the wheche wedding caused mony a monnus wonderyng' – but with no suggestion of malice, or even a sense of disapproval. Instead it indicates that the gossip arose merely from the unprecedented step of a duke marrying a woman when it was well known that she had been his mistress for many years: 'as hit was seyde, he haad holde heere longe before'. The tone is one of surprise that Gaunt had felt it necessary to do the decent thing. The *English Chronicle* quoted above is a version of the *Brut*, of which there are over 120 extant versions in English, plus several more in French. This multitude of available manuscripts suggests that the *Brut* was widely read at the time of its writing – surely these 120 extant manuscripts are only a small selection of those available at the time. They can be viewed, therefore, as offering a snapshot of public opinion at the time of the wedding. There may be little said of Katherine's character in the *Brut*, but this in itself is highly revealing. For example, the same cannot be said of Alice Perrers, the other famous royal mistress of the fourteenth century.[2] The *Brut* is much more garrulous about Alice, describing in detail the 'grete wronges and evel goveraunce that was done by her and by her counceyl in the reame'.[3] In contrast, the author of this particular *Brut* manuscript confuses Katherine with another royal female:

> Than kyng Herry sent to Dame Kateryn Swynfor, Countesse of Herforde, whiche was tho a wel-gouerned woman, and kept the most worshipful housolde, and the best rewlyd that was within

the londe; and to her he sent for men that were of good disposicyoun; and she sent him xij Ientylmen of sad gouernaunce and so this gracious kyng forsoke al wyldnes, and toke hym to good gouernaunce, and kept streytly his lawys with ryghtwisnes and Iustise.[4]

This is a most flattering portrayal of Katherine. However, it must be acknowledged that a mistake has been made on the part of the author. Katherine had been dead for a decade when this noble lady advised Henry V. The author has confused Katherine for Joan de Bohun, Henry's maternal grandmother. The fact that the deeds of Alice Perrers were well known, and her character displayed in the negative, while Katherine appears to be somewhat of a mystery to the *Brut* chroniclers, surely suggests that the lover of Gaunt was highly discreet, not involving herself at all in her suitor's political matters, or doing so in such a way that little was thought of it.

Other chronicles that are contemporary to the *Brut* strengthen this. Many do not mention Katherine or her relationship with Gaunt. *A Short English Chronicle* from the fifteenth century discusses Gaunt's politically important marriages to Blanche of Lancaster and Constance of Castile, but not his attachment to Katherine.[5] A similar lack of information is found in *The Chronicle of John Hardyng*. Hardyng was born in 1378 in the north of England. His initial career was as a soldier in the retinue of Sir Henry Percy (Hotspur), eldest son of the Earl of Northumberland. After the death of Hotspur, Hardyng joined the household of Sir Robert Umfraville and was constable first of Warkworth Castle and then of Kyme. He died here in 1465. Hardyng had another branch to his military career: he was a spy for Henry V, his mission being to uncover evidence that the English had the right of overlord of the Scots.

He started to write his chronicles in 1440 and presented them to Henry VI in 1457. He subsequently presented copies to Edward IV and Richard III but with revisions. His 'Yorkist' versions were missing a eulogy to Henry V. Instead, lines were inserted impugning Henry IV's right to the throne. The Yorkist chronicle also included hostility to John of Gaunt. Hardyng stated that Gaunt had forged a chronicle alleging that Henry III's second son, Edmund, was really his eldest child but was passed off as the second because he was a hunchback. If Edmund was the eldest, then the throne would have been Henry IV's by right through his mother, Blanche of Lancaster. Despite this hostility to Gaunt, Hardyng makes no reference to Katherine nor to her role in Gaunt's life. This is more remarkable when seen against the backdrop of Hardyng's political affiliations as a member of the Percy household. This family lost their lives in rebellion against the Lancastrian dynasty.[6] It would surely have been in Hardyng's interest to defame Gaunt's character through mention of his mistress if there had been any opportunity for scandalmongering on this subject. Equally, the Oxford academic Thomas Gascoigne did not hesitate in his criticisms of Gaunt, including one story alleging that Gaunt was ravaged by mortal disease as a direct result of his promiscuity! But there is no direct reference to Katherine, a remarkable omission.[7] Surely being able to name and shame the women with whom Gaunt had behaved so immorally would have added further spice to Gascoigne's text. Why did he not mention Katherine? Was he unaware of her presence?

The only hint of negativity towards Katherine's character in the fifteenth-century chronicles can be found in Capgrave. He writes that Gaunt married Katherine 'ageyn the opinion of many men'. John Capgrave, prior of the Augustrian friary at Lynn, wrote two major works. The first was *The Book of Illustrious Henries* written for Henry VI in 1446–7 and containing eulogies on any Henry who had a distinguished background. The second was *The Chronicle of England* dedicated to Edward IV. The two works had very different political outlooks. The first was pro-Lancastrian containing a eulogy on Henry IV. The second was pro-Yorkist, with Henry IV dismissed as a usurper. Capgrave appeared to have no strong political affiliation to either Lancastrians or Yorkists but wrote to please whoever was on the throne. His comment on Gaunt and Katherine's marriage suggests that it was inappropriate and therefore infers that Katherine's character and bearing were not suitable for the first lady of England, as she became on her marriage. At the very least, it suggests that the marriage caused a ripple in society. This demonstrates Capgrave's familiarity with the work of Froissart and his acceptance of the Hainauter's view of the court reaction to the wedding.[8] Froissart states that the Duchess of Gloucester, the Countesses of Derby and Arundel, and other great ladies descended from royal blood marvelled at how Gaunt had disgraced himself through this marriage. Capgrave himself, however, does not seem overly certain of the details of Gaunt and Katherine's relationship, as he states: 'of this woman cam many childrin, whech were aftir legittimat – so semeth it that thei were borne befor this marriage.'[9] This passage indicates that Capgrave knew only that the Beauforts were illegitimate because they underwent the legitimation ceremony. Was this just discretion on the part of the author? Katherine was not just connected to the Lancastrians through Gaunt; Edward IV was her greatgrandson!

Indeed, it can be said that the general decline in the quality and quantity of chronicles in the fifteenth century was due to the political situation. The changes in political climate led to a greater awareness of the need to tone down criticisms or animadversions against people in powerful positions.[10] This is one possible reason why information from this period on Katherine – with her unique position as both Lancastrian and Yorkist – is limited. Indeed, the only significant reference to Katherine made at this time was a statement made by one in a position of political power. Richard III discredited Henry Tudor's claim to the throne by issuing the following proclamation in 1485: 'for he [Henry] is descended of bastard blood both of the father's side and of the mother's side. For the said Owen the grandfather was bastard born, and his mother was daughter to John, Duke of Somerset, son of John, Earl of Somerset, son to Dame Katherine Swynford, and born of her in double adultery.'[11] This was obviously intended as a political slur against Henry Tudor, denying him royal blood. But it suggests that Richard believed people would not have been familiar with the background of the claimant to the throne. The lineage that Richard presents for Henry is correct. However, Richard is clearly trading off the assumption that the population at large would not recognise that he too shared this lineage. Richard was the son of Richard, third Duke of York, and Cecily Neville. Through his father he could trace a royal claim back to Edward III's third son, Lionel. But Cecily Neville was the daughter of Joan Beaufort, and therefore Richard shared this stain of bastardy with Henry Tudor. Richard also embellished the relationship of Katherine and Gaunt through the claim that both of them were married to other parties while bearing the child from which Henry was descended. However, the statement of 'double adultery' could be an error of translation. In the original fifteenth-century script the phrase is 'indouble avoutry', which could equally well be translated as indubitable, or undoubted, adultery.[12]

With the coming of the Tudors, Katherine's image, perhaps unsurprisingly, underwent a revival. Henry VII was anxious to promote his Lancastrian descendancy, as this formed the basis to his royal claim. This is evident through the development of the red rose as Lancastrian insignia. Before 1485 and the accession of Henry the red rose was the symbol of the Tudor family. However, after the rise of this family to the royal throne, its image was intensified to encapsulate Lancastrian loyalty.[13] And the chroniclers followed suit, emphasising the new king's Lancastrian descendancy. Francis Bacon, when enumerating the several claims of Henry, considered his right to the title of Lancaster as the most important.[14] Henry himself can clearly be seen to believe that the Crown was his birthright. The short Bill of Parliament passing Henry's claim declared:

> to the pleasure of Almighty God, the wealth, prosperity and surety of the realm, to the comfort of all the king's subjects and the avoidance of all ambiguities, be it ordained established and enacted by authority of the present parliament, that the inheritance of the crowns of the realms of England, France . . . be, rest, and remain and abide in the most royal person of our new Sovereign Lord king Henry the VIIth and in the heirs of his body lawfully comen perpetually . . .[15]

Indeed, the emphasis placed by Henry upon his Lancastrian heritage is most clearly demonstrated in the new epitaph that adorned John of Gaunt's tomb in St Paul's Cathedral during the first Tudor king's reign. The epitaph glorifies Gaunt, as one would expect, declaring proudly his many titles and riches, but it is the portrayal of Katherine that is most remarkable. She is described as:

> Tertiam vero uxorem duxit Catharinam, ex equestri familia, et eximia pulchretudine feminam; Ex qua numerosam suscepit prolem, uncle genus ex matre duxit Henricus Septimus Rex Anglie prudentissimus.[16]

> His third wife was Katherine, of a knightly family, and an exceptionally beautiful woman; they had numerous offspring, and from these came the maternal family of King Henry VII.

Katherine is here portrayed as an exceptional beauty, her lineage that of a knightly family. There is no indication that the Beauforts were born before the couple married nor while Gaunt was still married to Constance. Furthermore, the descendancy of Henry is proudly proclaimed, not just from Gaunt but explicitly linked to Katherine. The epitaph states that it was from her children that the maternal family of Henry VII was propagated.[17] From this publicly displayed arena Henry appears to have held no qualms about declaring his genesis from Katherine. Griffiths and Thomas have even suggested that Henry's daughter Katherine was named for her ancestress.[18] However, Henry may have believed that his royalty came from descent, but, despite this public declaration on Gaunt's tomb, Katherine is absent from the majority of the history from the Tudor period.

The most important of the Tudor chroniclers was Polydore Vergil. Born in Urbino, he came to England in 1502 with his patron Adriano de Castello of Corneto, who had been preferred to the see of Hereford. Castello became cardinal in 1503. Vergil enjoyed a favourable position – through Castello he obtained various preferments within the Church. He also acted as an ecclesiastical diplomat for the English court, but was out of favour in 1514 because of the ambitions of Wolsey. Vergil was imprisoned in the tower as a means of putting pressure on his friends in Rome. He was released when Wolsey became cardinal. After his release, Vergil lived quietly in England until his return to Urbino in 1553. He died in 1555.

It was as a result of a commission from Henry VII that Vergil wrote his history of England. He stated in his book that there was no adequate history of England; the medieval monastic chronicles were 'bald, uncouth, chaotic and deceitful'. Vergil stated his view of history and its recording as 'the only unique, certain and faithful witness of times and things, redounding as much to the glory of the author as to the useful of posterity'. But his purpose was to put a favourable interpretation on the rise of the Tudors and therefore, despite his anxiety to partake only of the truth, discretion was on occasion required. As he had already discovered at the hands of Wolsey, the political power of the Tudors demanded a circumspect approach to the history that he wrote. As a result, Vergil, in his descriptions of Henry Beaufort, states that he was son to Gaunt by his third wife, with no indication of Beaufort's illegitimacy or of Katherine and Gaunt's illicit affair.[19]

Instead, the myth was perpetuated that Henry was a gift from God to secure peace in England. This is the theme that the chroniclers adopted, and Katherine was not mentioned in any royal context. The Crowland Chronicler declared that 'Henry was praised by all as an angel sent from heaven, through whom God deigned to visit his people and free them from the evils which had so afflicted them'.[20] John Rous repeated this line that Henry came from God and proclaimed that, in accordance with an ancient prophecy, Henry would therefore be remembered with honour by future generations. This conflicts sharply with Rous's descriptions of Richard III, whom he portrays as a tyrant incited by the Anti-Christ.[21] Vergil elaborates upon the prophecy that Rous refers to. He states that Cadwallader, the last British king, proclaimed: 'Thie contrie shall fall into the hands of thine enemies, which thie progenie longe hereafter shall recover.'[22] But the Tudor kings Henry VII and Henry VIII commissioned Vergil's work. Therefore, to state that the Lancastrian line and the Tudor dynasty were of true royal value, not just from the Plantagenets but from ancient British kings, would certainly be the most pleasing line for this chronicler's patrons to read.

Robert Fabyan is the exception among the Tudor chroniclers. He too reflects the official line that Henry was the legitimate heir, blessed by God and the bringer of peace to England.[23] But his work also contains information on Katherine and her relationship with Gaunt. He notes how the Beauforts were base-born, and legitimised after their parents' wedding. Fabyan also displays his familiarity with the *Brut* as he, incorrectly, states that Katherine was made Countess of Hereford. This familiarity is perhaps to be expected. The *Brut* is connected closely to the London chronicles and Fabyan was a London man, an alderman, a member of the drapers' company and, in 1493, a Sheriff of London.[24] Uniquely, he also declares that the S in Gaunt's famous collar of esses stood for Swynford.[25] This is an extremely interesting assertion, as badges and insignia such as the collar were seen as intrinsic elements of identity and personality. However, it seems highly unlikely that Gaunt would have wished to celebrate the married name of his lover and equally unlikely that Katherine would have agreed to the step; her personal efforts were focused on producing an identity for herself that was firmly removed from her Swynford connections. Nevertheless, Fabyan's ponderings on this matter show that at least one chronicler was interested in the characters that surrounded the lineage of his king; he was known to be an ardent supporter of Henry VII. Moreover, given that he obviously obtained some of his information from the *Brut*, it can be safely asserted that he would have been familiar with other chronicles contemporary to Katherine's life and, therefore, aware of how she had been portrayed by others.[26] But he too continued the familiar Tudor line, describing Henry as a magnificent and excellent prince, and upholding the righteousness of the Tudor claim.

John Fisher described the myth that Henry was a gift from God in its fullest form in his tale of St Nicholas visiting Margaret Beaufort, mother of Henry Tudor and great-granddaughter of Katherine, with marital advice. Fisher does not refer directly to Katherine, but in his chapters on the many nobilities of Margaret he declares that the first came from the noble blood from which she was descended. He confirms that this noble blood was of Edward III, but also of John, Duke of Somerset, who was the grandson to Katherine.[27] However, Margaret was his patron, so a eulogy on her ancestors was perhaps to be expected. As the sixteenth century progressed, Katherine began to be included in the chronicles, but still no explicit connection to Henry VII was made. Edward Hall describes the lineage of 'the noble and haute' Henry from Gaunt in some detail, but without referral to Katherine or her character. She is mentioned only in 1403: 'In this year also died Lady Katherine Swinsford the third wife of John of Gaunt Duke of Lancaster'.[28] But, Hall does declare that Henry Beaufort was son to Gaunt by his third wife, so a Beaufort connection to Katherine is made in part.[28]

John Hayward includes similar detail in his chronicle. He writes that Henry VII is descended from Gaunt through the Earl and Duke of Somerset, but Katherine is again mentioned only as third wife of Gaunt when Hayward records her death.[30] However, what is noticeable in the texts of the sixteenth century is the favour granted to Gaunt. Hayward's portrayal of the Duke has Gaunt 'trying to act dutifully and honourably in difficult circumstances'.[31] Similarly, Shakespeare in *Richard II* makes Gaunt the play's voice of reason: 'one reason why Shakespeare apotheosised Gaunt in this way may have been his awareness (and that of his audience) that Gaunt was the progenitor of the Queen's paternal family, whereas she had no descent from the controversially rebellious Bolingbroke.'[32] The clear implication here is that it was well known that Gaunt's children had different mothers. However, direct mention of illegitimacy was obviously a delicate matter to be avoided at all costs. Thus it would seem that in the sixteenth century Katherine was just another wife or mother. No scandal was associated with her, but neither was she accredited with any character or worth. She was merely Duchess of Lancaster, wife of Gaunt, and it was up to the reader to connect her with the royal line.

The historians of the seventeenth century showed equal care in declaring Katherine as the wife of Gaunt, not his mistress, but were happier to link her directly to the royal line. The Stuart kings also owed their descendancy to Katherine. Joan, the daughter of John

Beaufort and granddaughter of Katherine, married James I of Scotland, a match that was negotiated by Joan's uncle Henry Beaufort, Bishop of Winchester. The marriage, however, would seem to have been a love match. James wrote Joan a poem in which he declared she was 'the fairest of the freshest budding flower that ever I saw'.[33] Perhaps, therefore, it is not surprising that John Weever, writing when Charles Stuart was on the throne, wrote of Katherine and her marriage to Gaunt in glowing terms. Weever describes how Katherine was daughter of Sir Paon Roet, king of arms for Guyenne, and continues:

> The abouefaid Katherine, eldeft daughter of this king of arms, was first married to Sir Otes Swynford knight, and after to John of Gaunt the great Duke of Lancaster; of whose issue by her is obserued to be descended a most royal and illustrious offspring; *videlicet*, eight Kings, foure Queenes, and fiue Princes of England; Six Kings, and three Queenes of Scotland; two Cardinals, aboue twenty Dukes, and almoot as many Dutches of the kingdome of England; diuers Dukes of Scotland, and most of all the now ancient Nobilitie of both those kingdoms, besides many other potent Princes, and eminent nobility of forraigne parts.[34]

Here Katherine is accredited with a royalty and respectability far beyond any previously granted her.

Also writing in the 1630s, Giovanni Francesco Biondi, gentleman of the privy chamber of Charles I, spoke of Katherine in unequivocally radiant terms. Biondi acknowledges that she had been Gaunt's concubine and that their children were illegitimate, but that Gaunt was wise to marry her, as she, although not nobly born, was of good condition. He continues that this marriage was fortuitous for England, enabling Henry VII to be king and, as a consequence, peace to reign in England. Biondi extends his praise to John Beaufort, whom he describes as a good scholar and 'perfectly wise'.[35] Later in the same century Thomas Speght connects Katherine with the wife of Geoffrey Chaucer, stating that she was sister to the 'gentle-woman' who became Chaucer's spouse.[36]

Katherine's familial links were again mentioned towards the end of the century by Richard Baker, who emphasised the royal descendancy from Katherine:

Henry Earl of Richmond, born in Pembroke Castle, Son to Edmund Earl of Richmond, by his Wife Margaret, sole daughter of John Duke of Somerset, which John was son of John Earl of Somerset, son of John of Gaunt Duke of Lancaster, by his third wife Katherine Swynford; and by this descent heir to the House of Lancaster.[37]

Thus the seventeenth century can be seen to have looked favourably upon Katherine. Writers of this period proclaimed her royalty; her position as mistress was either not mentioned at all or discussed as just a prelude to the fortuitous event of her marriage to Gaunt. Her character is displayed as one that was suitable, even desirable, for the medieval royal family to include within its ranks, and her descendants enabled peaceful times to be experienced in England.

But only a few decades later Katherine's reputation is portrayed in less glowing terms. M. Rapin de Thoyras declares that Katherine was Gaunt's mistress, and that her children were bastards. Thus Henry's claim to the throne was Lancastrian, 'but by a spurious branch', and, indeed, question arose over whether Richard II's legitimation of the Beauforts gave to Henry, 'derived from a bastard born in adultery, the right of succeeding to the crown'.[38] De Thoyras was obviously no supporter of Gaunt, declaring that 'the duke of lancafter was not beloved; he was charged with having abufed his power towards the latter end of the laft reign [Edward III's], and of having treated the fubjects with too great haughtinefs'. De Thoyras also asserts that even the Black Prince suspected that Gaunt had designs on the throne.[39]

A century later and this negative view of Katherine was gaining strength. Samuel Bentley deduced Gaunt's reasoning on marrying Katherine: 'As Lady Swynford was then upwards of forty, and had been the Duke's mistress above 20 years, it may be inferred, that gratitude and conscientious motives were his only inducements for making her his wife.'[40] A duke of the realm marrying his ageing concubine who was no doubt somewhat past her best was patently a dreadful business when measured against the conventions of nineteenth-century society. J.H. Wylie continues in the same vein as Bentley. He discusses Katherine in some biographical detail but asserts that it is only the success of the Beauforts that has allowed history to gloss over 'her deep dishonour'.[41] For Bentley it is the actions of Gaunt, and for Wylie the actions of Katherine's male children, that have 'saved' her reputation. No concession is made that perhaps she had a personal strength of character with the ability to control her own reputation; she was, after all, a mere woman, and, moreover, of somewhat 'loose' morals.

There was, however, some acknowledgement in these nineteenth-century texts that Katherine had a remarkable personality. Godwin, writing at the beginning of the century, declares that she must have been highly accomplished and that she was 'foremost in the possession of the confidence of the duchess [Blanche of Lancaster]'. But, despite these concessions, Godwin's view was that of the later authors. He includes this in his description of Katherine and Gaunt's marriage: 'John of Gaunt, whose mind was instinct with the domestic and social affections, had nothing now more nearly at heart, than the desire of making a respectable establishment, and providing in the most effectual manner, for this doubtful branch of his personal relations.' Godwin continues that, through the marriage to Katherine, Gaunt had 'thus paid homage he thought due to the woman to whom he had been so long attached'.[42]

These passages were of course written against a backdrop of the period, and, therefore, the style and tone of the texts are affected by the social conventions of the time of writing. However, it is astonishing to discover that these, somewhat quaint, views are also discernible throughout most of the following century. Radford, writing in the 1900s and therefore perhaps more of a nineteenth-century man than a twentieth-century one, continues the argument that it was as a reward for Katherine's faithfulness during their illicit connection that Gaunt married her and states that it was probably for the children 'that John braved the criticism and the resentment of the ladies at court'.[43]

It should be interjected here that there are some positives to be found in these declarations of Gaunt's honourable actions. The acknowledgement is made that Katherine's children, despite illegitimacy, are successful. And Katherine's 'faithfulness' was a remarkable feature of her character. Throughout her affair with Gaunt, despite not having the legal and religious blessing to wear the title, she can be credited with playing the role of the virtuous – and virtual – wife. Moreover, one scholar from this period of writing was a supporter of Katherine. Armitage-Smith, in his extensive biography of Gaunt, argues that 'the best answer to detractors who . . . attempted to class Katherine with adventuresses like Alice Perrers, is furnished by the new duchess of Lancaster herself'.[44] Furthermore, James Ramsay concurs that 'Katherine Swynford, no doubt, was a woman of superior manners and attainments, and capable of filling a good position in society'.[45] Unfortunately, this is tucked away in a footnote; the text itself criticises Gaunt for neglecting his wives in favour of Katherine.[46] Yet again, it would appear that the morals of a Victorian age filter through in the writings of the first part of the twentieth century. These are best summed up in the account of Philip Lindsay: 'When one considers the usual treatment of mistresses in those days Gaunt's act was a very noble one, and it brought much ridicule upon him. But he married for the children's sake.'[47]

Twentieth-century scholarship focused solely on Katherine rather than on her connections to Gaunt or the English court. R.E.G. Cole, whose 'Manor and Rectory of Kettlethorpe' was published in 1911, is a source of much useful information, especially in relation to the lives of the Swynfords and their landholdings in Lincolnshire.[48] An American scholar, Albert Stanburrough Cook, was also studying Katherine at this time. Cook's primary interest was the life of Geoffrey Chaucer, but, as with many Chaucerians since, his work expanded to include Katherine. His studies include much biographical detail of the lives of the Beauforts, discussing in detail the birth dates of these children of Gaunt and Katherine. Cook is the only academic to argue that the birth dates of the Beauforts must be considerably earlier than otherwise acknowledged. It is from his work that much is known about the background of Katherine's paternal Roet family.

Interest in Katherine continued into the 1920s, with correspondents in the *Times Literary Supplement* discussing her life, again in the context of her familial connections to Chaucer. It is the middle of the century, however, before the discourse on Katherine is again extensive. And it is from this period of time that there is a distinct downturn in the portrayals of her character. Works from previous centuries can be judged against their social and political background, and works of the early twentieth century show significant attempts at serious scholarship. But the 1950s witnessed the stereotyping of Katherine to an extreme. This is most evident in Anya Seton's novel about Katherine, first published in that decade. Seton states in her preface that she was anxious to ground her novel in historical fact, and indeed evidence of historical research is present. In many parts of her book there is some deal of accuracy in her portrayals of the past. However, the purpose of Seton's book was entertainment. It was intended to be a historical romance. And romance is certainly what occurs in the story. Katherine is beautiful, meek, virtuous, loyal and extremely religious. Gaunt is masterful, brave and proud, yet sensitive and loving. They both play their parts as romantic heroes extremely well.

But this romantic view of Katherine distorts the truth as much as any animadversions against her. It would be hard for any real person to be the perfect heroine that Seton illustrates through her tale. The book is intended as entertainment, and as such it is well written and enjoyable, and has certainly attracted much support. It has introduced Katherine as a strong and positive character to many people who would otherwise not have been aware of her existence. But there is much fiction present, and this, astonishingly, has appeared as history in other quarters. For example, Alison Weir describes Katherine and her life directly from the novel, including information that I have found only in Seton's fictional embellishments: 'Priests delivered sermons on her vices and the common people spat at her when she appeared in public.'[49]

Seton herself first discovered Katherine in the work of a Chaucerian, Marchette Chute, and it was in her study of Geoffrey Chaucer that she found the inspiration for her romantic tale.[50] Chute states that Katherine was the one great love of Gaunt's life, and that he was unfalteringly devoted to his mistress.[51] In the same period, Katherine was attracting attention from more Chaucerian scholars, most notably Margaret Galway, John Manly and George Williams.[52] Galway has researched Katherine's biography as part of her extensive quest to discover more about Chaucer's life and family. Similarly, Manly discusses Katherine where her life crosses that of the English poet. Williams, however, argues that Katherine exerted a larger influence on Chaucer than that of mere sister-in-law, suggesting that Gaunt and Katherine were the inspiration for a number of Chaucer's characters. He also suggests that Katherine is portrayed on the frontispiece of the Corpus Christi manuscript of *Troilus and Criseyde*. Williams discusses the Victorian image of Gaunt, stating that, to the Victorian mind, his affair with Katherine 'placed Gaunt outside the pale of decency', whereas to Chaucer and his contemporaries Gaunt would have appeared 'no worse than others in sexual behaviour, and better than most'.[53]

However, not all viewed the subject in the same way as Williams. The legacy of Victorian attitudes can be witnessed in the works of the second half of the twentieth century. McFarlane condescendingly declares of Gaunt and Katherine's liaison: 'The family life of the house of Lancaster must have been somewhat free and easy. It is perhaps not surprising that one of Bolingbroke's sisters, Elizabeth, went to the bad.'[54] Chrimes goes even further. Gaunt found Katherine 'in less distinguished quarters', and to make a women of her standing his wife was no light matter.[55] Rosenthal asserts that the fact 'that old John of Gaunt decided to marry his mistress of many years, Katherine Swynford, can perhaps be considered as the pleasant sentimentality of the elderly'.[56] The morals and beliefs of these scholars pervade their viewpoint, as did the beliefs of their earlier counterparts in the first decades of the twentieth century.

The last decades of the century provide some respite from a stereotypical view. Given-Wilson and Curteis discuss Katherine in some detail, providing biographical information with some analysis, and they acknowledge that Katherine's presence was perhaps not as scandalous as some would have us believe.[57] Anthony Goodman also attempts an analysis of Katherine, and indeed is the only historian to have produced any work solely on her. Both in his discussions of Katherine in his biography on Gaunt, and in the pamphlet that focuses on Katherine alone, Goodman attempts to see beyond the negative depictions of her.[58] He addresses issues of her education, her abilities and her status in society. But, despite acknowledging that Katherine's character was probably better than that of just ducal seducer, on the whole the work is based on documentary, biographical details. Little is uncovered of her personality.

Anil de Silva-Vigier discusses the character of Katherine in her work on John of Gaunt. She describes her as 'one of those fortunate women whose beauty was both physical and spiritual, a quality which she appears to have retained throughout her life'.[59] She also attempts a critique of Thomas Walsingham's negativity, saying of the reported public tour of 1378 described in the chronicler's work that 'perhaps we have here the usual exaggeration which was woven round the small incidents in his [Gaunt's] life'.[60] However, de Silva-Vigier's work is permeated with an extremely romantic view of both the couple and Katherine as an individual that leads to much of her findings having a somewhat unconvincing air. She reads the account in the *Anonimalle* of Katherine as 'une deblesce et enchantresce' as a compliment: 'it only confirms our suspicion that she was a fascinating woman.' The author of the *Anonimalle*, however, would surely have meant 'a she-devil and enchantress' as a derogatory term! Moreover, de Silva-Vigier reports speculative detail as fact: 'At first Katherine had insisted on absolute discretion because she certainly would not want to humiliate her husband; after his death, not knowing how John's marriage to Constanza would turn out, and before all her Beaufort children were born, she did not want to be openly humiliated either.'[61] It is impossible to know Katherine's personal views on the relationship and what efforts she took to conceal it.

It can be clearly seen that the historiography of Katherine Swynford is limited. Numerous references are made to her as mistress or wife of Gaunt or as mother of the Beauforts. But very little information on her character is to be found. And no scholar has discussed how Katherine was viewed by her contemporaries beyond a quotation from Froissart. Yes, the contemporary records are in themselves scarce, but information on Katherine is available, not just in these records but also in the histories of fourteenth-century court culture. It was against this background that Katherine was raised and lived as an adult; therefore a study of the lifestyles of the nobility of this time will provide information on Katherine's lifestyle. In addition, I believe that a rereading of the fourteenth-century chronicles will reveal more of Katherine and her personality than just a negative portrayal of her as a harlot.

CHAPTER 3

Contemporary Opinion

Condemnation then grew for his wicked and disgraceful behaviour, especially because he himself put aside respect for God's dread, deserted his military duties, rode around the country with the abominable temptress, seen as Katherine once called Swynford, holding her bridle in front of his own people, not only in the presence of his wife, but even with all his retainers looking on, in the most honoured towns in the kingdom. He made himself abominable in the eyes of God; and all people of the kingdom together, all feared divine vengeance on the whole kingdom to be near. Every inhabitant of the whole of the kingdom despaired that they would be able to resist enemies under such a duke.[1]

Thomas Walsingham (*c.* 1340–*c.* 1422) was a monk of the abbey of St Albans for most of his adult life; the records list him as a member of the abbey when he was ordained priest on 21 September 1364. His family background is unknown, but, given the expense of entering an abbey such as St Albans, his people must have been of some standing. He may have studied at Oxford – Abbot Thomas de la Mare encouraged a number of St Albans monks in this pursuit. De la Mare is also known to have encouraged Walsingham in his chronicle writing, and the resulting chronicle is one of the major contemporary sources for the fourteenth century. Walsingham started to write his contemporary history, the *Chronica Maiora*, from around 1380. It extended to 1420 and included a retrospective section from 1272 as a continuation of the work of the thirteenth-century St Albans chronicler Matthew Paris.[2]

Walsingham's earliest mention of Katherine is in the passage quoted above. In it he refers to a public tour made by Katherine and John of Gaunt in 1378, but he is notably the only contemporary chronicler to describe this occasion. Walsingham's opinion of Katherine and her relationship with Gaunt is made explicit throughout the piece. Katherine is denounced as an 'abominable temptress', and Gaunt's blatant showcasing of his mistress in front of not only his wife, but also his retainers and the wider public, can only bring God's vengeance to the kingdom.

Although this was the first appearance of Katherine in Walsingham's text, he had previously condemned John of Gaunt for his immorality and the repercussions that this would have on the land and its people:

O unlucky and piteous duke, who by your treachery and folly betray those you are leading to war, and are by devious means enticing and conducting to their destruction those whom you should be leading in the ways of peace by the example of your good works! Then, although God, or Nature, the mother of all things, as it were, has given you a soul and discretion, and nothing is superior to these, you nevertheless so dishonour and degrade yourself as to make one think that there is no difference at all between you and the beasts. Most wretched of men, who think you are prosperous, and believe you are blessed, look how your troubles oppress you, and your lusts torture you, for you are never satisfied with what you have and are fearful that even that will not last long. You are pricked in your conscience by the things you have done wrong: If only you were as frightened of the law and the courts as other people are! Perhaps then you would amend your ways, albeit unwillingly.[3]

This diatribe refers to Gaunt's actions in 1376, and it is odd that Katherine is not mentioned by name here – Walsingham would not willingly have missed the opportunity to berate Gaunt. Indeed, the passage that precedes this tirade lists the Duke's lavish promiscuity in some detail:

Although he was willing to stir up hostilities against his enemies, he did not dare to do what would appear to be foolish and unscrupulous, despite the fact that he was without conscience and his character dishonoured by every kind of outrage and sin. Indeed, a fornicator and adulterer, he had abandoned lawful wedlock and deceived both his first wife who was the daughter of our most noble lord Henry, the first duke of Lancaster, and [his second] the daughter of Pedro, king of Spain. He not only dared to do such things secretly and privately, but also took the most shameless prostitutes to the beds of these wives, who, grief-stricken as they were, did not dare to protest.[4]

Walsingham wrote about the events of 1376 with hindsight, as it is generally believed that he did not start to write his chronicle until 1380. Why did he mention Katherine by name in the passage referring to 1378 but not in the one referring to 1376? He knew of her presence when writing the earlier passage. Castigating Gaunt for his relationship with Katherine, however, would not have had the impact of the scene that Walsingham chose to depict – that of multiple adulterous relationships with prostitutes. His aim here was clearly to denounce Gaunt, not Katherine. It perhaps also suggests that Katherine's reputation was such that a castigation of her in this way would not ring true to the contemporary readers of his work.

It is well recognised that the force of Walsingham's condemnation in his early work was directed at Gaunt: 'Walsingham, who started to write history *c.* 1380, vilified Gaunt in his original account of events from 1376 to 1381 as immoral, unscrupulous, anti-clerical, consumed by pride and ambition.'[5] Many examples of this can be found in Walsingham's text, including allegations of plots against the throne and the suggestion that Gaunt was not of royal birth:

Standing alongside his colleagues he began to speak as follows before the nobles, the greatest of all was John duke of Lancaster, a man whose deeds always belied his name, for he ever lacked the divine grace, it is believed, as well as human grace.[6]

He further requested that, following the example of the French, they should pass a law forbidding a woman to succeed. He reflected upon the age of the king [Edward III], whose death was close, and the youth of the son of the prince, whom, it was alleged, he contemplated poisoning if he could not himself attain the throne any other way: if these two were removed from the scene and a law such as he had requested were passed in parliament, he would himself be next in succession to the throne.[7]

The cause of all this ill will was the bishop's [of Winchester, William Wykeham] remark that the duke was not the son of the king or queen, but that during her pregnancy at Ghent she had given birth not to a son but a daughter, but the queen had concealed this. Fearing the king's anger, the queen had ordered the baby boy belonging to a Flemish woman to be substituted for her baby girl. She had accordingly nursed a baby she had not given birth to, and this became the man called John of Gaunt, the duke of Lancaster. All these facts, the bishop said, she had revealed to him upon her deathbed under the seal of confession. But she had begged him most insistently that if the time should come when he sought the throne, or that the throne passed to him for any reason, the bishop should reveal the facts of his descent so that he should not inherit the throne of England as a false heir.[8]

On the face of it, it is hard to justify Walsingham's attacks on Gaunt; Gaunt was, after all, a considerable patron of St Albans Abbey, the place where Walsingham lived. He frequently granted gifts of wine and money to the abbey church and assisted in matters of business.[9] Any propaganda or bias in monastic chronicles was generally in favour of the monastery. Therefore, surely Gaunt's attentions to St Albans should have secured him a somewhat more respectful place in its recordings? However, it would appear that not all Gaunt's actions were favourable to the abbey. The Duke took thirty oak trees from one of the abbot's estates for work on his castle at Hertford – the Abbot's response was that he would have paid £30 to save them. Moreover, Walsingham was friends with Sir John

Philpot, Mayor of London in 1378–9. Philpot defended the liberties of London against Gaunt in 1377 and was instrumental in the subsequent reconciliation between the King and the Londoners.[10] It would seem that Walsingham and Gaunt held opposing political beliefs, which provided a reason for the chronicler's animadversions against the Duke.

But it was not just politics that affected Walsingham's writing. The passage referring to the events of 1376 is just one example of how the tradition of preaching can be seen to have influenced Walsingham's literary style: 'he writes tirades against the moral failings of great men, with frequent animadversions on the sins of pride, avarice and adultery.'[11] Walsingham's monastic background is evident here, with the clerical commonplace that God rewards the good and punishes the bad emphasised throughout his work and clearly visible in the passages under discussion. In both respects the sins of Gaunt will rebound on the country, the behaviour of the leader affecting wider failures for his subjects. Walsingham had great faith in the natural hierarchy of society and believed that the stability of society therefore rested on the good conduct of leaders. This belief, coupled with his clerical mores, led Walsingham to condemn illicit sex in the lives of political leaders. Such condemnation was not just reserved for Gaunt but can be witnessed in Walsingham's discussions of Edward III and Richard II's confidant Robert de Vere.[12] The presence of Katherine in Gaunt's life provided further fuel for the monk's abuse. The depiction of the 1378 tour is graphic. Walsingham portrays a public exhibition by the couple. Gaunt's hand is described as openly resting on Katherine's bridle, and the insulting reference to Katherine's surname, 'Katherine once called Swynford', leaves no doubt as to the nature of their relationship and to Walsingham's view of it as entirely inappropriate. The affair is flaunted, not only, shamefully enough, in front of Gaunt's wife, but, worse still, or so Walsingham infers, in front of the country, including those in the retinue, and therefore under the direct influence of, the Duke.

But can Walsingham's real agenda be seen to be the condemnation of Katherine and her relationship? Was not the main intent of the passage to highlight Gaunt's neglect of his duties and his perceived inability to lead his men, and his country, in a correct manner rather than to castigate the nature or character of Katherine herself? Indeed, does this passage contain any information on Katherine? The depiction of her as temptress merely emphasises the well-known clerical standard of woman as Eve, the seducer of men. The passage tells nothing of Katherine's behaviour or self; she is merely a player in a wider narrative. These narratives of 1376 and 1378 emphasise Gaunt's military errors: Katherine's role is to highlight the moral failings that demonstrated Gaunt's unsuitability for, and his dereliction of, his duties in France. Walsingham supported the French war, and a recurring theme in his work was the condemnation of weak government and poor campaigning that left the English defenceless.[13] Against this, Katherine becomes the universal woman whom Walsingham, as a cleric, knew to be the enemy of sense, reason and authority, the enemy of the usual strength of men.

Walsingham's literary background is well known to us, and his library at St Albans contained many texts that are familiar to us now as providing a misogynistic tradition from which the medieval clergy could draw their knowledge of woman. As Christiane Klapisch-Zuber states: 'Much of our evidence about medieval women derives from the fantasies, certainties, and doubts of the clergy . . . Since much of their knowledge came from books, their portraits were caricatures more than true likenesses.'[14] Certainly, the portrait of Katherine in Walsingham's work can be read as a caricature. She plays the role of the temptress, the beguiling woman who uses her many dubious charms to persuade the man from his logical, reasoned path. Within this reading the relationship of Katherine to that of the ultimate seducer Eve is manifest. Walsingham is not describing the direct personal action or behaviour of Katherine but is saying 'here is yet another woman responsible for the downfall of men'.

Walsingham did not have biblical references alone to support his belief of the power of females. Classical works had long formed an image of woman as a creature to be wary of, and, of course, the increasing emphasis on clerical celibacy arising from the Gregorian reforms of the eleventh century resulted in many texts warning of the evils of the opposite sex. And it is clear from these texts that women were viewed not as the opposite sex but as the inferior sex: 'The fact remains that in the Middle Ages women were largely identified with the unofficial culture, with temptation to sin, distraction of the ongoing masculine intellect, disorderliness.'[15] If women were the unofficial culture, the Church and its beliefs were the official. Examples of the texts that were circulating at the time, and of those that they influenced in later centuries, emphasised clearly the nature of womanhood as viewed by the clergy:

> Countless are the traps which the scheming enemy has laid throughout the world's paths and plains: but the greatest of all – and the one from which no one can escape – is woman. Woman, the unhappy source, evil root, and corrupt offshoot, who brings to birth every sort of outrage throughout the world. She starts arguments, conflicts, terrible disagreements; she instigates fighting between two old friends. But this is nothing: she unseats kings and princes from the throne, makes nations clash, convulses towns, destroys cities, multiplies slaughters, brews deadly poisons. She hurls conflagration as she rampages through farms and fields. To sum up, there is no kind of evil lurking in the universe, in which woman does not claim some part for herself . . . Armed with these vices, woman subverts the world . . . spreading honey on her sword to transfix the hearts of the wise.[16]

> What else is a woman but a foe to friendship, an inescapable punishment, a necessary evil, a natural temptation, a desirable calamity, a domestic damage, a delectable detriment, an evil of nature.[17]

The latter extract suggests a conflict in the view of woman. She is both natural, desirable, delectable, and evil, a punishment, a danger. This depiction of pleasing temptation hiding inner evil was a method used frequently to impose ecclesiastical celibacy. Woman was associated with the material not the spiritual on the authority of Aristotle, in whose works men were portrayed as morally and intellectually superior and women as purely physical creatures. Medieval authors reproduced this view. Of course, it is possible with this theory to argue that men were then the culpable party – if theirs was the stronger reason, then surely their fall was all the greater for succumbing to the guiles of the inferior intellect?

Perhaps some of this can be read in Walsingham; he certainly sees Gaunt as weak for allowing Katherine to have a hold over him greater than that of his military duties. But it was Woman whom the Church viewed as guilty, and Woman's greatest sin was centred on sexuality, hence the necessary separation of the clergy from them. The irony, therefore, is that the clergy moralised about women and their dangers yet lived removed from this half of society, their actual knowledge of women non-existent. But, 'because anti-female statements were found in authoritative texts they were thought to represent the truth, especially when they were used in parallel with biblical quotations concerning women'.[18]

Can the reader of these medieval clerics, therefore, have any faith in the truth of their depictions of women? Walsingham was removed from the society of women, had never spent any time with Katherine, and most probably did not witness for himself the purported tour of the couple through the countryside. As librarian of his abbey and reader of many of the classical and patristic works that condemn the seemingly many faults of women, can Walsingham be seen as reporting Katherine's nature and character? Indeed, the very emphasis of Gaunt holding the bridle of Katherine's horse may not have been just to highlight the unseemly intimacy between the two but may have held a deeper meaning for medieval readers. In medieval iconography a horse could represent woman or flesh,[19] and therefore Gaunt holding the bridle may have been a more vulgar reference to his relationship with Katherine than the mere literal meaning immediately implies.

In addition to this, the question remains how true Walsingham's description of the event was. Walsingham places the tour at the time Gaunt was indeed delayed from his French campaign. But this delay was due to naval problems, not to the luxury of immoral public adventures with his mistress.[20] Walsingham represents the tour as being explicitly public, yet no other extant chronicle records it. Either it did not happen, with Walsingham inventing it for the numerous reasons outlined above, or it was not public enough to draw the attention of other writers, or only Walsingham was sufficiently outraged at the event. Whichever of these three speculations is correct, the conclusion is the same: at this time Katherine was not deemed an important issue in herself. Her behaviour drew the venom of Walsingham only as far as she suited both his clerical, moral purpose and his political agenda towards the French wars. It is clear that Walsingham's attacks on Katherine were not because of her personality, or of anything she had done that was witnessed by Walsingham, but because her presence provided him with yet another means of condemning the Duke of Lancaster, whom he saw as failing the country in the French campaigns. Goodman has argued that 'it is likely that Gaunt's adultery in the late 1370s had a negative effect on his political standing'.[21] However, it is my belief that Gaunt's political standing had a negative effect on how his adultery was both perceived and tolerated and therefore on how it was ultimately portrayed in the contemporary records. Arguably Walsingham criticised the adulterous relationship not because he believed it really affected Gaunt's political decisions but because the affair added weight to the negative opinions Walsingham already held and expounded about Gaunt and his politics. Indeed, Walsingham's text can be seen as an example of the increasing use of sexual slurs as a tool of political propaganda. Of course, the basic belief in official Church doctrine was that all sexual relations, whether within marriage or without, were unclean, though in general lay attitudes were more tolerant, and royal mistresses were not seen as an unusual, or disconcerting, occurrence by the majority. Therefore, it is perhaps something of a triumph for the official mores of the Church that increasingly slanders revolving around sexual impropriety were used to discredit political opponents in the late fourteenth and fifteenth centuries.[22]

It was not only events of the 1370s that drew Walsingham's interest. Further evidence of Walsingham's use of Katherine as a literary standard and an example of clerical discourse on the horrors of women can be found within his text on Gaunt's reaction to the 1381 Peasants' Revolt:

> And, it is written, 'when you understand what you hear, it will cause you distress,' so then for the first time the duke turned to religion, and began to revile his former way of life not only by private confession but by acts of public confession: one moment he was ascribing the causes of the misfortunes which had befallen him to his sins, at another he blamed himself for the deaths, not only of the nobility, but also of others who at that time had been laid low by impious violence; at yet another moment he reproached himself for his liaison with Katherine Swynford, or rather renounced it. So by his tears and his expressions of grief he seemed to produce the fruits of true repentance; by these devices, so he believed, he placated the Lord's anger.[23]

Again Katherine is clearly assigned the role of temptress, but on this occasion she was not successful. Gaunt's masculine, and therefore greater, reason is turning from her and converting to a moral, religious path. The sins of his former life are deemed responsible for the horrors of the revolt that had just occurred, and Katherine, symbolic of this past evil life, is cast off, a decision that appeased the Lord's anger. Gaunt was in Scotland at the time of the peasants' revolt; news of it was carried to him by messenger. The horror of hearing of the looting and burning of the Savoy, John of Gaunt's great London palace, and the fleeing of Constance and her ladies to the north, where they were refused entrance to his own castles, had obviously shocked the Duke into reason, or so Walsingham would have us believe. Walsingham states that this conversion to a more religious and honourable path was announced with both public and private confession, and it could be argued that this was the case. John of Gaunt's register includes a recording for February 1382 of a 'quitclaim', a lengthy and legally couched document that released Katherine, addressed as the former governess of Philippa and Elizabeth, and any of her future heirs, from having any claim on Gaunt or his heirs, or of him on her.[24] This officially documented split, as it would appear to be, was clearly widely known, as two other chroniclers, Henry Knighton and the author of the *Anonimalle Chronicle*, include details of the parting in their discussions of the aftermath of the Revolt.[25]

However, evidence from the 1380s contradicts this parting, and it would appear that Katherine continued to be firmly attached to the Lancaster family unit.[26] It therefore seems that this parting was an official ploy only. Indeed, after the 1381 revolt it was politically expedient for Gaunt to concentrate on his Castilian ambitions channelled through his wife, the Castilian Queen Constance, and it is tempting to speculate that the parting was an example of medieval 'spin', and the quitclaim was leaked to the 'tabloid press' of Walsingham and his fellow chroniclers as a means of controlled political propaganda. Constance suffered greatly during the revolt, fleeing north to the safety of Gaunt's castle at Pontefract only to be refused entry by the constable there. She would surely have been deeply offended by the insult to her rank and frightened on her journey to escape the rebels. As Gaunt would not wish to upset this politically important figure, key to his valued role of King of Castile, what better way to appease her than through a shifting of allegiance, if only in the public eye, from his mistress to his desire to secure the Castilian throne. Walsingham can certainly be seen to have regarded Constance as a victim of the Duke, and therefore can only have accepted such actions positively. Indeed, the chroniclers in general took the bait of the quitclaim as intended. In Walsingham, Knighton and the *Anonimalle Chronicle* the denouncement of Katherine by Gaunt is portrayed as evidence of a positive change in Gaunt's political and moral character. This positive change in Gaunt continues throughout Walsingham's work post-1381, with the monk's attitude becoming decidedly neutral compared to the venom of previous years:

At first he had suffered misfortune in Spain, but in the end he enjoyed great success, not because of the strength of his forces, or in the number of his fighting men, but because of the conspicuous support of God.[27]

With his customary good sense, the duke persuaded the people of Lancaster to accept the peace.[28]

Henry Knighton (d. *c.* 1396), canon of the abbey of St Mary of the Meadows, Leicester, was the kindest of the chroniclers in his attitude towards Gaunt, and throughout his chronicle the author is explicitly pro-Lancastrian. But, then, the patrons of St Mary's abbey were the Dukes of Lancaster and the Earls of Leicester: 'thus Knighton's bias in favour of and interest in the house of Lancaster were mainly the result of his loyalty to St Mary's abbey and to the town of Leicester.'[29] Along with Walsingham's, Knighton's chronicle is the only monastic chronicle of the fourteenth century whose author is known. Very little, however, is known of his life beyond his title and home. His chronicle extends from the tenth century to his death, and it seems most likely that he started to write the history of his own lifetime in about 1390.[30]

On describing Gaunt's reaction to news sent to him in Scotland of the revolt in the south, Knighton declares that the Duke was

not moved by anger, because he had betrayed no one, not struck by frenzy, because he was conscious of no fault, but as he showed himself in all actions, that is to say good and gentle, he heard the tidings with a cheerful countenance, as though he were unmoved by them, and kept them to himself.[31]

A few months later, after his duties in Scotland were complete and he could reflect on the Revolt, Knighton again describes the actions of the Duke:

Amongst other matters one which he [Gaunt] often turned in his mind was that he frequently had heard, both from churchmen and from members of his own household, that his reputation was greatly tarnished in all parts of the realm, and that he had paid no attention to what was said to him because he was blinded by desire, fearing neither God, nor shame amongst men. For in his wife's household there was a certain foreign lady, Katherine Swynford, whose relations with him were greatly suspect. And considering those things, and inspired by the Grace of God, he turned about and, committing himself wholly to the divine mercy, and promising that he would reform his life, he vowed to God that he would, as soon as he was able, remove that lady from his household, so that there could be no further offence. And when he returned to his own estates he at once took occasion to send her away, so that she should no longer dwell with him.[32]

As with Walsingham, Knighton describes the parting from Katherine as being to the benefit of Gaunt and his religious and moral conduct. But, again, any information on Katherine's character or bearing is absent. She is, once more, merely the universal woman whom clerics know will deceive and seduce men, and here she has caused Gaunt to forsake his usual strong male reason, as he was 'blinded by desire'. Knighton does concede that Katherine is not the only cause of Gaunt's sullied reputation: she is one 'amongst other matters'. But she becomes symbolic of all faults, and Knighton even alludes to the quitclaim that provided these chroniclers with the confirmation of parting. Knighton describes Gaunt's vow to distance himself from Katherine as an immediate decision in the aftermath of the Peasants' Revolt, but the actual parting would be 'as soon as he was able' when he had returned to his estates and therefore had the opportunity to formalise the split with documentation. This would fit with the later date of the quitclaim. Katherine, or rather Gaunt's renunciation of her, is key to Knighton's vindication of the Duke after the revolt, and allows his pro-Lancastrian praise to remain intact:

For he [Gaunt] had many who were jealous of him, and were his enemies, both rich and poor, who would rather speak evil of him than good, thinking evil of him, and mediating injustice towards him when he had not observed it of them. Yet God always sustained him, and turned his enemies' deceits to his advantage, and at all times repressed their malice, and delivered him from their hands.[33]

It was not just Knighton who conceded that Katherine was not Gaunt's only sin; Walsingham implied as much also. Knighton's 'other matters' related to the far bigger issue of Gaunt's patronage of John Wyclif and his consequent support of Lollard beliefs. The Church viewed Wyclif and his Lollard followers as heretics. The Lollards wished to translate the Bible into English, denied the authority of the Pope, and believed that saints and relics had no powers of intercession and should not be prayed to and worshipped. A Lollard tract provides evidence that Gaunt had advocated the reading of the Gospels in English and Gaunt summoned Wyclif as his counsel against the bishops.[34] This would have been wholly unacceptable to men so firmly embedded within the Church as Walsingham and Knighton. Indeed, Knighton even cited William of St Amour, a thirteenth-century theologian who included changes made in the text of the Gospels among the signs that would portend the end of the world.[35] Obviously Gaunt's support of such heresy was an important matter. But, again, for Knighton, this was not the fault of Gaunt. He stated that the Duke was deceived in this matter as well, believing the Lollards to be 'God's saints, because of their bland words and expressions'.[36] Moreover, Gaunt's innate goodness – Knighton frequently referred to him as the pious duke – protected the heretics: 'He [Wyclif] had the notable support of the good duke of Lancaster, who was an invincible guardian to him and his followers in all their needs, for otherwise they would have fallen into the pit of destruction.'[37] God never neglected Gaunt despite his failings, and this divine support led the Duke to recognise the deception of both Katherine and Wyclif.

Walsingham, in contrast to Knighton, included reference to many unsavoury rumours in his text that served to condemn Gaunt. The chronicler stated that Gaunt poisoned the sister and co-heir of Blanche of Lancaster, his first wife, to claim the full Lancastrian inheritance, as well as claiming that Gaunt sought to poison Richard II, and, if this was to prove unsuccessful, plotted to have the King declared illegitimate.[38]

The sin of Gaunt that provoked Walsingham to circulate gossip of this nature was the Duke's support of Wyclif's attacks on the Church:

> In the mean time the duke, so it is said, did not cease plotting with his accomplices ways of enslaving the Church and of subjugating the kingdom to himself by some means or other. He hoped to bring to fruition with greater freedom and licence a plan he had long been mulling over in his mind. But he was aware that while the position of the Church remained strong it would be very difficult for him to achieve his designs, and that it would be very dangerous to venture publicly upon the actions he had contemplated while the power and customary rights of London remained intact. He therefore went to great pains especially to overturn the liberties of both the Church and the city. He therefore recruited the services of a false theologian, or, to describe him better, a true adversary of God.[39]

In the chronicler's depiction of the aftermath of the 1381 revolt Gaunt weeps and sobs violently because of the evil that had previously seized him and therefore becomes worthy of the fruits of penitence.[40] This level of contrition was surely depicted by Walsingham as a suitable apologia by Gaunt for his direct sins against God's word rather than his inability to control his worldly sexual lusts. The emphasis of the passage is the Duke's conversion to religion, the implication being that previous behaviour was heretical.[41] Whereas his relationship with Katherine could be described as immoral in the eyes of the Church at the time, condemnations of heretical behaviour would have been reserved for his patronage of Wyclif. The sin of the mind and reason that Gaunt displayed in his support of Wyclif was far greater than the

71

sin of the flesh that he committed in his illicit relationship with Katherine. Walsingham manifestly portrays this distinction elsewhere, stating in relation to 1376: 'O unlucky and piteous duke, who by your treachery and folly betray those you are leading to war, and are by devious means enticing and conducting to their destruction those whom you should be leading in the ways of peace by the example of your good works!'[42] Surely this is a discernible reference to the Duke's public support of Wyclif and his tolerance of Lollard beliefs among his retinue. Indeed, Walsingham has been described as seeing 'Lancaster playing Beelzebub to Wyclif's Lucifer'.[43] Walsingham called Wyclif 'the mouthpiece of the devil, the enemy of the church, the confuser of commonfolk, the idol of heretics, the mirror of hypocrisy, the incitor of schism, the sower of hatred, and the inventor of lies'.[44] This has still greater meaning when Walsingham's attitude to Gaunt changes post-1381 to a more positive view. Although this could be seen as a reaction to Gaunt's supposed repudiation of Katherine with the 1381 quitclaim and therefore the removal of immorality from Gaunt's life, surely Walsingham would have soon been aware that the couple were still in close contact during the 1380s. However, Gaunt's support of Lollardy was publicly abandoned in the months following the 1381 revolt. This would fit perfectly with Walsingham's declaration that Gaunt had undergone religious conversion.

Walsingham's references to Katherine can therefore clearly be seen to be heavily influenced by his assessment of Gaunt on both a political and a religious basis. Walsingham's monastic background is made manifest throughout his text as he displays for his readers the innate immorality of both women and poor leaders, both, of course, being the perceived faults of Gaunt. Throughout his work no discernible or accurate reference to Katherine's actual character or countenance is present, presumably because it was irrelevant to Walsingham's purpose – the depiction of her as one of Eve's sisters was enough for his intent of castigating Gaunt. In the work of Henry Knighton the monastic influence is also clearly present, but in this pro-Lancastrian work Katherine has a slightly different role. She is still Eve, capable of deceiving the Duke with her feminine beauty and guile, but here she plays a symbolic role as the source of Gaunt's sins. Again no direct commentary on the actions of Katherine herself can be detected in this monk's work.

The reference to a parting by the couple in 1381 appears in another contemporary chronicle. But its recording in the *Anonimalle Chronicle* is expanded upon and embellished by the author beyond Walsingham's and Knighton's depiction. Again the chronicler illustrates Gaunt's reasoning for the spilt:

> he supposed that God wished to chastise him for the misdeeds and the evil life which he had for long led, namely in the sin of lechery, in which he had particularly associated with dame Katherine Swynford, a she-devil and enchantress, and with many others in his wife's household, against the will of God and the law of holy church.[45]

Katherine is again seen as temptress, and she forms the now familiar stereotype of the clerical view of base and lewd woman. But, significantly, the *Anonimalle* credits Gaunt with a sexual appetite that Katherine alone could not satisfy, portraying the Duke as having affairs with many women, implying that the relationship with Katherine was not in itself enough to present Gaunt as leading a sufficiently evil life for the author's purposes. The reality needed additional spice to be truly shocking – Gaunt's sin had to be greater than this single relationship. Interestingly, this implies that the burden of sexual sin lay much more with Gaunt than with these females, and echoes Walsingham's tirade of 1376, where he accuses Gaunt of many liaisons with prostitutes.

The piece continues with Gaunt making peace with God and with his wife Constance:

> and then with the lord Neville he went to Northallerton where the Duchess was with her household; and when she saw her lord she descended from her horse and fainted on the ground, three times in different places before she came to the place her lord

stood; the Duke took the lady by the hand and kissed her, and commiserated with her and she with him about all the circumstances they had suffered and the Duke asked pardon for his misdeeds to her. She forgave him willingly and there was great joy and celebration between them and with their companions that day and night . . .[46]

The political bias made manifest in Walsingham and Knighton is not clear in the text of the *Anonimalle*. There is no reference of war or Gaunt's patronage of Wyclif. The passages emphasise sexual sin only, and, uniquely, the *Anonimalle* chronicle describes in detail a scene of apology between Gaunt and his duchess. Gaunt, weeping, kisses Constance's hand in a noble fashion, and begs pardon for his faults, seen by some as echoing 'the conventions of courtly romance'.[47] The style of the passage conveys some information on the author. The *Anonimalle* was written at St Mary's Abbey, York, and, therefore, the obvious suggestion is that the author was one of the abbey's monks.[48] But the style and terminology of the passages on the Peasants' Revolt suggest that they were written by someone more closely in touch with the events in London, and that the St Mary's chronicler copied them into his work from another text. Indeed, it is possible that the unknown author of the *Anonimalle*, Thomas Walsingham and Henry Knighton had access to the same source for the parting of the couple and adapted the information to suit their own purposes. If this was the case, it suggests all the more strongly that it was the support of Wyclif that was Gaunt's biggest sin in the eyes of Walsingham. Walsingham viewed Constance as one of Gaunt's victims, and surely, if his greatest concern had been with Gaunt's conduct with Katherine, then this apology to Constance would have found its way into Walsingham's text.

Galbraith states that the passages in the *Anonimalle* relating to 1381 are 'more dramatic than anything else in the book'.[49] It would, therefore, seem highly probable that the compiler of these passages was a layman. The 'courtly' scene does indeed portray a more secular view of infidelity than the writings of Walsingham and

Knighton; no doubt they found it more appropriate to amend these parts than the author of the *Anonimalle*. It seems that the treatment and function of the 1381 official parting of Katherine and Gaunt provided an opportunity for monks to denounce Gaunt's sins, and for a secular author to write chivalrous, romantic prose.

The *Anonimalle*, therefore, differs in tone from the writings of Walsingham and Knighton in that a seeming political impartiality deters the author from criticising Gaunt's campaigning and patronage, while secular influences lead him to convey the 1381 parting in quite different terms. However, despite the differences in these chronicles, the depiction of Katherine is still negative in tone; she is the 'other woman' who harms the actions of the man, towards either his wife or his country. But I strongly believe that the condemnation of Katherine in no sense provides an accurate representation of her. Too many issues, styles and stereotypes cloud the passages to allow us to accept the role of sexual temptress assigned to her in these texts. I believe that Walsingham's unique portrayal of the 1378 tour and the discourse that followed an official 'parting' in all three chronicles manifestly demonstrate that Katherine was not seen in the disparaging way that the texts would have us believe. If Katherine was responsible for Gaunt delaying the French campaigning, why did no other chronicler see fit to mention it? Moreover, for Knighton and the author of the *Anonimalle* it is only the implementation of an official discourse in the form of the quitclaim that leads to their mention of Katherine; before this she is absent from their chronicles.

Goodman argues that Katherine offended convention by her lack of discretion within the relationship.[50] The texts of Knighton and the *Anonimalle* do not support this, and Walsingham's 1378 passage, which does condemn the public nature of the relationship, was written specifically to criticise Gaunt. Indeed, it can be strongly argued that the textual evidence suggests that Katherine was very discreet and was not seen to play a large part in Gaunt's public life. For example, in comparison to his depictions of Alice Perrers, Walsingham's description of Katherine as a sexual temptress is positively restrained.

Alice Perrers was the mistress of Edward III and was unique among the mistresses of medieval English kings in that 'her behaviour became a national scandal'.[51] Little is known about her; we do not have the details of her place or date of birth, nor of her parentage. We do not know how she came to be part of the royal household. Her biographer, F. George Kay, states that 'the tenuous details of her life contained in memorial documents, Parliamentary rolls, and municipal records set down her actions but say nothing of the woman herself'.[52] Clearly, parallels can be drawn here with Katherine. And, as with Katherine, Walsingham discussed Alice and her relationship with her royal lover.

At that same time there was a woman in England called Alice Perrers. She was a shameless, impudent harlot, and of low birth, for she was the daughter of a thatcher from the town of Henney, elevated by fortune. She was not attractive or beautiful, but knew how to compensate for these defects by her seductive voice. Blind fortune elevated this woman to such heights and promoted her to a greater intimacy with the king than was proper, since she had been the maidservant and mistress of a man from Lombardy, and accustomed to carry water on her own shoulders from the mill-stream for the everyday needs of that household. Even while the queen was alive, the king loved this woman more than he loved the queen.[53]

Alice's actual parentage and background are unknown. This claim of Walsingham's is probably false, as Alice was in the service of the Queen. Would it be possible for someone of such low birth and associations to be a member of the Queen's household? It seems unlikely. Walsingham made many claims about Alice and her hold over the King:

After Alice Perrer's love affair with the king began, she gained such a hold over him that he allowed important and weighty affairs of the realm to be decided on her advice. Once she had begun to make a fool of the king and perceived that he was enthralled by her, she began to act unjustly in all matters, to support wrong causes, to appropriate possessions wrongfully wherever she could for her own uses and, if opposition was planned anywhere against her, she would go immediately to the king and supported, justly or unjustly, by his protection, she would achieve what she desired . . . Indeed, so great had her insolence grown in harming others, and so abundant was the patience and humility of the English, that this woman felt no embarrassment in taking her place on the bench of judges at Westminster; and she was not afraid to speak there, either on her own behalf or on that of her friends, or even on behalf of the king as though she were promoting his business . . . It is no surprise that the judges, motivated by fear of the king or, more likely, by fear of this harlot, did not dare on most occasions to pass judgement that differed from what she had determined.[54]

In the course of these events parliament was informed that Alice had over a long period of time kept in her company a man who was a brother in the Order of Preachers who displayed the appearance of a physician, and professed that skill; but he was an evil magician, dedicated to evildoing, and it was by his magical devices that Alice had enticed the king into an illicit love affair with her, or to be more truthful, into that 'madness'. For a lecherous youth sins, but a lecherous old man is insane.[55]

The whole populace desired Alice's condemnation when they saw that no action was being taken to remedy her wrongdoings, but realised that this evil enchantress, exalted above the cedars of Lebanon, was enjoying extraordinary favour; and the people of the realm passionately longed for her downfall.[56]

Evidence suggests that Alice was an intelligent woman, and she was certainly astute in her business dealings. Bothwell argues that Alice was one of the wealthiest land-owning women in the later fourteenth century: 'More importantly, unlike many male royal favourites of the period, she did so primarily not through direct royal intervention but of her own initiative – making free use of the funds available to the king, but letting her own business sense determine the form their conversion into landed wealth would take'.[57] Alice had jewels worth in excess of £20,000 and had control of over fifty manors in twenty-five different counties and of numerous smaller properties. One of the manors of which she felt she had control was Oxhey Walround in Hertfordshire, but this right was in heated dispute with another claimant – the abbey of St Albans.[58] This is one possible reason why Walsingham was so hostile towards Alice – he certainly would not have praised a woman who was in dispute with his abbot. But other chronicles can be seen to be equally hostile towards Alice. The *Anonimalle* also criticises her relationship with the King and the influence she appeared to have over him.[59]

Walsingham's depictions of Alice differ considerably from those of Katherine. Alice is disparaged as an individual – Katherine only as an appendage of Gaunt. Far stronger language and phrasing are used to criticise the mistress of the king, suggesting that her position was felt to be problematic in a way that Katherine's was not. Indeed, several important chronicles of the time contain no mention of Katherine, most notably *The Westminster Chronicle* and Adam of Usk.[60] This may, of course, have been because the authors were not interested in tales about women, preferring to focus on politics. But both chronicles contain scandals surrounding other women of dubious repute, or accounts of men who should have known better than to be influenced by the evil of woman. Adam of Usk discusses the rumours surrounding the illegitimate birth of Richard II with the comment that his mother, Joan of Kent, was 'given to slippery ways', a reference to her clandestine marriages.[61] *The Westminster Chronicle* describes an event closer to Katherine, that of the scandal of Gaunt's daughter Elizabeth and John Holland. The author states how this daughter of Gaunt and Blanche of Lancaster

had been betrothed to the earl of Pembroke, a child of tender age, before, having herself come to womanhood, she was introduced into the royal court to study the behaviour and customs of courtly

78

society. Here Sir John Holland, the present king's uterine brother, fell violently in love with her at first sight and pursued his wooing night and day until at last his constantly renewed campaign of enticement led to such folly that by the time her father the duke left for the coast she was with child.[62]

Both chroniclers are generally viewed as being well informed, so their omission of any reference to Katherine is significant.[63] It is hard to believe that they were not aware of the relationship, so it would seem that the issue was not scandalous or politically important enough to warrant discussion. *The Westminster Chronicle* in particular, while containing praise for Gaunt and his mediating abilities, did not refrain from making disparaging comments on the Duke's political standing. The chronicler states that Gaunt and the Commons were at odds over Gaunt's plans for Castile, and this led to the Duke acting in irritation towards the Commons, setting them 'in a ferment'. He also calls Gaunt a traitor for desiring peace with France.[64] But, unlike Walsingham, the monk of Westminster, writing more or less contemporaneously with the events he recorded, restricted his criticisms to politics, not personal morality. His omission of Katherine in this context would surely indicate that Gaunt's mistress was not seen as politically active or influential, or even as showing indiscretion in any way regarding the politics of her lover. Furthermore, the monk of Westminster did not object to including information in his chronicle on other scandalous sexual relationships of the time. Robert de Vere, favourite of Richard II and player of a prominent role in the politics of the 1380s, left his wife in favour of another woman. The following passage is contained in *The Westminster Chronicle*:

This Robert de Vere, duke of Ireland, had married the daughter of Euguerrand, sire de Coucy, by the lady Isabel daughter of King Edward III; but he grew to detest her, and sent the clerk John Ripon to the Roman curia to secure a divorce terminating the marriage – a task at which he worked to such effect that through perjured witnesses, hired for the purpose, he came away with the pronouncement of a sentence of divorce. These proceedings greatly displeased the lady's uncles, the dukes of Lancaster, York and Gloucester. When she had eventually been thus repudiated this Robert de Vere, duke of Ireland, to his ever-lasting disgrace and reproach committed the iniquity of taking to wife a Bohemian chamber-woman of the queen's, named Lanecron, and this in face of the queen's unremitting protests.[65]

Walsingham too records this incident:

> It was at this time that Robert de Vere, who had grown arrogant because of the high office that the king had bestowed on him, divorced his wife, a noble and beautiful girl, the daughter of Isabella, who was herself the daughter of the illustrious King Edward. He married another girl who had come with Queen Anne of Bohemia and was said to be a saddler's daughter of decidedly low rank and ugly. This, therefore, provided a great opportunity for scandal to spread. The name she was given was 'Lancecrona'. The king supported him in all this, not wanting to upset him in anything, or rather, as men say, being unable to oppose his wishes in any way, because he was prevented by the wickedness of a certain friar who was a companion of this Robert and, as a result, was in no way able to see and pursue what was good and honourable.[66]

The Latin term Walsingham used to describe Agnes Lancecron is 'foeda', which translates as foul, filthy, vile, loathsome, disgraceful and disgusting.[67] Here, as with Alice Perrers, Walsingham is prepared to dismiss her character outright in a way that he does not with Katherine. In fact, Agnes has been done a disservice by the chroniclers, for she apparently did not agree to the match, being abducted by two of de Vere's men, and moreover, as a lady-in-waiting to the Queen, she cannot have been of such a low birth as claimed, but this only provides yet more evidence of Katherine's discretion. It was not the fact that the chroniclers were afraid to castigate women in such abusive ways that led to such limited discussion of Katherine, but rather that Katherine did not provide them with any sound reason to castigate her. Much more condemnation is heaped upon other women than on Katherine. In contrast, it would seem that Katherine's actions were not of sufficient scandal to merit attention.

However, the attention of the chroniclers was drawn to Katherine by the marriage of the couple – as with the quitclaim, it can be seen that only the release of news surrounding an 'official' event prompted discussion. In the main this 'discussion' was limited to a brief recording of the wedding having taken place. For example, the *Historica Vitae et Regni Ricardi Secundi*, written by a monk of Evesham abbey during the lifetime of Richard, includes the following: 'After this time Katherine Swynford became the wife of John Duke of Lancaster. The which mistress he for a long time during the life of his wife Constance was acquainted with carnally.'[68] While acknowledging the illicit relationship of Gaunt and Katherine, the author does not intimate scandal or malice. Of course, after the legitimisation of their relationship it would not have been politic to abuse the Duchess of Lancaster in the lifetime of her husband, so the reference to their 'carnal knowledge' may be as far as the author dared to go in any description of the couple's relationship. But the little space that the Evesham chronicler gave to Katherine is again an indication of how little interest she generated. Certainly Walsingham's claim that the couple blatantly offended public taste is not echoed in any other chronicle. And, indeed, Walsingham himself can be seen to reduce his criticisms as political expediency demanded.

Different manuscripts are available for Walsingham's work. The Royal Manuscript is the major contemporary one, comprising a history from 1272 to 1392. This manuscript contains evidence of revision undertaken during the 1390s. A section of the text relating to 1376–7 was removed; the survival of other fourteenth-century manuscripts provides evidence of this. Parts of the text were then replaced with those found in *The Short Chronicle*, a manuscript condensation of the main work of Walsingham.[69] The revisions affected Walsingham's animadversions towards Gaunt. The harshest passages were removed:

What we can trace throughout the whole reign is a transformation in Walsingham's attitude towards John of Gaunt. His early bitterness was perhaps already softening before 1388, but the events of the crisis of that year evidently hastened his change of view. Henceforth John of Gaunt was a pillar of the state, and the flagrant inconsistency between the old John of Gaunt and the new is characteristically explained by a miraculous change of heart. There was no conscious reconsideration of old verdicts on his conduct in the early part of the reign: but the simple assumption that John of Gaunt, who was a bad man until he went to Spain in 1386, was, by divine grace, a good one afterwards. The change of view, therefore, showed itself not in suppression but almost unconsciously in the alteration in successive recensions of words and phrases merely, which seemed on each revision to have lost their point.[70]

In the political field, Gaunt was no longer the enemy but the hero, and Walsingham altered his text to reflect this. The 1378 passage depicting Gaunt and Katherine's public tour is entirely edited from the Royal manuscript, presumably for fear of insulting the new Lancastrian regime in addition to no longer wishing to condemn Gaunt so harshly.[71] The passage that remains reads: 'While these events that concerned the duke were taking place, as we have said, and he was to be in no particular hurry to take to the sea but was rather delaying his departure from day to day . . .'.[72] Followed by: 'The duke of Lancaster still delayed in England, unwilling to try his fortune at sea either in the spring or in early summer, the time being limited. No one knows what obstacles held him back.'[73]

This reads very differently from Walsingham's original text and his proclamation that Gaunt delayed so he could tour the country with his mistress! Other derogatory remarks concerning Gaunt and his policies in London and France were also omitted or altered. The passage referring to the events of 1381 takes on a new context in this light. The depicted repentance of Gaunt came with Walsingham's realisation that the political scene had shifted and that Gaunt was no longer the villain. It is interesting that in the Royal

Manuscript no amendment is made to this passage. It clearly did not need to be with regard to Gaunt's newly found religious temperament, but Walsingham obviously saw no reason to omit the role of Katherine in this passage. His editing of the 1378 passage suggests that he considered his condemnation here as too extreme, but his continued inclusion of the 1381 denunciation of Katherine, especially in the light of the power of Katherine's Beaufort children and, indeed, of Thomas Swynford around Henry IV, suggests that Walsingham felt vindicated in his depiction. However, this does not necessarily lead to the conclusion that Walsingham truly considered that it was the public recognition of the relationship that was scandalous; his clerical beliefs would still have been a catalyst for the stereotyping of Katherine as symbolic of Gaunt's sin. As Gransden states, 'it is not for rationality that Walsingham deserves his reputation' but for vivid prose: 'few chroniclers can rival his dramatic narrative.'[74] The passage would certainly lose dramatic impact if Katherine was deleted from it. Perhaps the deletion of the 1378 passage is further evidence that this tour did not take place. The quitclaim, however, does suggest that, publicly at least, there was a split between Gaunt and Katherine. Walsingham would presumably have felt vindicated in keeping the passage because of the presence of this official documentation.

So far we have seen how little the monastic chroniclers mentioned Katherine in their texts. The secular chronicler Jean Froissart is by far the most garrulous on Katherine, particularly in regard to her character. It is he who provides the background information of Katherine's parentage and childhood, his place at court allowing him access to this knowledge, and, presumably, his secular background leading him to consider this information of importance. Froissart became a clerk of Queen Philippa in 1362 and spent the rest of that decade at the English royal court, where he very probably became personally acquainted with Katherine. However, he was not in England during the 1370s and 1380s and therefore did not witness at first hand Katherine and Gaunt's relationship nor the public reaction to it.[75] This lack of first-hand knowledge is evident in the passages of Froissart's work that relate to the children of Gaunt and

Katherine, even though Froissart wrote these passages after a trip to England in 1395. Froissart states that the couple had three children, not four, and he confuses their names, recording that it was Thomas Beaufort who became Bishop of Lincoln, not Henry. He also declares that the relationship started in the lifetimes of Blanche of Lancaster and Hugh Swynford.[76] It is possible, however, that Froissart witnessed at first hand the reaction to the couple's wedding. He claims that 'from affection to these children, the duke married their mother, to the great astonishment of France and England, for Catherine Swynford was of base extraction in comparison to his two former duchesses, Blanche and Constance'.[77] He recounts in detail how the news was greeted by the noble ladies at court, stating how the Duchess of Gloucester, the Countesses of Derby and Arundel, and other great ladies descended from royal blood marvelled at how Gaunt had disgraced himself through this marriage. The marriage made Katherine first lady of England until Richard II remarried, and the royal ladies said 'it should be a great shame for them that such a duchess, come of so base a blood, should go and have pre-eminence before them; they said their hearts would break with sorrow'.[78]

Whether this really happened we do not know. However, as there was no Countess of Derby at the time of Gaunt and Katherine's wedding (Mary, wife of Henry of Bolingbroke, had died two years earlier), it seems unlikely to have been an event actually witnessed by Froissart. However, his knowledge of the English court would suggest that his portrayal was accurate in tone if not in detail. The objection at court, as portrayed here by Froissart, would appear to be based on status, with the disgrace lying, as Philips has argued, not in Katherine 'being the mistress of a great man . . . but in getting above her baseborn station by presuming to marry the man she slept with'.[79] The great ladies of the court have no sense of outrage at any previous immoral liaison, but have a heightened sense of the damage done to their personal prestige, having to give way to a woman of lower status. The conclusion can be drawn that, had Katherine been of noble birth, there would have been no objection to the marriage from the ladies of the court – but the *affair* may then have been more of a scandal. Katherine was good enough to be a mistress, but not to be Gaunt's official consort, whereas a woman good enough to be a duchess would surely not have paraded publicly as a mistress: 'English elite society was materialistic and pragmatic enough to tolerate marriages between merchant and gentry, or gentry and aristocratic, groups, if worldly ambition were served thereby, but powerful taboos, born out of intense class consciousness, lurked just below the surface.'[80] Indeed, males of the gentry and aristocratic classes had mistresses without suffering condemnation, but the women were either prostitutes or women of lower status who were themselves married or widowed and presumably therefore considered women of the world. Certainly the class issue can be seen to arise when marriage occurred. Elizabeth of Lancaster's elopement with Holland was a scandal until they married, whereas de Vere's conduct with Agnes Lancecron became a scandal when his noble wife was unceremoniously dumped for a woman who was a mere waiting maid. It was on the marriage of Agnes to de Vere, and Katherine to Gaunt, that both women were emphatically described as being of low birth.

But Froissart suggests that the manner in which Katherine conducted herself was in actual fact of the standard desired in noble ladies: 'Catherine Roet, however, remained duchess of Lancaster, and the second lady in England, as long as she lived, and she was often with the king. She was a lady accustomed to honours, for she had been brought up at court during her youth.'[81] This implies that Katherine was able to hold her own among the highest ranks of society. And surely Gaunt would not have married a woman unable to carry out duties by the side of the King. But Froissart's style is problematic – his flowery and chivalrous prose shows he was influenced by romance literature. Furthermore, 'he was always reluctant to criticise the wealthy and influential, especially if they came from his native Hainault'.[82] In this respect, it is notable that, when being disparaging about Katherine, Froissart calls her Swynford, but when being complimentary he calls her Roet. The maiden apparently cannot be faulted, but the widow can. Moreover, the mistakes Froissart made with regard to her children, and to the presence of the Countess of Derby, cast doubts over the accuracy of his comments on Katherine. However, it does seem highly likely that the royal ladies at court would have found it objectionable to make way for a mere knight's daughter, while at the same time it is highly probable that Katherine did excel at court etiquette, as a result of both her court upbringing and her role as governess. Therefore it is possible to conclude that here we are dealing with the truth, despite the literary style.

The texts examined so far have been chronicles, either monastic or secular. But suggestions have been made that Katherine was portrayed in literary texts as well, notably those of Chaucer: 'Echoes of division and disquiet over Katherine may be faintly signalled in two passages written by her highly discreet brother-in-law, Geoffrey Chaucer, in *The Canterbury Tales*.' This refers to Chaucer's discussion of governesses in *The Physician's Tale*, and his panegyric on Pedro of Castile in *The Monke's Tale*. In the middle of his eulogy to the beautiful and virtuous Virginia, Chaucer writes:

> And all you ladies that in middle life
> Are put in charge of younger gentlefolk,
> Pray do not think that I speak as to provoke
> Your anger; think that your appointment springs
> From either one or other of two things,
> Either that you were chaste and did not fail
> To guard your honour, or that you were frail,
> And therefore, knowing well the ancient dance,
> You have forsaken your intemperance
> For ever. Teach them then for Jesu's sake
> And never slacken; virtue is at stake.
> Just as a poacher who forsakes his crimes
> And leaves his trade in villainy betimes,
> Makes the best gamekeeper – he's just the man –
> Keep you your charges; if you will you can.
> Never belittle or connive at vice
> Lest you should pay damnation as the price;

For those who do are traitors, never doubt it,
And so give heed to what I say about it.
Top of all treason, sovereign pestilence,
Is the betrayal done on innocence.
    You fathers and mothers, let me add,
However many children you have had,
Yours is the duty of their supervision
As long as they are bound by your decision.
Beware lest the example you present
Or your neglect in giving chastisement
Cause them to perish; otherwise I fear,
If they should do so, you will pay it dear.
Shepherds too soft who let their duty sleep
Encourage wolves to tear the lambs and sheep.
One parable's enough, you understand;
Let me return to what I had in hand.
    This girl who is the theme of my address
Was such as not in need a governess.[84]

Larry Benson comments that 'this digression on the responsibilities of parents and guardians has often been regarded as unduly obtrusive, and historical explanations have been sought'.[85] This 'digression', if it should be seen as such, has for many years been taken as a caustic reference to Katherine and the scandal of the relationship of her charge Elizabeth with John Holland.[86] The link has been made because of the familial relationship of Chaucer's wife Philippa with Katherine. Nicholas Orme argues that Chaucer's 'encounters with a mistress well known for her *frailty* were close ones and give interest to his writing', choosing 'frailty' to refer to sexual indiscretion.[87]

I realise that I am on dangerous ground assessing this source. Chaucer's works are infinitely multilayered, and many conflicting readings can be found within them. Which of these readings was the one intended by the author, if any, and the one understood by the medieval audience is unknown to us, and I am far from confident in my abilities as a Chaucer scholar to claim that I have found the elusive grail of full understanding. However, it seems to me that any argument linking this passage with Katherine is made from a point of convenience, an argument constructed because Chaucer must have known of her position and therefore must have held an opinion on it and consequently must have wanted to make veiled reference to it in his writing with the belief that his audience would link the two. But would this have been the case? The passage is deemed inappropriate in the context of the tale, and therefore seen as necessarily related to a contemporary occurrence.[88] Indeed, the dating of *The Physician's Tale* has been established as 1388, because of the presumed links between the passage and the elopement of Elizabeth and Holland.[89] But is the passage inappropriate to the *Tale* and should it necessarily be read as a negative portrayal of governesses? Indeed, should it be taken literally, or is it another example of Chaucer's overriding concern with authority and responsibility? Chaucer states that governesses take on their role as either honest or reformed creatures, but that both are equal to the task of protecting the virtue of a charge. However, Virginia needs no such protector, as her virtue shines through, goodness being innate to her character. In this context the passage is neither inappropriate nor negative but a tool to emphasise the girl's purity. The discourse that follows on the authority of parents and elders, and the important responsibility that accompanies this authority, emphasises the neglect of the judge Apius, who failed to honour the obligation that came with his magisterial position, more than any neglect on the part of governesses.[90] Lynn Staley argues that 'through the [Canterbury] tales Chaucer continues to debate and explore his own relationship as a poet to the social body and to its most visible embodiment of authority and order'. She continues that Chaucer was 'far more than a passive transmitter of cultural and social ideas and symbols. Though oblique, he was a shrewd social and political analyst, one capable of asking genuinely provocative questions about the figuring of authority.'[91] In *The Physician's Tale*, is the question about the authority of a governess over her charge, or about the intrinsic worth of people behind roles of status such as the Physician or the Judge?

There are scholars who have viewed the passage as perfectly in keeping with the rest of the tale and therefore *not* of any historical significance, nor a reference to a 'real-life' situation or person. Brown suggests that:

Had Chaucer been seriously concerned about the breakdown of domestic surveillance that led to the liaison between Gaunt's daughter, Elizabeth, and John Holland, however, he could have built his covert chastisement of Gaunt and Katherine into a tale in which parental laxity was directly responsible for some dire result. *The Physician's Tale* demonstrates that no matter how perfect a child is and how free she is from the need of a 'maistresse', she can still be destroyed by wicked forces beyond her or her parents' control. That hardly seems an exemption calculated to keep parents and governesses on their toes.[92]

Therefore, it can be seen that the passage is fully in keeping with the rest of the tale, with the tale read as a satire against physicians. Although the story of Virginus and Virginia was well known and the cause of Virginia's death would have been more than obvious to the audience of pilgrims, the Physician himself appears to struggle to understand the cause of her death, providing a literary tool with which Chaucer shows that Physicians do not know all the causes of human illness or death. And the last two lines of the passage quoted surely establish that this discourse on parents and governesses was not a criticism of Katherine. Here, Chaucer states that the maiden in his tale was of such worth that she was 'not in need a governess', an obvious suggestion that it was not a governess who was responsible for her downfall. Moreover, at the time of elopement in 1387, Elizabeth was a full 23 years of age, and therefore long out of the care of governesses. Indeed, the quitclaim from 1381, six years before the elopement, describes Katherine as the former governess of Elizabeth. And Katherine was certainly not a lady 'in middle life' when she was governess. Furthermore, the evidence in the chronicles suggests that Holland was dogged in his pursual of Elizabeth and that Elizabeth was not a culpable party in the elopement.

The Physician's Tale is not the only Chaucerian text to be linked to Katherine. Goodman suggests that Chaucer wrote his panegyric on Pedro of Castile as a partisan of his daughter, Duchess Constance, and therefore intended to be hostile to Katherine, implying that the relationship between Constance and Katherine was hostile in nature. It may be that this tells us more about Goodman's reaction than that of the medieval court, believing that a relationship between wife and mistress can only be hostile. The medieval court, however, may have held different views on the matter. *The Monke's Tale*, which is focused on the activities of the Roman goddess of Fortune, who was thought to govern fate, in which the panegyric to King Pedro can be found (lines 2375–90), was written in the early 1370s, at a time when Philippa Chaucer was one of Constance's ladies-in-waiting.[93] Perhaps Chaucer was thinking more of his wife's welfare than his sister-in-law's when writing this tale. And there was a possibility that Chaucer had met the King himself, travelling to Spain in 1366 on an embassy to Pedro's court. Personal knowledge may have led him to his laudatory discourse on the King, rather than a desire to be hostile to his sister-in-law.

Some links have also been found in the *Man of Law's Tale*, if not of Katherine directly, then of people around her. This tale, written *c.* 1390–1394/5, relates the story of an exiled princess named Constance who marries because she has to, and dislikes the attentions of her husband. Rickert suggests that it was written for Constance of Castile.[94] The date of writing could support this view – at this time Gaunt had relinquished his Spanish ambitions and had returned to England, dropping the arms of Castile and Leon from his livery. It would also appear that Constance was living apart from her husband at this time. A description of an exiled princess would therefore not be too unfitting for the Duchess. But, as with the discourse on Pedro of Castile in *The Monke's Tale*, does evidence of Chaucer's apparent support for the Castilian queen mean hostility towards Katherine? Surely this would speak of more current sensibilities and the modern belief that wives and mistresses must be natural enemies. In the fourteenth century, at court, opinions may have been very different. Marriage was seen as a matter of political advantage and monetary and land gain – within this context there must have been frequent loveless marriages and consequently many adulterous relationships.

The Chaucerian text discussed most in connection with Gaunt and Katherine is *Troilus and Criseyde*. This text is indisputably connected with the couple, in that a manuscript of the tale belonged to Anne Neville, daughter of Joan Beaufort and therefore granddaughter of Gaunt and Katherine. This manuscript, held at Corpus Christi College, Canterbury, has a glorious frontispiece that appears to show Chaucer reading his work to an assembled audience of Richard II and other fourteenth-century notables at the English court. Brusendorff believes it is probable that this manuscript was transcribed on the order of the Countess of Westmorland from a family copy of the *Troilus* originally produced for John of Gaunt in the 1380s. He suggests that the frontispiece was also a copy from this assumed original.[95] Two scholars in particular, George Williams and Margaret Galway, have undertaken to establish who the personages displayed in the frontispiece are, believing the depiction represents a situation that occurred regularly at the court of Richard.

Williams concurs with Brusendorff that the manuscript was a copy of an older illuminated manuscript because of the unfinished nature of the Neville copy; there are many blank spaces in the Neville manuscript to allow for the insertion of pictures, presumably to have been copied from the original.[96] Galway was the first of the two scholars to identify figures in the frontispiece, stating that it is 'rich in portraits of fourteenth century celebrities'.[97] She identifies Richard II as the figure dressed in gold with the face rubbed away, conjectured by Galway as occurring at the hands of the Lancastrians who owned it. Williams agrees with Galway on the identification of this figure, but the pair disagree over the identification of John of Gaunt. Galway suggests that he is the figure with the red cap on the far right, recognisable 'partly because of his striking resemblance to the portrait of Gaunt in a stained-glass window in the chapel of All Saints College, Oxford'. Williams, however, disagrees:

It is extremely unlikely that any contemporary artist would have represented the richest, most highborn, most widely celebrated, most personally influential, and most powerful nobleman in England during Richard II's reign as the humble figure at the right-hand edge of the frontispiece.

He also points out that the image of Gaunt in stained glass dates from around forty years after his death. Williams places Gaunt as the figure in blue on the orator's left, because of the prominence of this figure in the piece and due also to the style and colour of his dress – blue and white were the colours of Gaunt.

The three prominent female figures in the bottom left of the picture also produce differing opinions from the two Chaucerian scholars. Galway believes the figure at the front dressed in blue and white is Joan of Kent. Williams, in contrast, believes it is Constance of Castile. They agree, however, that the figure in blue next to this lady is one of the Roet sisters, Galway opting for Philippa while Williams argues that this figure is Katherine herself. If so, this is the only near contemporary likeness of her in existence. It is also interesting to speculate that the two figures were wife and mistress, both wearing Lancastrian blue, standing, presumably chatting, together. Williams gives her reason for identifying this figure as Katherine:

> Since this particular picture was probably meant to please Anne Neville, granddaughter of Katherine Swynford, and since the Troilus itself may be, in some ways, an allegory of the affair between Gaunt and Katherine, this second woman, obviously important in the eyes of the artist, may well be Katherine Swynford herself.

Troilus and Criseyde is a tragic love story, written by Chaucer sometime from the late 1370s to the mid-1380s, most likely during the period 1382–5. His main source was Giovanni Boccaccio's *Filostrato*, written in the late 1330s. It seems that Chaucer's edition of the *Filostrato* was a French prose version, and, although it was the main source, it would have been studied alongside many other sources; during the medieval period there were many available tales of the Trojan legends.[98] But was he, as Williams suggests, also influenced by the affair of Gaunt and Katherine, with which he must have been familiar? Is Criseyde a literary depiction of Katherine? Can this work of Chaucer's be read as providing information on the character of Katherine?

Williams certainly believes so. He states that Chaucer would have regarded Gaunt as 'a man of honour' as 'there is no record of his ever having betrayed a friend, or swerved in loyalty to a supporter', and from this conjectures that Chaucer's reason for writing the *Troilus and Criseyde* was based on the fact that 'the court gossiped about Gaunt and Katherine; Gaunt did not like the gossip; and Chaucer tried to defend the lovers'.[99] Williams links the authorial defence of Troilus and Criseyde from gossip and slander as providing evidence of an authorial defence of real lovers in a similar situation.[100] He assumes that Gaunt was Chaucer's patron, and that this, linked to the familial ties between the two men, led to Chaucer's wish to write favourably about the couple. Williams lists in detail sections of the text and how this supports his argument, asserting that Chaucer changes the Italian Cressida from a rather bold wanton to a woman, 'more innocent, less experienced, less sensual, more modest than her Italian prototype', and continues that there is 'constant reiteration' of the honourableness of Troilus' love.[101] He argues that Chaucer went out of his way to excuse Criseyde for her unfaithfulness and that, when forced to present his heroine unfavourably, he apologises for her in a way not to be found in *Il Filostrato*.[102]

Furthermore, Williams does not believe the *Troilus and Criseyde* to be the only work by Chaucer about the lovers. He believes that the *Complaint of Mars* features Gaunt as Mars and Katherine as Venus.[103] Of course, this again was written in defence of the couple:

The actual 'complaint' of Mars, for which the entire poem is constructed, is essentially a plea for tolerance of Mars' illicit love that has been harshly rebuked. In making his plea, Mars points out the 'gret excellence' of his mistress (ii. 169–81) and says that he loves her because he cannot 'help it' (ii. 218–71).[104]

Yet should these poems be read in this way? Was this Chaucer's true intention? As stated before, the poet's true meaning is impossible to uncover, and his works can be interpreted in many different ways – who is to say which is the correct interpretation? But should Chaucer's Criseyde be seen as unusual because she was different in character from Boccaccio's heroine? Does this difference mean she was based on a real woman, based on the true character of Katherine? Shepherd argues of Criseyde that,

> Though her appearances in the poem are covered with a continuous sheen of sentiment and charm so that at the slightest encouragement we are willing to lead her out of the poem as if she were a particular woman whom we delight to know, yet she is the familiar, if never commonplace figure of every English romance, of every woman's magazine, another Emily or Felice, the passive pole in this story of a struggle for possession . . . She is set alongside Nature's mean, she embodies the virtues that all heroines of romance exemplify, the beauty of figure, face and hair; discretion, fairspokeness, kindness in word and thought, a dignity, liveliness and gentility, sentimentality and fearlessness. These are characteristics that had been tabulated centuries before Chaucer's time, for example by Hugo of St Victor in his *Summa Sententarum* VII, I, as the moral and social gifts in a woman that draw men's love.[105]

From this it would appear that Chaucer's Criseyde is a standard fictional character and therefore can tell us nothing of Katherine's personality – or the way that Chaucer viewed Katherine's personality. But she is still a positive female character in the virtues that she embodies. The faults that clerics assign to women, those of vanity, garrulousness, indiscretion, are not found in Criseyde. In this the text is of value; maybe not in describing details that are specifically personal to Katherine, but in offsetting the misogynistic tone of the clerics – clerics, of course, who were by necessity distant from the females whom they described. Chaucer, in contrast, would have known many of the ladies who frequented the King's court. Perhaps the positive traits of Criseyde are those seen in the high-born and educated ladies of the English medieval nobility, and, therefore, at least some of these characteristics can be assigned to Katherine. Perhaps Criseyde does tell us more of Katherine than Walsingham *et al*. Indeed, Criseyde does seem overly concerned with reputation, and, as will be demonstrated in the following chapters, this was also a concern of Katherine's.

The story of Troilus and Criseyde was well known in fourteenth-century England – Trojan history was a popular subject and formed the setting of many tales of courtly love. Could Chaucer's audience have seen a significance in the change of Criseyde's character from that of the *Filostrato* and the other versions of the tale known to them? Would this significance be linked to Katherine? Chaucer's Criseyde is much less interested in sexual encounters, is much more cautious and concerned for her honour – would this have led the audience to think of Katherine, a woman who, after all, had been the mistress of a man for more than a decade at the time of writing, and had borne him at least four children?[106] Furthermore, to what extent would the audience have thought it possible that the poet had written with the intention of real people being linked to fictional characters? After all, a tale of tragic love such as *Troilus and Criseyde* would hardly have been listened to or read as an edifying tale. Surely the *Troilus and Criseyde* would have been deemed as entertainment only, heard as a tale of tragic love rather than a description of lovers they knew? Sources such as Edward IV's Household Book demonstrate that gatherings for the purposes of leisure, for listening to music, singing, hearing tales, were common in the fifteenth and presumably the late fourteenth century.

Williams is not alone, however, in viewing *Troilus and Criseyde* as encapsulating the story of Katherine and Gaunt. De Silva-Vigier argues that 'it is not unthinkable that, when writing *Troilus and Criseyde*, he [Chaucer] was not influenced and inspired by John's long and deep love for Katherine'.[107] But Benson states that

Williams's work is an 'unconvincing attempt to prove the pervasive importance in Chaucer's world of his relation to John of Gaunt'.[108] And, indeed, there are elements in Williams that lead to a lack of conviction in his argument. He states that 'a good writer seldom forces his allegories to fit actual fact down to the last detail; and medieval writers were notoriously inconsistent in such matters'.[109] This nicely deals with any questions over the parts of *Troilus and Criseyde* that do not fit with the story of Gaunt and Katherine! Williams continues: '*Once we start noticing it*, Chaucer's insistence on the honourable obligation of Troilus and Criseyde seems to leap from almost every page of the poem.'[110] Undoubtedly it is easier to find reference to something if you search believing it will be there. And Williams does acknowledge that 'no doubt Chaucer was moved by a pure creative impulse to write his poem' as 'people seldom do anything for only one reason'.[111] Furthermore, he appears to have a very romantic view of Gaunt and Katherine's relationship. He discusses how Philippa Roet would have been a very fine catch for Chaucer because of her background and the status of her connections, but, mere pages later, refers to Katherine as a waiting maid who enraptured a great prince.[112]

And not everyone views *Troilus and Criseyde* as an exemplarly tale:

> To speak of it as 'courtly love' would be to take a very small-minded and cynical view indeed of the *mores* of our chivalric ancestors. The book furnishes us with a vivid picture of 'manners' but they are the manners of the less noble of Chaucer's noble contemporaries, and are by no means intended as a model to be followed. The activities in the parlour, in the garden, and in the bedchamber combine, in fact, to form one of the finest comedies of manners in English.[113]

Within this context, if Troilus and Criseyde are Gaunt and Katherine, then surely the couple would have been insulted by the connection. Indeed, Robertson views Criseyde's character as flawed in many ways: 'her conception of honour is pitifully inadequate, as is her understanding of virtue and truth.'[114] He continues that Chaucer recommends the reader to look on her with compassion as she is a 'pitiable creature'.[115] The description of the poem as a comedy would surely fit with the view that the work was intended as a tool of entertainment, to be listened to, as the Troilus frontispiece infers, by a large gathering eager to pass a happy hour at leisure.

It seems we are back at our original caveat. Perhaps all we can be sure of about Chaucer's writing of the *Troilus and Criseyde* is that he intended the characters to be different from those of Boccaccio. To uncover why can, it seems, lead us into going round in circles, following arguments and counter-arguments. What was Chaucer's style of writing? When he was sitting writing a tale of love, did his thoughts wander to those around him in love, and did the characters of those he knew were in a similar state to his fictional heroes and heroines influence his writing? Or, upon reading the *Filostrato*, did he merely feel that, though the premiss of the tale was good, the characters of Troilus and Criseyde were in need of amendment, regardless of, and unaffected by, any real people he knew?

At most Gaunt and Katherine must have been only a small influence on Chaucer. It is possible that Gaunt, or even Katherine herself, was a patron of the poet and therefore may have been in his thoughts when writing. Indeed, *Troilus and Criseyde* may have been commissioned by one of them, especially as it appears highly possible that one of them owned a splendid manuscript of the poem. But, if commissioned, surely this would have been because the tale was a favourite of the couple rather than from a desire to have people think more favourably of illicit relationships! Possibly the character of Criseyde was softened at the request of Katherine; she may have thought that Boccaccio was too hard on his leading lady. But, as with so much concerning the inspiration of Chaucer, we can offer only conjecture as to the reason for the poem. At best, we can view it as a source for the concerns and virtues of noble ladies, but, bearing in mind opinions such as that of Robertson, even this may not be a straightforward issue. Indeed, to what extent would Chaucer have written with any intent beyond that of entertainment?

Do poems have a purpose beyond that of mere art-form? The medieval audience was accustomed to texts that had an edifying message, for example in courtesy or religious texts. From these they would surely have tried to draw meanings and intent. But would they have done so from a poem or tale of courtly love?

So at the end of this chapter what has become clear about the personality of Katherine? It would seem difficult to extract any solid evidence of Katherine's actual character or bearing, or of the way courtly society, or indeed the wider medieval society, judged her from the information contained in the chronicles and literary texts of her lifetime. Thomas Walsingham, the monk of St Albans, and the author of the *Anonimalle Chronicle* appear to be disparaging about Katherine, suggesting that she was viewed in a negative way and was indiscreet in her actions. But Walsingham's 1376 and 1378 passages provide clear evidence that his object was the condemnation of Gaunt's moral status within a context of perceived political weakness and religious heresy. Katherine was merely a pawn in this play of Walsingham's; he clearly felt no need to discuss her character in detail, or to offer any information on her actions. From this can be drawn the conclusion that, in the early 1380s at least, it was Gaunt's position that affected Katherine's press, not Katherine herself or her public conduct. In 1381 the quitclaim led to discussion about the relationship, and again Gaunt's position in the author's thoughts dictated the portrayal of Katherine, his renunciation of her being symbolic of his renunciation of sin. It would be easy to deduce from this (and many, it would seem, have done so) that Katherine was seen as Gaunt's downfall, but the chroniclers were clearly influenced by the official information fed from the top, in the form of the quitclaim, and not the opinion from the bottom. In other words, the depiction of Katherine as representing Gaunt's sin was not a reflection of an actual societal rejection of Katherine. If so, surely the condemnation that Alice Perrers faced, where Walsingham actually wrote that the public were against her, would have been Katherine's fate too.

Chronicles such as the *Brut*, Adam of Usk, and *The Westminster Chronicle* contain no suggestion whatsoever that Katherine was indiscreet or viewed as offensive by society, either courtly or otherwise. Indeed, their lack of discussion, especially in the context of their discourses on other women of the period, suggests the opposite to be true, that Katherine did not flout convention. Froissart indicates that Katherine's chief fault, as seen by the nobility, was her lowly birth, not her 'immoral' position, differing in tone from the moralistic line of Walsingham *et al*. And, indeed, would not the eventual marriage of the powerful Duke of Lancaster to a woman who was not of noble birth be seen as pleasing to the majority of the low-born English public?

The supposed links and references to Katherine in Chaucer's works seem immediately dubious. If the search is for some historical context to the poet's work, then it is easy to argue that the discourse on governesses in *The Physician's Tale* does not fit the remainder of the poem and therefore must have been an allegorical reference to a specific event or specific people that his audience would have found significant. But equally, as has been shown, the text fits firmly into a purely literary context. And for Criseyde to be the embodiment of all that is Katherine seems equally dubious. An influence may have been present, but would Chaucer have seriously set out to write a tale of star-crossed and illicit lovers to be read to a courtly audience consisting of Gaunt and Katherine's family while intending this same audience to recognise the hero and heroine to be that couple who were so well known to them, and, moreover, intend the poem to plead for the audience's understanding, support and compassion?

What an investigation of the possible sources on Katherine's character does reveal, however, is how inaccurate it is to view her as a condemned character, unaccepted at court and disapproved of in general, based on the information of the contemporary chronicles. A literal reading of Walsingham *et al*. can only mislead. Read again, these sources do not directly disclose any information or opinion on Katherine's self, her conduct or bearing, and do not reflect a horror in society towards this woman or her influence on Gaunt. Katherine's role in the chronicles is to provide yet more evidence of

Gaunt's character. She is one more example of Gaunt's weaknesses to Walsingham and provides an opportunity for Knighton to denounce his patron's actions as due to the influences of others. The chronicles clearly talk about the man not the woman. The lack of information on Katherine in the chronicles can only suggest that she was not a condemned character, was not despised by the court or wider public but was discreet in her liaison, creating no malicious court gossip or public defamation.

CHAPTER 4

Katherine's World

The fourteenth-century chroniclers did not write about Katherine's character. They merely assigned to her the familiar monkish view of Woman as Eve, the one who seduced and betrayed. Too many modern accounts of Katherine include information from these chronicles as literal truth without acknowledging the view of the medieval Church towards women. No attempt has been made to investigate the character of Katherine beyond these contemporary portrayals. An obvious reason for this omission is the lack of documentary evidence. But there are other sources available for an investigation of Katherine's life. The context of her social setting is an important area to search. Katherine grew up at court, among the highest ranks of medieval society. Her character will have been formed in part by the influences around her. An investigation, therefore, of how noble girls were raised and educated will reveal much that influenced Katherine as a girl. Furthermore, the reactions of other nobles towards Katherine and their acceptance, or otherwise, of her within the courtly environment will provide a setting against which to measure her behaviour. The same approach applies to the roles her children, both Swynfords and Beauforts, played in royal circles. These children would not have been accepted as members of royal society if they were incapable of displaying appropriate behaviour and character. Above and beyond these issues is the relationship between Katherine and Constance. How did the legitimate Duchess of Lancaster and Queen of Castile react to this third member of her marriage? Was there a tacit acceptance of Katherine by her lover's politically important and powerful wife? If so, what can this reveal about Katherine's diplomacy and discretion?

Indeed, how did consorts of the time view their husband's mistresses? Does our modern aversion to wife and mistress being openly and happily aware of each other's presence cloud our view of a medieval situation that was commonplace?

Katherine's character was ignored by all the commentators of the time bar Froissart. He states that 'she was a lady accustomed to honours, for she had been brought up at court during her youth'.[1] Katherine was a member of Blanche of Lancaster's household, a fact disclosed both by Froissart and by the records of Bishop Buckingham of Lincoln when he granted Katherine the right to witness the celebration of divine service privately.[2] The details of how Katherine came to be in the Lancastrian household are unknown. Indeed, the records of Bishop Buckingham provide the earliest confirmed dating of Katherine's presence here. Payne Roet, Katherine's father, may have entrusted the care of his daughters to Queen Philippa on his departure from England early in the 1350s.[3] The English Queen was known for her willingness to care for the children of those in her service. Almost all the letters of Philippa that are extant were written on the behalf of others.[4] If Payne was a favourite in Edward III's retinue, then it would seem highly likely that the Queen's good and kind nature would have led her to place his daughters in suitable positions. Of course, Katherine would have been a mere babe at this time, but it was commonplace for the children of valuable servants to be brought up at court, taking their place alongside noble children.[5] Nothing is known of Katherine's mother, but it is probable that she was also in the employ of the King and Queen, most probably as one of the Queen's ladies. Perhaps Katherine's mother died during childbirth and this added to the Queen's desire to ensure that Payne's daughters would be well looked after and secure within the atmosphere of a royal court.

Philippa Roet was certainly in the service of Countess Elizabeth of Ulster, daughter-in-law to the Queen through her marriage to Philippa's second eldest son Lionel, by 1357, listed as a 'damoniselle' in the records for this year.[6] It is possible that Katherine herself started life in this household, transferring to the Lancastrian household when she was old enough to carry out a serviceable role.

St Catherine, from John Beaufort's *Book of Hours*. *(© The British Library)*

The Neville family in prayer; Joan Beaufort is on the right, with Cecily Neville on her left. *(Bibliothèque Nationale, Paris.)*

An initial containing a portrait of Chaucer from *The Canterbury Tales*. *(© The British Library)*

John of Gaunt from *The Golden Book of St Albans*. *(© The British Library)*

The frontispiece to Chaucer's *Trolius and Criseyde*. *(The Master and Fellows of Corpus Christi College, Cambridge)*

Sir Geoffrey Luttrell mounted, from the Luttrell Psalter. (© *The British Library*)

The Wilton Diptych. (*National Gallery, London*)

Above: Fragment of an altar frontal made for Lady Catherine Stafford. *(Victoria & Albert Museum)*

Right: Wall painting of St Catherine, Hardley Street, Norfolk. *(www.paintedchurch.org)*

Far right: Wall painting of St Anne teaching the Virgin to read, Corby Glen, Lincolnshire. *(T. Marshall/ www.paintedchurch.org)*

A picture of Katherine's tomb by Gervase Holles. *(Lincoln Cathedral Library)*

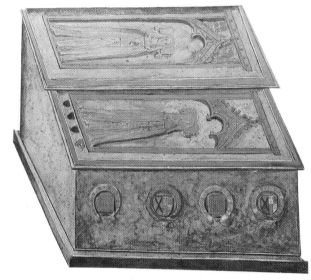

Katherine's arms, as seen on her tomb. *(Lincoln Cathedral Library)*

Katherine's tomb as it is today, seen through the chantry arching. *(Lincoln Cathedral Library)*

The Angel Choir at Lincoln Cathedral. *(Lincoln Cathedral/Bridgeman Art Library)*

Kettlethorpe Gate. *(Author's collection)*

Left: Medieval cross in Kettlethorpe churchyard. *(Author's collection) Right:*
Henry Beaufort's tomb at Winchester cathedral. *(Hulton Archive/Getty Images)*

Froissart suggests this to be the case, stating that Katherine first entered the Lancastrian household in 1359 upon the marriage of the Duke to Blanche of Lancaster.[7] Katherine would, of course, have still been very young in age, in her early teens, but there were many roles that young girls could carry out in a household, particularly that of a royal child, who would have been provided at birth with his or her own retinue. This would include a young girl known as a 'rokestare' whose chief role was cradle rocking. On the marriage of John and Blanche, their household may have been expanded to include provision for future children. Katherine was certainly fully ensconced in the household by 1365, the year in which the Bishop of Lincoln records her request for private mass, describing her position as 'ancille' or servant.[8] If 1359 is too early a date for her transference between households, then 1362 must have been the latest date, as this is the year that Elizabeth of Ulster died.

However, whichever date is correct, it is certain that Katherine was brought up in the household of a royal from a very young age, aware of the importance and standing of the people around her and aware of her position, and that of her family, in serving these powerful personalities. Her upbringing, however, would have equipped her to do more than serve. The Lancastrian household was known for its belief in education, and this would not have been reserved for the highest members only. In many households references can be found to both boys and girls as wards and pages undergoing formal or informal education.[9] Katherine would almost certainly have been taught how to read, would have been educated in the arts of embroidery, music and dancing, and would, of course, have undergone religious instruction. Desirable personal traits, such as refinement of manners, and the social skills needed to associate with the highest echelons of society, would also have been accomplishments that Katherine would have been shown from a young age.

Indeed, medieval education was focused more on attributes than on letters, particularly for girls. Accomplishments such as dancing, music making and riding would have been taught. These skills were bound up with the medieval idea of good manners. Social etiquette and correct behaviour were the mainstay of the feudal rankings; it was vital to know one's place in society and to be able to demonstrate a worthiness for one's station in life. The nobility and those connected with it were expected to be all that was good and graceful. Fine manners and elegant deportment were of prime importance, and the education offered to children within noble households reflected this.

It was commonplace for maids and knights within households to marry, and this was true for Katherine. Her first husband, Hugh Swynford, was a knight in John of Gaunt's retinue, and this marriage firmly cemented her Lancastrian links. It is probable that, on her marriage to Hugh, Katherine also became a member of the Confraternity of Lincoln Cathedral.[10] This would also have confirmed her Lancastrian solidarity, but personal devotion to St Katherine may have influenced her decision to join. Mass was said daily at St Katherine's Altar in the cathedral for the Brethren and Sisters of the confraternity.[11] The Swynfords certainly seem to have been respected members of the Lincoln Cathedral community. Two of the canons, Thomas de Sutton and John de Warsop, stood godfather to Thomas Swynford.[12] The Swynfords' daughter Blanche was goddaughter of the Duke of Lancaster, and was probably also goddaughter of the Duchess and therefore given her name in honour of the spiritual relationship. The role of godparents in the fourteenth century was a more serious commitment than for their modern-day counterparts. The bonding of the godparent to the family was significant. Indeed, the relationship precluded that of marriage, and Gaunt and Katherine had to petition the Pope to confirm their marital status because of this previous spiritual bond. The Duke would not have entered the relationship lightly, and his agreement to stand godfather indicates the high esteem in which both Hugh and Katherine were held by Gaunt. Katherine should therefore be viewed as a respectable woman in her early life, a valued and educated member of the distinguished Lancastrian retinue.

It would also appear that Gaunt engendered loyalty in all his retinue. Knighton records incidents of the Duke showing forgiveness and kindness to all in his employ.[13] Furthermore, the editors of

John of Gaunt's Register report that, 'John of Gaunt does not seem to have been a severe landlord'.[14] The regard felt towards Gaunt by his retainers is perhaps best displayed in a letter written to him by Maud, the former nurse of his eldest child, Philippa. Noble children had nurses from birth to around the age of 6 or 7, when they graduated to a tutor or governess. Nurses were usually of artisanal status.[15] Maud appears to have been the nurse only of Philippa – it would appear that Elizabeth and Henry had their own nurses – so would have been in the employ of Gaunt from 1360 to *c.* 1366/7. There is no evidence that she took another position in the household, yet in 1376, nine years after leaving the service of Gaunt, her regard for him led her to write a letter warning him of political unease:

Most redoubtable, excellent and powerful lord, I recommend myself most humbly to your exalted lordship, desiring especially to hear good news of your noble lordship, and pray to our sweet Lord Jesus Christ that he protects you out of His great pity; and because, very noble lord, the ancient proverb says in this manner, that he who is forewarned is not shamed, I wish to warn you of any enemies that I have perceived by my own experience; note that the brothers, Hugh Brandon and John Drynkestor of the order of the Friars Minor [Franciscans] of Canterbury, and the brothers, John Pykeworth, John Robert and brother John Hill of the order of preaching friars [Dominicans] of Canterbury aforesaid, have wickedly and treacherously spoken of you, my very redoubtable lord, as I heard to the great misery of my heart, so I beseech you, my very powerful lord, that you protect yourself well from them and all others, in God's name and as an act of sacred charity. Very redoubtable and very powerful lord may the Holy Trinity protect your lordship for a long time and grant you victory over your enemies.[16]

This letter reveals much of Gaunt's personality and his attitude towards those in his retain. For this woman to feel the need to warn Gaunt of the fact that some friars had spoken against him demonstrates the goodwill with which Gaunt was held by his retinue. This goodwill was generated by Gaunt himself and his treatment of those in his household – he was obviously a kind and caring lord. With this in mind it seems natural enough that the Duke stood sponsor to the children of hard-working and loyal couples.

It is unclear exactly when, or on whose appointment, Katherine became the governess of Philippa and Elizabeth of Lancaster, but this appointment reveals a great deal about Katherine's bearing and reputation. There have been suggestions that the appointment was merely one of convenience, allowing the relationship between Gaunt and Katherine to blossom on the Duke's trips to the nursery. However, Katherine must have held a certain level of education and accomplishment to have been considered for the post. The education of aristocratic girls was of considerable importance. They were not claimants to royal titles themselves but were nevertheless the means by which valuable alliances were cemented. They remained under female supervision until married, and the office of governess or mistress was the female equivalent of a boy's master or tutor. Katherine's own education can be assessed most clearly here. She must surely have possessed considerable personal traits to be given the charge of ducal daughters. The expectation of the behaviour of noble women, and of those of lower status, is well documented. Numerous texts are extant that outline the guidance a parent or guardian should give to daughters – for example, *The Goodwife Taught her Daughter*, *The Good Wife Wold a Pilgrimage* and *Book of the Knight of the Tower*, all texts from the late fourteenth or early fifteenth centuries. These instructional texts are invaluable at providing information on which virtues and accomplishments were valued in medieval society. They became an increasingly common phenomenon from the mid-fourteenth century and were widely circulated. Of course, how closely they were followed is unknown, and the visions of womanhood displayed in the texts were, on the whole, of meek and virtuous women who obeyed their husbands and fathers, following what is traditionally seen as the misogynistic medieval view of the inferior sex. But much practical advice was contained in these texts on how to manage households and servants and how to aid one's husband in the running of an estate.

The education of noble women did not necessarily happen within their own household. Children of even the highest rank were often sent to other households to gain their education. Gaunt himself sent his own children to the houses of other aristocracy in the 1370s, accompanied by their own retinues. Katherine, as governess, would have been present in the retinues of Philippa and Elizabeth.[17] Her role would have been to teach a range of accomplishments, intellectual, artistic and physical.[18] The intellectual would have covered the ability to read basic Latin, for the purposes of reading liturgical texts, but also to read English and French for more practical and pleasurable reasons. Katherine would also have been responsible for what is termed in the modern curriculum personal and social education, covering matters of dress, table manners, etiquette, music and dancing. The skills of tapestry and embroidery were also deemed of value to keep ladies from idleness. Aristocratic girls would also have been taught the physical arts of hunting and hawking. It is clear from the job role that Katherine herself was accomplished in all these areas: 'Gaunt would only have appointed as governess to two of his daughters a lady of serious demeanour, who possessed a well-informed piety and a knowledge of romantic literature and household economy, as well as a delight and aptitude in the more frivolous courtly accomplishments and games.'[19]

Indeed, these accomplishments took on a greater significance under the court of Richard II. Richard took a delight in art and fashion, and this greatly influenced the culture of his court. Fashion, luxury, etiquette and patronage, the mainstays of the court, were all determined by the preferences of the monarch. Richard loved the use of heraldry, promoting livery collars and badges. This emphasis on the feudal links between lords and retinue led to an increased focus on behaviour. Knowledge and appreciation of art and literature were seen as desirable and noble traits. Women were welcomed into his court, with music making leading to elaborate dancing. The court was decorated with heraldic symbols but also with scenes from courtly romances portraying heroines as wise, lettered and self-controlled. These depictions undoubtedly presented a fashion that the women of the time admired and strove to achieve.

The religious instruction of noble children would have been the job of a cleric. However, masters or governesses would have been expected to assist in this and therefore would have been required to show a pious nature themselves. Again, the record of Bishop Buckingham provides useful information on Katherine and her piety. The licence granted by the bishop gave Katherine the right to witness the celebration of divine service privately. Private chapels increased in importance in the later Middle Ages. Whether this was symbolic of a growing sense of internalised, privatised religion, or merely an element of status definition, is debatable. Mass was the centre of the symbolic nature of medieval Catholicism and empowered the priesthood with the ability to perform the holy transformation of bread and wine into flesh and blood. But there is an argument that, despite its all-important position in the centre of worship, mass was somewhat distanced from the laity. In many churches the high altar where mass was celebrated was separated from the nave by the rood screen, physically distant and partially obscured. However, most churches had more than one altar, and daily, less elaborate, masses took place here for the more pious among the parishioners for whom the weekly celebration was not enough. These smaller altars were often controlled by the laity, paid for out of chantry funds, or from bequests. Here, the prayers could focus on more immediate concerns – to help family and friends and to address issues of personal concern and favourite saints. From this grew the ability for the more financially secure of the laity to have private chapels and altars and for the more literate to mediate over devotional handbooks. For some, this may have been a posturing of status, for example, giving the new gentry the opportunity to enforce their superiority on their tenants and workers. However, for most, mass was a time of private prayer and reflection that they preferred to attend in their own chapel away from the prying and distracting eyes of other parishioners. The opportunity to have one's own priest performing mass at a private service in a chapel in one's own living accommodation was a natural extension of this. That Katherine, at a young age, should desire this for herself suggests that mass for her was a service she attended often, with much private reflection and prayer.[20] Further evidence for this is provided in the records for 1376, when she received an indult from the pope to have a portable altar.[21] Indults were normally granted for a privileged altar – for example, one dedicated to a local saint or to a saint for whom one had a particular devotion. The fact that Katherine could hold a private service meant that she could personalise it, specifying particular prayers and devotions. Her desire to have her own altar confirms this, indicating specifically her wish to focus her devotion towards particular saints.

So it seems very clear that Katherine would have been extremely accomplished. Of course, throughout the later Middle Ages the household and court environments of royalty were important centres of education and of educated people, and Katherine would have been exposed to this atmosphere in her youth in Blanche's household as well as later in life as governess to the two girls.[22] It was the individual family or household that limited the education of noble women and girls to what was deemed necessary or desirable in their daughters' learning.[23] John of Gaunt was known as a promoter of education and learning through his patronage of Wyclif and of Lollard texts. His own education was scholarly; he could read Latin and was familiar with the classics, as well as having a taste for courtly literature.[24] Little is known of the actual books owned by Gaunt. Bequests in his will include manuscripts, but these are mainly religious in character described, for example, as *Livres de la Chapelle*. Much debate has raged over Gaunt's conjectured patronage of English medieval literature, most notably that of Chaucer, with scholars claiming that Gaunt authorised several works by the poet including *The Complaint of Mars* and *The Complaint of Venus*. Brusendorff also suggested that Gaunt owned a copy of *Troilus and Criseyde*.[25]

Gaunt's literary accomplishments can be further observed within his family. His father, Edward III, owned many books and seems to have been a lover of Arthurian romance and chansons de geste. Many of these books were passed on to Richard II (and were possibly previously owned by his grandmother Queen Isabella). However, it would seem that Richard had different tastes from his grandfather, as eleven of the fourteen books that Richard inherited were either pawned or sold within the first year of being in the new king's possession.[26] Richard's testament does not include mention of any books, but this is not in itself unusual. Testaments are a major source for the ownership of books. However, at least half of the books mentioned in wills are liturgical or devotional in nature. This does not mean that the same proportion of all books were of a religious character. Bequests were limited to items of value, so only books of significant value were listed. These tended to be, for example, Books of Hours or Psalters that were heavily decorated and gilded. Comparisons between booklists from wills and those from other sources such as inventories show that testators frequently omitted mention of some or even all their books.[27] There are a number of records that show the range of books in the possession of the crown during Richard's reign. These books were often gifts from other royals – for example, a breviary in two volumes presented by Charles VI of France on the marriage of Richard to his daughter Isabella in 1396 – but there are also wardrobe accounts showing the purchase of manuscripts by the King. It appears that several works were dedicated to Richard or his queens, and may even have been written on royal command. Chaucer's *Legend of Good Women* bears a dedication to Queen Anne and Gower's *Confessio Amantis* declares it was written on command of the King. Froissart too brought Richard a gift of a book containing works of romance on his visit to England in 1395. Richard also granted books as presents himself, notably a book of the Miracles of Edward, late King of England, to Pope Urban in 1394/5.[28] This love of literature was no doubt encouraged by his tutor Simon Burley, who was himself a considerable book-owner. An inventory of 1388 lists twenty-three books, and it is possible Burley owned more besides. Among those listed were a book of the romances of King Arthur, a book on the government of kings and princes, works of philosophy and a copy of the *Brut*.[29] Other members of Edward III's family can be seen to be literate. His granddaughter Philippa de Coucy, the unfortunate wife of Robert de Vere, owned a number of texts, including *Les Voiages que Saint Antoine fist en la terre d'outremer* and *L'Estoire de Balaam et de Josaphat*.[30]

Closer still to Gaunt is the Bohun family. Humphrey de Bohun, father-in-law to Gaunt's son Henry, commissioned the writing of many Psalters and Books of Hours. We know of six manuscripts that were made for Humphrey or others in his family. Indeed, the Bohun group of manuscripts has been called 'the most important English illuminated manuscripts of the second half of the fourteenth century'.[31] His wife, Joan FitzAlan, may have been the owner of the Symeon manuscript, which is moralistic in nature. Hoccleve dedicated several works to her, including the *Complaint of the Virgin*. Humphrey and Joan's eldest daughter Eleanor, Duchess of Gloucester, owned several books, including a *Cronike de Fraunce* and *Pastorelx Saint Gregoire*. She bequeathed several books in her will. Her daughters benefited from these bequests; Isabella received six religious books including a French bible, while Joanna was bequeathed a Psalter and Anne a collection of saints' lives. Eleanor's younger sister Mary, wife to Henry Bolingbroke, owned a copy of *Lancelot du Lac* and commissioned several Psalters and Books of Hours. Her copy of *Lancelot* bears the arms of England, Bohun, and Leon and Castile, suggesting that Gaunt had been a previous owner of the manuscript.[32] Her husband, the future Henry IV, was another Lancastrian book-owner. Again, as with Richard II, no books are listed in his testament, but household accounts record amounts paid for the mending or purchasing of books. He was known for his scholarly abilities and was a principal benefactor of Oxford University library. He also invited Christine de Pisan to reside at his court.[33] His own children were well educated. The household accounts include much information on this, from the names of the tutors and mistresses of his four sons and two daughters, to details of books purchased to aid their learning. His eldest son, the future Henry V, benefited in 1396 from the acquirement of seven books of Latin grammar. A year later another son, John, was bought a Latin primer. In this same year his daughters, Philippa and Blanche, when only 3 and 5 years old, were bought copies of a Latin ABC from which to learn their alphabet.[34]

Gaunt's daughters, Katherine's charges, were as well educated as one would expect given the learned atmosphere with which they were surrounded. Indeed, it has been conjectured that they were the first ladies at court who knew how to write, and they certainly were interested in literature and the production of texts.[35] Philippa, who became Queen of Portugal through her marriage to Joáo I, was credited with inaugurating a new era at the Portuguese court through the education of her children, and was herself regarded as a model of womanly goodness for her piety and household management.[36] Eustache Deschamps also speaks of Philippa as the English patron of *The Flower and the Leaf*, a secular poem that celebrates love and honours Philippa as a partisan of the Order of the Flower through the love match of her marriage with Joáo and her knowledge of the joy of secular love.[37]

The Portuguese queen is also depicted on her tomb as holding a book.[38] This is highly significant. The design of a tomb was a serious matter, and much thought went into the carvings and decoration. As Ward states: 'The burial of the noblewoman may be viewed as her last public appearance and one which she often appeared eager to make the most of and prepared for carefully.'[39] Medieval views of death (and reputation) are far removed from modern ideas, and the tomb was believed to be on display for perpetuity. That Philippa wished to be remembered for her literacy is clear and denotes much of her personality.

Her sister Elizabeth also wished to associate herself throughout perpetuity with piety, education and literature. Her fame surrounds her scandalous relationship with John Holland, half-brother to Richard II. However, her last public appearance has her lying with hands clasped in prayer with a book by her side. A window of Ampthill church also portrays her in a humble reverent pose with a book on her lap.[40] Ampthill manor was one of the landholdings of Elizabeth's husband, Sir John Cornwall, and he financed much work in the church there.[41] It would, therefore, seem likely that the couple commissioned this window and the pose contained within it. Nothing is known of her own literary collection or, indeed, of which works she was patron, but, as with her sister, she was surely influenced by the atmosphere that surrounded her.

Not only was Elizabeth's father's family immersed in education; her maternal family was also involved: 'Blanche [of Lancaster] belonged to a family in which education seems to have been the norm.'[42] Henry, Blanche's father, actually composed a devotional treatise as an act of penance.[43] Blanche is credited by Froissart as being his patron, and he directs some of his poems to her. Speght's edition of Chaucer also claims that Blanche was the patron of the poet's ABC or *La Priere Nostre Dame*. This consisted of alphabetically ordered stanzas dedicated to the Virgin Mary. It was used for private devotion, but is also known to have been used to teach children to read.[44] It is easy to picture Katherine using this book to assist her charges in their learning, and, certainly, it has become very clear that within this environment any governess would have been required to be literate in French and English, to have good economic sense and to excel in many feminine courtly attributes such as embroidery and dancing.

Katherine's own children also demonstrate how educational influences affected the Lancastrian family. Joan Beaufort, in particular, was a highly literate woman. Katherine's youngest child owned works of piety, including Rolle's *Meditations on the Passion of Christ*, and played hostess to Margery Kempe.[45] In 1431 Sir John Morton of York bequeathed to Joan 'unum librum de Anglico vocatum Gower pro remembraneia',[46] and Hoccleve dedicated a work written 'in honur and plesance of yow ladyes' to Joan with the following inscription:

> Go, smal book to the noble excellence
> Of my lady of westmerland and seye,
> Hir humble seruant with al reuerence
> Him recommandith vn-to hir nobleye;
> And byseeche hire on my behalue, and preye,
> Thee to receyue for hire owne right;
> And looke thow in al manere weye
> To plese hir womman hede do thy might.[47]

Joan also had copies of *The Chronicle of Jerusalem* and *The Voyage of Godfrey de Bouillon*, which she lent to Henry V, and her brother Thomas left her a copy of the Arthurian romance *Tristram*.[48]

Romance in general was obviously something that moved Joan. In a letter to her half-brother Henry IV she pleads the case of a Christopher Standish and his wife Margaret. This couple are 'lodged very uncomfortably', as Christopher's father has dismissed him from his service 'merely because he and his wife married each other for downright love'.[49] However, Joan was also pious in nature. Dobson has described her and her children as 'the most influential of all aristocratic patrons known to the Durham monks'.[50] She also shared an interest in the convent of Durham Priory.[51] It is possibly because of this piety that she valued a Psalter, which warranted a separate mention in her will. This Psalter was to go to her son, William. Another reason why it was of obvious value to Joan is evident in the description of the book as formerly belonging to 'the illustrious lady and my mother, lady Katherine, duchess of Lancaster'.[52]

Joan's literary interests were shared by her daughters, Anne and Cecily Neville, described by Carol Meale as 'significant figures in the history of piety and book-patronage in the fifteenth century'.[53] Much work has been done on the household of Cecily, and her daily activities are known. Included in her routine was the reading-aloud at dinner of devotional works such as saints' lives. Cecily bequeathed a large number of books in her will, the majority of which were religious in nature. A book was more likely to appear in a medieval will if it had an intrinsic monetary value or if it was devotional or liturgical in nature. Cheap, popular manuscripts, the best-sellers of their day, were not considered suitable bequests. Books that had a high monetary value, normally arising from their decorative nature, will have appeared for obvious reasons. Books of a religious theme were, of course, highly suitable bequests, as they demonstrated the piety of the deceased and therefore promoted their worthiness for prayers and mass to help their passage though purgatory. Several of the books that Cecily bequeathed were left to her granddaughter Bridget, who was a nun.[54] Her sister Anne also bequeathed large numbers of books. She was the patron of *The Nightingale*, an allegorical commemoration of Christ's Passion. Anne's daughter was also known for her patronage of literary works.[55]

Mary Erler states that 'for both men and women the exchange of books in a manuscript culture depended heavily upon whom one knew'.[56] This is one of the reasons why whole families can be seen to be literate. Networks across family bonds and between generations allowed the passing of knowledge and culture and, of course, of the actual manuscripts themselves. These networks appear to be particularly strong between females. Indeed, women were strongly linked to the teaching of reading in the fourteenth century:

One of the earliest stories in English history about a boy and his reading in Asser's Life of King Alfred, tells how Alfred's mother showed him and his brothers a book of English poetry and promised it as a gift to the first one who learnt it. Alfred took the book, went to his 'master', learnt it, and recited it to his mother. The account does not say that his mother taught him, nor that he learnt the book except by memory, but it features her as a benign and positive influence. In less important families, without specialist teachers, a mother's role in this respect may have been still greater.

By about 1300, the linkage of women with children's reading was familiar enough for a poem comparing men and women to include the statement 'woman teacheth child on book'.[57]

Cavanaugh's research on medieval book ownership has revealed that 'women were among the more important consumers of vernacular literature'.[58] Furthermore, Barrett argues that 'women were certainly consumers of the products of others' literacy, or there would not be so many books, such as *Ancrene Wisse* and the associated texts of the Katherine group, specifically directed at women'.[59] I believe it is clear that female literary networks in the families surrounding Katherine were alive and strong, and she would surely have participated in this, being involved in the patronage of works and the sharing of texts with the educated females around her.

But it is not just the daughter and granddaughters of Katherine who can be seen to be immersed in a literary culture, nor even her children with royal blood. Her son with Hugh Swynford is another of Katherine's children who appears to have been highly learned. Thomas was fluent in Latin, evidenced by his request when negotiating with the French commissioners as Captain of Calais in 1404 that the French counsel write to him in Latin not French – although, of course, this may have been a posturing of power, an insult to the French language rather than direct evidence of his own Latinate standing; someone may have translated for him.[60] But it would seem highly likely, given the level of learning and literary taste at the English court, that Thomas was able to read, and possibly to write, Latin. Thomas's cousin and Katherine's nephew, Thomas Chaucer, is another male from Katherine's family who was literate, as may be expected given his father's abilities. His father's friend John Lydgate addressed a poem to Thomas, 'Balade at the Departyng of Thomas Chaucyer into France', and possibly wrote 'My Lady Dere' for him as well.[61] Lydgate also dedicated works to Thomas's daughter, Alice, notably his 'Virtues of the Mass'.[62] Alice, possibly influenced by the literary friends of her father and the heritage of her grandfather, showed much interest in literary pursuits. Indeed, a letter written by Alice expressed concern over her books.[63]

Finally, Katherine's Beaufort sons are known to have been highly educated and owners of numerous manuscripts. Henry Beaufort was university educated and, as befits his role as cleric, owned many religious texts. John owned an illustrated Book of Hours that he probably commissioned himself. As previously mentioned, Thomas owned a copy of *Tristram* that he bequeathed to his sister Joan. One of the Beauforts appears to have owned a work of Boccaccio; an extant manuscript of this contains the Beaufort coat of arms.[64]

Katherine and her children can therefore be seen to be fully enveloped in the Lancastrian court and its learned atmosphere. And it would appear that both Richard II and Henry IV accepted the Beauforts and the Swynfords as members of Gaunt's family. Richard II refers to the Beauforts as kinsmen during the 1390s[65] and uses glowing terms to describe the offspring of Gaunt in their patent of legitimation:

Richard by the grace of God, king of England and France, and lord of Ireland, to our most dear cousins the noble men, John the Knight, Henry the Clerk, Thomas Domicello and to our beloved the noble woman Joan Beauford Domicelle, the most dear relations of our uncle the noble John Duke of Lancaster, born our lieges, greeting, and the favour of our royal majesty. Whilst internally considering how incessantly and with what honours we are graced by the very useful and sincere affection of our aforesaid uncle, and by the wisdom of his counsel, we think it proper and fit that, for the sake of his merits, and in contemplation of his favours, we should enrich you (who are endoured by nature with great probity and honesty of life and behaviour, and are begotten of royal blood, and by the divine gift are adorned with many virtues) with the strength of our royal prerogative of favour and grace.[66]

Describing royalty as being endowed with virtue by nature fitted in with Richard's belief and promotion of kingship and royal status in general. Moreover, if the Beauforts owed their status directly to the King, he could reasonably expect to gain their loyalty too. However, for the Beauforts to be legally enveloped into the royal sphere was the ultimate acceptance of the family and an unprecedented move in English history.

The details of the legitimation ceremony itself are revealing. The Beauforts took on the role of mantle-children. Mantle-children were so called as they were covered with a mantle or care-cloth at their parents' wedding, and the Beauforts were placed under the care-cloth with Katherine and Gaunt in parliament. However, the Beauforts were not strictly speaking mantle-children. This designation was usually saved for children who were born out of wedlock to two single parents who subsequently married, not for the offspring of an adulterous relationship. This speaks volumes about the way Gaunt and Katherine perceived their relationship.[67] They obviously did not view their relationship as stained with the sin of adultery but were happy to proclaim it as a love match entered into freely by both, with marriage as a natural and desirable end to a honourable relationship.

Gaunt's fondness towards his children is manifest through his inclusion of them in his regime, and through his gifts to them. Given-Wilson and Curteis argue that such affectionate relationships between fathers and bastard children were highly common; 'after all, they were often the product of genuine love-matches, whereas legitimate sons often were not'.[68] The household rolls of Gaunt show the Beauforts in attendance with Gaunt's legitimate children, with them all appearing very much as one family unit.[69] Throughout the 1380s and 1390s the Duke showered his children with gifts, both directly from his own resources and indirectly through the King and the royal exchequer.[70] This generosity extended to the Swynfords, with, for example, Thomas and his wife Joan Crophill granted an annuity of 100 marks in 1393.[71] Gaunt also referred to Thomas in his will as 'mon tres chere bacheliere'.[72] The future Henry IV continued these gifts, and explicitly stated his trust in the family: 'To the treasurer of the barons of the exchequer. Writ of *supersedes omnino* in respect of any process against John, earl of Somerset, whom the king, trusting in his loyalty and prudence, lately appointed his lieutenant of Southwales . . .'.[73] Henry also emphasised his family ties with the Beauforts, referring to them regularly as the King's brothers and sister in the official records.[74] The King also stood godfather to John Beaufort's son Henry, presumably named for his half-uncle.[75]

Perhaps it is the sensibilities of the historians who wrote during the Victorian era that prompt our surprise at the apparent ease with which illegitimate children were accepted into a medieval family. These historians discussed the adulterous relationship as a shameful affair and the resulting offspring as children who should have been hidden away. However, church moralists in the fourteenth century stated that men had a duty to all their children, legitimate or otherwise. Medieval fathers were expected to provide for, and claim as their own, all children, whether born within wedlock or not. As Given-Wilson and Curteis argue:

> It does seem true that at all social levels, there was no great stigma attached to bastardy in the Middle Ages. It is true that allegations

of bastardy were commonly used for political slander, particularly in the later middle ages, but such allegations nearly always had a specific purpose: they were designed to show that a man or woman was not entitled to claim a particular office or property. That is very different from using the allegation of bastardy to cast a slur on a person's character or reputation.[76]

Furthermore, although English common law stated that an illegitimate child could not inherit as of right, fathers were able to ensure that their children were financially secure through grants and bequests. Gaunt certainly ensured that the Beauforts were provided for in this way. And other magnates were obviously influenced not by the Beauforts' bastard status but by their royal one – it would seem certain that part of Joan's attraction to Ralph Neville was her ability to bring royal blood and royal connections to his family. Moreover, other notables surrounding Gaunt and his family were of illegitimate status.[77] Indeed, Constance herself was the daughter of Maria de Padilla, the mistress whom her father married in secret. And Gaunt was happy for his daughter Philippa to marry João I of Portugal, who was also illegitimate. João had illegitimate children himself during his marriage to Philippa, but his queen accepted these children at court.[78] The significance of royal blood was obviously greater than that of bastardy. There is no evidence of the Beauforts suffering because of their status, and, indeed, they can be seen to have lived and worked at the highest social level with ease. No doubt that was due to personal abilities as well as to royal blood. John Beaufort, for example, showed his political astuteness in his careful backing of both Richard II and Henry IV in 1399. The most telling action is that of Henry V in granting to Thomas Beaufort responsibility for the upbringing of his young son, Henry VI. To be judged capable of fulfilling such a role intimates the high regard that the Beauforts gained.

It was not just the Beauforts who benefited from royal regard. Katherine's son from her first marriage, Thomas Swynford, was one of the closest of Henry IV's friends. This friendship was demonstrated in a number of ways. The choice of a king's chamber knights was a personal matter, and Henry chose Thomas for this role.[79] Perhaps more importantly, Adam Usk in his chronicle accredited Thomas Swynford with the role of Richard II's jailer at Pontefract.[80] Documentation is extant for Thomas's claim for expenses for a journey undertaken at speed from Pontefract to King Henry, presumably with the message that Richard was dead.[81] This in itself speaks volumes of the close-knit nature of the Swynfords, Beauforts and Lancasters, as only the most highly trusted Lancastrian would have been entrusted with the role of Richard's warden. This friendship between the King and Thomas appears to have stemmed from childhood. When Thomas was only 15 years of age he was present in Henry's retinue. He went to Calais with him in 1390, and, when Henry was banished by Richard II, Thomas travelled with him to Prussia and the Holy Land. The two were obviously in close contact in England as well as abroad. Henry's accounts record expenses incurred for the bringing of two of Henry's horses from Thomas's Kettlethorpe home.[82]

Henry also spoke on Thomas's behalf over an inheritance dispute. The Patent Rolls contain the following entry for 1411:

> Notification, because on account of a doubt as to the legitimacy of the king's knight Thomas Swynford certain persons of the parts of Henaud have hitherto not permitted him to have divers inheritances in those parts which have descended to him on the side of his mother Dame Katherine de Roet, late duchess of Lancaster, that he is her son and heir and born in lawful matrimony and a writing of his annexed to these present letters, sealed with his seal of arms, is his deed and he and his father and all his ancestors on his father's side have borne the arms and used the seal.[83]

In the letter from Henry IV to his subjects that accompanied this entry Katherine is described as 'the most renowned lady', and Thomas as 'our beloved and trusty knight'.[84]

Thus the evidence demonstrates that Katherine was a highly educated and accomplished lady, and that her children were perceived similarly, enveloped into the royal sphere in England, taking on public roles alongside their legitimate family. However, there are also indications that Katherine had a reputation as an adulteress that rebounded on Thomas Swynford. But this dispute over Thomas's inheritance seems odd. It would be understandable if the doubt was over his right to Swynford property, but the details explicitly state that it was his claim to his mother's Roet inheritance that was at stake. How any doubt over his father's identity would have affected this claim is unclear. It would therefore seem most likely that this was merely a political smear, an attempt by an unnamed person to keep land that was not his by trading on a perceived reputation. Indeed, would not this land have already been Katherine's and passed from her to Thomas? If Payne had owned lands in Hainault, then they would have passed to his son Walter on Payne's death, unless Walter's death preceded that of Payne. If this was the case, then on Payne's death the lands would have been split between the succeeding daughters, with Katherine surely receiving her share at this juncture. The letter of Henry IV does suggest that Katherine had succeeded in inheriting the lands herself ('divers inheritances in those parts which have descended to him on the side of his mother'). If this was so, how could a third party claim these lands on Katherine's death because of Thomas's illegitimacy on the part of his father? It would make more sense if the claim was that he was not Katherine's son, but, again, the letter intimates that it is due to doubts over his paternal ancestors given the emphasis on Thomas's legitimate use of the Swynford seal.

Another possibility is that these lands in Hainault did have some tenuous claim to be Roet lands but that Katherine herself did nothing to claim them. However, Thomas, possibly from greed, or to get himself out of a financial tight spot, decided to claim the lands. Indeed, there are some suggestions that Thomas suffered financial hardship at various points in his life. In 1409 a notice records his outlawry on account of indebtedness to a London draper. In 1421 he is granted pardon by the council of all his debts, arrears and fines.[85] The person or persons claiming ownership might have been equally prepared to use whatever means necessary to stop

Thomas's claim and therefore used knowledge of Katherine's status as adulteress. This would, of course, have meant that Katherine had a reputation as mistress that crossed the Channel to the land of her father – or that the people involved had done some digging of their own. A further possibility, though, is that it was pure coincidence – the persons in Hainault may have been completely ignorant of Katherine's status, surely a more likely scenario given that seven years had passed since her death and fifteen since her marriage to Gaunt. The Hainault party may have used the convenient charge of illegitimacy to weaken Thomas's claim without any idea of whether this was true or even possible. Whichever is correct, though, there is the suggestion that Katherine's status was deemed as dubious under certain circumstances.

This same negative view is detectable elsewhere. It has already been discussed how, in clerical circles at least, Katherine was accepted as a respectable woman in the county of Lincolnshire. The civic population, however, appears to have held a different view. Katherine's houses at Lincoln and Grantham were broken into, her goods stolen and her servants assaulted. The same people are accused of both crimes, including Robert de Saltby, Mayor of Lincoln.[86] To what extent these were personal attacks or were merely robberies of a woman known to have wealthy connections and who would therefore have riches on the property is unknown. The double attack suggests a personal vendetta, but the same people were also accused of breaking into other people's property.[87] Moreover, Katherine was able to rent cathedral property only two years later, which suggests that there was no strong or widespread resistance against her in the town. Cole suggests that she incurred the hostility 'for some breach of municipal regulations, as the outbreak was headed by the civic authorities'.[88]

In royal circles again there are some mixed messages over Katherine's acceptance. Richard II clearly agreed to the wedding and proceeding legitimation, and as first lady Katherine escorted Richard's new bride, Isabella, from France.[89] After his seizure of Lancastrian estates on Gaunt's death, Richard restored Katherine's entitlements from the estate, clearly not perceiving her as a political enemy despite Henry's close relationship with his stepmother.[90] When Henry IV was on the throne, he referred to Katherine in gifts to her as 'the king's mother'.[91] As Henry was not king until after the death of Gaunt, this terminology could not have been at the request of the Duke but Henry's own choice.[92]

While aristocratic males were happy to embrace Katherine into the fold, aristocratic females appear to have been more dubious. Froissart's recording of the court reaction to the wedding of Gaunt and Katherine states:

> When this marriage was announced to the ladies of high rank in England, such as the duchess of Gloucester, the countess of derby, the countess of Arundel, and others connected with the royal family, they were greatly shocked, and thought the duke much to blame. They said 'he had sadly disgraced himself by thus marrying his concubine'; and added, that, 'since it was so, she would be the second lady in the kingdom, and the queen would be dishonourably accompanied by her; but that, for their parts, they would leave her to do the honours alone, for they would never enter any place where she was. They themselves would be disgraced if they suffered such a baseborn duchess . . . and their hearts would burst with grief were it to happen'. Those who were the most outrageous on the subject were the duke and duchess of Gloucester. They considered the duke of Lancaster as a doting fool for thus marrying his concubine, and declared they would never honour his lady by calling her sister.[93]

There is some artistic licence in this passage. Froissart has the ladies declaring that Katherine would dishonourably accompany the Queen. However, there was no queen when Gaunt and Katherine married – Richard's wedding took place by proxy two months later. Surely the ladies knew of Gaunt's marriage prior to Richard's own wedding? It is also interesting that, of the three ladies mentioned by name, two of them were directly connected to Gaunt's legitimate son, Henry Bolingbroke. Could it possibly be not the actual marriage but the subsequent legitimation of the Beauforts that troubled Henry's sister and mother-in-law? If Henry were to suffer in any way from the legitimation, then surely these two ladies would suffer too? Concerns for their own future may have been the catalyst for their dissension. Mistresses had no legal protection, and their illegitimate children no right to inherit – in this situation Katherine was no threat to the status quo at court and therefore readily accepted. However, the unprecedented legal confirmation of her position changed this.

This is echoed elsewhere. When Robert de Vere left his royal wife in 1387 for his mistress, a mere lady in waiting, he faced hostility from the court, which felt he had brought dishonour on the royal family. One of the notables who were offended by this affront to the Crown is the Duke of Gloucester; presumably his wife shared his dismay.[94] Status was obviously an issue, not just in how royals were affected by these unusual liaisons but also in the fact that the two ladies involved, Katherine and Agnes, were of low birth. Froissart implicitly states that the fact that Katherine was 'baseborn' was a major argument against her acceptance by the court ladies. He has the ladies crying that 'they themselves would be disgraced if they suffered such a baseborn duchess'. It would appear that the horror was someone of low birth having pre-eminence over them rather than a censuring of the adultery. As Chamberlayne argues, 'the bias of monastic and chivalric chroniclers on questions such as adultery makes it impossible to ascertain court attitudes conclusively, but a trend of increasing condemnation for the woman the lower her status is evident'.[95] This is also true of Alice Perrers. Alice, of course, was somewhat unusual as a royal mistress in that she was publicly tried and convicted in parliament for her influence on the King. Moreover, Walsingham claimed that she offended not only because of her social status but also because of her manly attributes, which did not tally with the way women were expected to behave.[96] But, again, the chroniclers emphasised her lowly birth, claiming she was the daughter of a mere tiler.

Perhaps this issue of status being more important than actions is best seen in the case of Joan of Kent. The mother of Richard II had been married twice before marrying Edward the Black Prince, and scandal surrounded these marriages, one of which ended in divorce and at least one of which was clandestine.[97] The chroniclers did mention the unsuitability of the match for Edward because of Joan's history, but her reputation was also proclaimed by the chroniclers as one of peacemaker, with much positive influence over the magnates around her. Walsingham imputed to her 'a high degree of initiative, of individual will, and of success'.[98] But Joan was an heiress and not of the low birth of Katherine, Agnes and Alice; her indiscretions were viewed with less denigration because of her social standing. The reaction of the court ladies to Katherine's marriage does not have any bearing on her unsuitability to carry out the post because of her character or accomplishments, but instead shows the snobbery that was innate in court society. This was probably intensified by the fact that Katherine was, for a time, first lady of England.

Katherine's fame is due to her relationship with Gaunt. This relationship was in itself unique. Medieval royal affairs were on the whole more casual in nature.[99] For a relationship to survive twenty-five years was unprecedented. The gifts that Gaunt granted to Katherine, as well as traditional presents such as wardships and annuities, emphasise his deep affection for her. Included in these are the gift of a silver chafing pan, and, during Gaunt's absence on campaign in 1373, deliveries of venison, fuel and timber to care for Katherine's well-being.[100] Goodman has also suggested that Gaunt rewarded an annuity of 5 marks to Katherine's former nurse.[101] However, it is possible that the lady concerned, Agneys Bonsergeant, was not Katherine Swynford's nurse but the nurse of Gaunt's daughter to Constance, also called Katherine.[102] Gaunt was also concerned with Katherine's spiritual well-being. In 1398 he founded a chantry in Lincoln Cathedral for the good estate of his duchess.[103] In his will Gaunt bequeathed to his 'most dear wife Katherine' a large quantity of jewels and money together with more personal bequests: 'The bed and appurtenances, with all the copes, tapettes, cushions, closet oreillers etc which he bought of the Duchess of Norfolk; his large bed of black velvet embroidered with a circle of fetterlocks and garters, all the beds made for his body, called in

England "trussing beds".'[104] It may seem unusual for beds to be bequests in wills. But beds were luxury items and ranked high on the list of bequests in medieval wills to favoured friends or relations. The monetary value of these items was high. For example, Simon Burley, tutor to Richard II, had a bed valued at £13 6s 8d and Robert de Vere had a bed valued at a remarkable £68 13s 4d, excluding the mattress, blankets, sheets and pillows.[105]

Should we be surprised that Gaunt could show such loyalty to his mistress, to support his children openly and to marry Katherine when politics allowed? Perhaps not, as loyalty seems to have mattered a great deal to the Duke. He had a great political skill, an ability to manipulate and use duplicity to his end, but he was tireless in his efforts to protect those in his patronage. He had a luxurious lifestyle, loved hunting and delighted in chivalrous sports, but for much of his adult life Gaunt was deeply committed to giving service to the crown through military, conciliar and diplomatic means. The Duke enjoyed his pleasures, but duty and the demands of his titles, both as the mighty Duke of Lancaster and as lord of individual manors, always came first.

For over twenty years of the illicit relationship Gaunt was married to Constance of Castile. How would this woman have viewed and treated Katherine? Sydney Armitage-Smith has argued:

> From the first she [Constance] had a rival; it must have been difficult for her, even allowing for a different standard of taste in such matters, to do the honours of the Lancastrian household, while everyone paid court to the Duke's mistress, and Katherine Swynford's position was openly acknowledged not only at the Savoy or Hertford, but at the state ceremonies of Westminster and Windsor.[106]

But would Constance and Katherine have been rivals? The marriage of Gaunt and Constance was of political importance, the ambition of both to recover the throne of Castile, to which Constance was rightful heir. Would Constance have been affected by Gaunt's love interest outside this relationship? Certainly Katherine could not be accused of interfering in the politics of Gaunt's Castilian campaigning. Indeed, she did not appear to interfere in politics at all. Goodman also suggests that Constance's position would have been compromised by Katherine's presence, stating that Katherine provided an alternative means of approaching the Duke to the 'proper' one associated with his wife.[107] It has been acknowledged that the Mayor of Leicester approached Katherine for patronage purposes in 1375–6. But it seems unlikely that this was a common experience. There are no other records to suggest that Katherine was approached directly for patronage, and surely, if Katherine was involved in politics, the chroniclers would have reported this, especially given the condemnation directed at Alice Perrers for her politicising. Indeed, this may have been the reason that Katherine did not interfere in politics. It may be more than coincidence that the only record of Katherine being approached as a channel of patronage fell before Alice Perrers's impeachment in the Good Parliament of 1376.

The Duke made no apparent efforts to separate his wife and mistress. Katherine was the messenger assigned to inform Edward III about the birth of Catalina or Katherine in 1372, and this daughter of Gaunt and Constance shared a name with the Duke's mistress.[108] In addition, both ladies attended ceremonies surrounding the Order of the Garter. Constance was granted robes in 1378, 1379, 1381, 1382–90, 1393 and 1394. Records show that Katherine was granted robes for the feast of St George in 1388, 1389, 1390, and 1395–8.[109] Therefore, on at least three occasions both wife and mistress were present at this eminent festival.

When Gaunt's Castilian ambitions finally ceased in 1389 Constance was pushed from the Lancastrian court and Katherine fully embraced.[110] As both relationships of the Duke appear to have started at the same time, it is possible to speculate that it was Katherine who was compromised by Gaunt's necessary marriage to Constance, not Constance who was compromised by Katherine.[111] Constance brought to Gaunt the prestigious title of King of Castile, and this was the reason that Gaunt married her. But Gaunt married Katherine purely because he wanted to. I do not believe that

Katherine was a rival in Constance's eyes, but that the Castilian queen tacitly accepted that Gaunt's duty and Gaunt's desire were split between two women. Her role and duty as a member of royalty were to ensure an alliance that would aid her country. Constance married Gaunt for political reasons, not for love, and was surely aware that in many political marriages one or both partners had lovers. Her own father had had a mistress. On her arrival in England she was no doubt soon aware that the King had a mistress and that the wife of the heir to the throne had a dubious sexual history. The mere knowledge that her husband had a lover cannot have affected her – it was almost to be expected when marriages were based purely on politics and not on love.

The nature of the relationship between Gaunt and Katherine may, however, have affected Constance. This was not just some 'bit on the side' but a woman whom Gaunt loved and respected immensely and with whom he had children, three sons to the one daughter that Constance produced. To our modern eyes it seems inevitable that the two women must have been rivals, their demands of Gaunt irreconcilable. And Constance may have wished that Gaunt and Katherine were not so public in their affection, and probably worried over the Beauforts sons, concerned that these children would have pre-eminence in Gaunt's affection over her daughter – the natural mothering instinct for protection. We can never know how the two women viewed each other – there is no record in the chronicles of the two meeting, of conversations, even of how household responsibilities were shared. The nearest to this we have is speculation that two of the figures in the Troilus frontispiece are Katherine and Constance. There is no way of ascertaining who the two figures are. Certainly major figures such as Chaucer, Gaunt and Richard II can be identified with some degree of certainty. But the group of women in the bottom left of the depiction is problematic. There are simply too many notable women at court who would have been invited to listen to readings and entertainments in castle grounds on a balmy summer's evening.

However, as already stated, Gaunt did not try to keep wife and mistress apart. Indeed, during the 1370s it would have been expected that Katherine and Constance were in each other's company. Surely, when in residence in England, Gaunt would have wanted his wife and her children with him; Katherine as governess to his two girls and part of his children's retinue would have been present also. Would a governess be invited to take part in outdoor entertainment? With her charges she probably would have been. But would Katherine and Constance have talked, chatted, made social small talk? Constance, as Queen of Castile and consort of Gaunt, would no doubt have treated Katherine as another servant; after all, Katherine *was* a servant, albeit a high-ranking one, of the Lancastrian household. And Katherine would have had to treat Constance with the deference and respect her position commanded.

Did Constance try to get Gaunt to end his relationship with Katherine, or at least to be more discreet? Again, we do not know. If she did, she was obviously unsuccessful. Indeed, once Constance had lost her political importance, it was she who was effectively removed from Gaunt's life. We can only speculate here, but it is pleasing to imagine that wife and mistress lived in harmony. Gaunt obviously regarded loyalty as a virtue. His loyalty to the Crown and to the divine right of kings is above question, his loyalty to friends and followers likewise. Any doubts Constance may have had over Katherine's children would surely have been settled by this attribute of Gaunt. Furthermore, Katherine's obvious wish not to interfere in politics would again have been a comfort to the Castilian queen – she did not have to fear that her husband's mistress would keep him from honouring his promises to her country. And perhaps Katherine's personality was a comfort – accomplished in social etiquette, discreet in political matters, well read and educated, would not this woman have been a companion to a queen far removed from her own lands?

It would seem that the quality that Katherine held most in abundance was discretion. The chroniclers could find nothing on a personal level with which to discredit her, and her upbringing and environment heavily suggest that, as Froissart romantically declared, she was a lady that knew all honours. The Lancastrian, Swynford and Beaufort families of which she was the link were all accomplished in education and literacy. Surely Katherine shared these characteristics and that is why she was granted the post of governess. Moreover, she did not overstep the mark when mistress. She was not politically active, her children both legitimate and illegitimate associated happily with royalty, and she appears to have waited patiently for her man to fulfil his public duties through marriage and campaigning. There is some indication that it was not all smooth sailing, with the problems of Thomas Swynford's inheritance and the attacks on her property. But these seem to be minor issues when compared to the positive portrayal that is clearly evident through Katherine's lifestyle and the widespread acceptance of her in court circles.

However, as much as we know of Katherine's accomplishments, and as much as we can speculate as to her discretion, we still know little about the specifics of her personality. Was she kind, gentle, warm, blessed with a good sense of humour? This we do not know, beyond the conjecture that her personality must have been of merit to hold Gaunt's attention and love for so long. But we can speculate further as to Katherine's character. We have already ascertained her piety. This piety and its specific links to the popular medieval saint Katherine of Alexandria suggest much about the way Katherine viewed herself and wished to be viewed. It seems that Katherine desired to create an identity and reputation for herself based on the identity and reputation of St Katherine. The ways in which she did this, and the significance of it, will be discussed in the next chapter.

CHAPTER 5

Construction of Identity

The documentary evidence for Katherine's life is limited to the writings of monks. Probable scenarios for Katherine's upbringing and education can be uncovered using information known about other medieval notables at court or throughout the country. Attitudes towards Katherine can be gleaned from the lack of information that is available about her. But the issue of how Katherine viewed herself, or how she wished others to view her, cannot be uncovered from these sources. Personal letters, a journal, or even her testament would be crucial sources here, but none of these is extant.

This whole issue is, of course, a troublesome concept. How does one capture the essence of another's identity as she saw it and wished it to be seen? This is made more problematic because of Katherine's gender and status. Her sex means that we have no accounts of her direct actions; her sexual conduct and marginal role as mistress further this lack of information – she did not play a public role that led to documentation. The nature of the medieval period, and the means by which documents survive, means that we have no diary, letters, or personal accounts of any kind that inform us of Katherine. We are in general heavily reliant on wills with regard to the investigation of people's beliefs, customs and desires, but even here there remains the problem of the scribe and the common model that he followed. People did not write their own wills, merely gave instructions to a scribe, and he transposed these instructions in standard form. However, the clearest indication of any self-perception, or desire to promote a certain image, would have come from Katherine's testament. Unfortunately, and frustratingly, this is not extant. She does appear to have written a will. The chapter accounts of Lincoln Cathedral record that in 1403, the year of Katherine's death, the Clerk of the Common together with one of the chapter messengers journeyed to Liddington to confer with the Bishop, Katherine's son Henry Beaufort, concerning the probate of her will. Puzzlingly, Katherine's will was not copied into Beaufort's episcopal register, nor is any copying apparent in the Prerogative Court of Canterbury or the Lincoln Consistory Court.[1] Was there some reason why Henry did not record its details, or was it merely a mistake, a forgotten instruction?

A further problem is to what extent there was a sense of self in the fourteenth century. Modern times are focused on the expression of the individual. 'Self' is all: we do things generally because we want to; personal desire is seen as enough to override problems or constraints to achieve what we want; self-belief is the key to success. Was this a possible, or even a desirable, scenario for a medieval woman? Were the ideas of self-belief and personal goals present in medieval society? Interpretations of sources for this information are nuanced. What we see as important now in medieval texts and art may have been of little significance then, and the contrary position is equally true; that which seems of little import to our modern eyes may have been of greatest significance at the time of creation. As much as we try to recapture a 'medieval mindset' when reading sources, both textual and pictorial, the frustration remains that much of what was significant is now lost to us.

What control could Katherine have had over her identity and the creation of a public construction – that is, a personality specifically created to promote a certain image to others? What factors influenced her self-perception and provided elements she could adopt that would allow for a public understanding of what she was trying to achieve? The frustration of Katherine's missing testament does not mean that these factors cannot be uncovered. Katherine's coat of arms and her epitaph, indeed her tomb in general, are extremely revealing about the identity promoted by this lady, particularly when coupled with gifts made by her to Lincoln Cathedral. I believe that Katherine's perception and construction of her own self were strongly linked to the ideas and associations of the popular virgin martyr St Katherine of Alexandria. This is manifest in her armorial, *Gules, three Katherine wheels, Or*. The imagery of St Katherine, the most popular saint in late medieval England, was associated with royalty and queenship and Katherine can clearly be seen to be trying to promote herself as a worthy first lady of England through the adoption of the Katherine wheel.[2] It is also possible that the martyrdom of St Katherine played a part in reassuring Katherine of her own worth – the saint defeated her enemies because of her innate goodness and worthiness in the eyes of God, and through her intellectual abilities and her more material attributes of nobility and bearing. Perhaps when gossip at the court suggested that Katherine was overstepping her mark, being able to remember the saint's suffering sustained her.

Issues of identity were important to John of Gaunt, and, indeed, to other members of the Plantagenet family. The fourteenth century saw a growth in significance and popularity of the livery badge, a device adopted as a mark of allegiance. This first became widely used under Edward III and flourished under Richard II, but, as Gaunt's was the largest retinue in England, the Duke's promotion of badges and insignia among his men was of considerable significance.[3] The most familiar of Gaunt's insignia was the Lancastrian collar of esses. The allegiance collar was a device introduced into England by Gaunt.[4] Social differentiation was marked among his retinue, with different cloths and badges awarded according to status and role, and this has been described as having the cultural impact of advertising – an active promotion of identity and association.[5] The SS collar was not the only symbol associated with Gaunt. The traditional sign of St John the Baptist, the eagle, was adopted by Gaunt as an extra crest on his armorial, and records show that in 1373 he presented as a gift an eagle in gold enamelled in white.[6] Indeed, the eagle was commonly recognised by contemporaries as a symbol of Gaunt in an age when 'heraldic symbolism carried a vital meaning and importance to everybody'.[7] It is important not to underestimate the significance of such symbols:

'notions of reality were then quite different from ours and were inseparable from the importance accorded to symbols and signs.'[8]

Although the symbolism of the collar of esses as a badge of livery and mark of association is clear, its origins are not. The original meaning of the word 'livery' was the act of giving or taking possession, and thus 'livery came to be used for all that was given or taken away at pleasure, not only badges or collars, but eventually the dress of domestic servants'.[9] A 1391–2 wardrobe account of Henry of Bolingbroke records the SS collar as the livery of the House of Lancaster, but Richard II also wore the collar, making a payment for a gold collar with seventeen letters of S and for another made with esses and the flowers of 'Souvenez vous de moi' (forget-me-not).[10] Indeed, on his return from Spain in 1389, Gaunt was wearing a collar of esses. On greeting him, Richard removed the collar from Gaunt's neck and placed it on his own, a clear symbol of trust and friendship. Furthermore, in 1394, the Earl of Arundel complained in parliament of the King's penchant for wearing the livery of Gaunt and for encouraging his own retinue to do so. Richard's reply was that he wore it as a sign of love.[11]

Many examples of people wearing the SS collar can be found on tomb brasses and effigies, the earliest being that of Sir John Swinford, who died in 1371. John Gower, the poet, is also depicted in his effigy as wearing the collar and he wrote the following about the livery:

> He who wears S I see
> At length in the same company
> Noble is he forsooth
> That same illustrious youth
> As though from the very heaven
> That faithful one had been given.[12]

Gower's collar on his effigy also depicts the Bohun swan. Henry IV on his accession can be seen to have promoted the collar, treating it almost as an order of chivalry; in 1400 he granted ten marks annually to a squire for the purposes of maintaining the dignity of the Order of the Collar.[13] During his reign it was usual for the collar and the swan badge of Bohun to be seen together, for Henry had been married to Mary de Bohun when Earl of Derby. The swan was adopted as a badge of the Bohun family because of their supposed origins from Loherangrin, the swan knight, who was son of Lady Blanchefleur and Sir Percivale, knight of King Arthur.[14] It was perhaps this connection that led Henry to adopt it as part of the collar and associate it with chivalrous acts. Of course, his model for doing so was Edward III's famous Order of the Garter, also based on Arthurian legend and a model of chivalry and nobility.

The collars appear to have been made out of different materials. The esses themselves were either lead, pewter, bronze, silver or gold and were fastened together by either silk, velvet or leather. The materials could alter in colour but seem usually to have shown either family colours, the blue and white of Gaunt, or the colours of the Crown. The collar was adapted by many beyond Gaunt and became a royal livery – although, notably, the Yorkist kings Edward IV and Richard III did not favour it. Henry Tudor, on his accession, used the collar to emphasise his link with the Plantagenet kings and used it as a symbol of unification of the Yorkist and Lancastrian lines by adding white and red roses and garter knots to the esses. A further link to Gaunt himself and not just the Plantagenets in general was the addition to the collar of the portcullis, another badge by which Gaunt was known.[15] The collar, although adopted by other royals, was still clearly linked to Gaunt through the additional use of his symbols and badges alongside it.

What the S itself stood for is unknown. Both Purey-Cust and Fletcher summarise the most favoured arguments. Fletcher believes that the meaning may have changed over time, the symbol therefore being more important than one single significance. The earliest known use of an S symbol was by Gaunt's mother, Queen Philippa, in 1348. She had a set of wall hangings of red Sindon stamped with esses. Furthermore, accounts for 1350–2 show that the Queen possessed a cloak 'powdered with gold roses of eight petals and bordered with white pearls, in the middle of each rose an S of large pearls'.[16] Under Henry IV the clearest meaning of the S is seen – his tomb is decorated with the repeated word *Souveragne*. This word was obviously of significance to him, and the S in his collars probably represented this word. What the S meant to Gaunt is unknown. The Tudor chronicler Robert Fabyan suggested uniquely that the S stood for Swynford and the collar was therefore in honour of his mistress. It seems unlikely, however, that Gaunt would have wanted to honour the married name of his mistress.

It is interesting to speculate whether Katherine herself wore the collar. Given the apparent widespread use of it throughout Gaunt's retinue, this was more than likely. It is known that women wore the collar as well as men – again, evidence from tomb brasses and effigies confirms this. The extant depictions of Katherine's monumental brass are not clear enough to establish whether she is portrayed as wearing one. However, we do know that her daughter wore one. On the Neville tomb at Staindrop, Joan Beaufort is clearly wearing the collar, as are both her husband and his first wife.

Within this context of badge wearing, and the widespread use of livery symbols at court and within Gaunt's retinue, it was perhaps inevitable that Katherine herself was concerned with issues of identity and image. This concern is most evident in her armorial: *Gules, three Katherine wheels, Or.* Coats of arms as heraldic devices increased in significance, as we have seen with livery in general, under the Plantagenets: 'Coats of arms made their appearance, at least from the middle years of the thirteenth century, not just on the accoutrements of the mounted knight, but displayed in ways in which they could be seen by all.'[17] This aspect of social display appears to have been the primary purpose of coats of arms in the fourteenth century; heraldic devices appeared on vestments, liturgical vessels, domestic plate, household objects, seals, architecture and funereal monuments. It was possibly out of this growth in heraldry that the badge found significance as a simpler form of the armorial that could be used as a distinct device for allegiance.[18] The heraldic device had a deeper significance than mere art and display, however, as seen most clearly in the contest of Scrope versus Grosvenor for the right to bear arms *Azure, a bend Or.* Scrope discovered that Grosvenor was using the same arms while on campaign with Richard III. He successfully argued that his family had been associated with the armorial since the Norman Conquest. Grosvenor was ordered by the courts to change his armorial. The symbolism of arms was obviously close to the foundation of identity and construction; it was not just a mere device to stamp possession on items, but a statement of who one was. This had not been the first time that Scrope had contested the use of his arms in court.

As coats of arms began as a matter of convenience, a means of recognition on the battlefield, they are most clearly associated with men. Women did not bear arms in their own right but displayed them as an extension of their male family, either father or husband: 'they were rarely, unless they were heiresses, manifest heraldically as separate personalities.'[19] This makes the matter of Katherine's armorial all the more interesting as it can be clearly seen to represent Katherine alone, separate from the males around her. It has been suggested that Katherine wheels were the arms of her father, Sir Payne Roet. For example, Bentley states that Payne's arms 'in allusion to his name were *Gules, three Catherine wheels, Or*', and Given-Wilson and Curteis state that Katherine shared her paternal Roet arms, the French *roue* meaning wheel.[20] However, I believe that this is incorrect.

Katherine wheels were clearly the armorial of Katherine, recorded as such from her tomb detailing by both William Dugdale and Gervase Holles in the seventeenth century.[21] However, the Roet arms were plain wheels, as adopted by Thomas Chaucer and visible as such on his tomb. They are also portrayed as plain wheels originating from Payne Roet on the 'Progenie' page of Thomas Speght's edition of the *Workes* of Chaucer.[22] Moreover, and perhaps more significantly, the Roet arms are portrayed as *Argent, three wheels, Or* on the tomb of Lewis Robsert, standard-bearer to Henry V and mentioned in the will of Thomas Beaufort.[23]

It is interesting that Thomas Chaucer chose his maternal Roet arms over his paternal Chaucer arms, these being *parti per pale, a bend over all*.[24] Indeed, of the twenty coats of arms represented on his tomb, the only male ones are those of the Beauforts. The rest represent the female side of his family, a clear sign of Thomas's ambitions, as the female side was of more political and monetary significance than the male. This affiliation to the female side of his family allows the differentiation between the Roet arms and Katherine's own to be made. The significance of Katherine wheels over plain ones may now appear lost to us. We can all make the association of Katherine and the wheel, but, beyond the allusion to her name, the reasons why Katherine adopted these arms may appear clouded. However, she made the deliberate choice to change them, an unusual step in itself for a woman to display her own arms, and it would appear that she adopted them on her marriage to Gaunt in replacement of her Swynford arms. The exact date of the change in arms is unknown. In the Sanderson edition of Dugdale, an editor's note states that:

> In an old pane of glass the arms of John of Gaunt and Katherine Swineford are expressed:
> (1) France and England, quarterly, a label of three points ermine.
> (2) Argent, on a cheveron sable, three boars heads cupped, or. (Swynford)
> Under which is written – John of Gaunt and Katherine Swynford his third wife has essew John of Beaford.[25]

This would appear to be a 'non-official' image. It is hard to imagine that Katherine kept only her Swynford connection prominent after marriage to Gaunt. However, on her marriage to Hugh she would have adopted his arms and in her widowhood would probably have continued in her use of these, if only for the ease of association with her Lincolnshire estates, which she held in wardship for her son Thomas. On her marriage to Gaunt, therefore, she faced a choice: her armorial could now be changed, but what to change it to? It is interesting to speculate as to why she did not adopt the arms of Gaunt, and did not keep some allusion to Swynford. It was usual for women who remarried to combine arms of fathers and husbands. For example, Elizabeth de la Plaunche married five times; 'the shield on her seal is divided into equal divisions with her paternal arms in the centre. However, the husbands have been re-ordered according to their social significance regardless of the chronology of her marriages.'[26] The most natural outcome would have been for Katherine's armorial to form a combination of Swynford and Gaunt, with possibly a reference to Roet. The fact that Katherine decided to adopt wholly new arms, with no reference to husbands or father, is of considerable significance. It demonstrates both that Katherine was aware of the strength of armorials as a badge of identity and that the Katherine wheel was a significant symbol to her. This link to St Katherine is strengthened by the general level of piety shown by Katherine, and by other connections that can be found between Katherine and the saint.

Devotion to the saints was an integral part of medieval religion. Images associated with them decorated parish churches, cathedrals and monastic institutions. Saints' lives or *Vita*, the recording and retelling of the legends of the saints, were extremely popular, and many manuscripts were produced, seen both through testamentary bequests and the number of extant manuscripts. The virgin martyrs, classical saints famed for their steadfastness in keeping their purity despite immense pressure through torture, were a highly popular genre of saints in the fourteenth century, second only to the fast-growing devotion to the Virgin Mary. Indeed, the virgin martyrs were often depicted in association with the Virgin Mary and can be seen to have formed a female community around Christ. Within this context St Katherine of Alexandria was the most popular medieval saint: over fifty parish churches were dedicated to her, and she appears constantly in manuscript collections of saints' lives and in wall paintings and other decorations.

The *Vita* or life of St Katherine follows many of the conventions of the virgin-martyr legends. She was of noble birth, beautiful, educated and deeply devoted to her Christian religion and to Christ in particular. She faced pagan opposition in the form of Roman male authority, which attempted to persuade her away from her path through torture and threats to her virgin status. These males, of course, failed in their attempts, and, indeed, Katherine was responsible for the conversion of many of them to Christianity. The method of torture chosen to break her was a spiked wheel, but at the crucial moment angels destroyed it. Winstead states that by the late medieval period the saints were distinguished from each other by the methods of torture used against them: 'although St Katherine could be and was identified by some combination of a book, a crown, a trod-upon Emperor Maxentius, or a sign of her mystical marriage, her wheel is almost never omitted.'[27] She continues that 'the paradox of the virgin's triumph is distilled in their emblems, where instruments of torture designed to erase identity are used to proclaim identity'.[28] The wheel was meant by Maxentius to kill Katherine and to destroy her ability to convert his followers to Christianity. Instead the wheel became her symbol, emphasising her holiness and worth before God.

The wheel therefore became a symbol uniquely and unequivocally associated with St Katherine. Indeed, one of the most frequently portrayed images of the lives of the virgin martyrs was the destruction of the wheel in Katherine of Alexandria's story.[29] The symbol proclaimed the virgin's power and inability to be harmed. And medieval people, on seeing the wheel, would have thought of St Katherine and have been reminded of her story, with which they were so familiar. As a consequence, Katherine's adoption of the Katherine wheels for her own armorial and emblem would have been perceived as a clear desire to be associated with the legend of the saint and would have evoked images from the saint's lives in medieval minds:

> Livery badges deriving from such sources as names, family mythology, or individual devotions were certainly very popular in this period, and were often a way of establishing both one's identity as part of a wider group, and loyalty towards the head of that group. Katherine Swynford therefore marks herself out as a loyal follower of St Katherine's, and perhaps as part of the saint's 'entourage'.[30]

But what would this association say about Katherine Swynford? Which elements of St Katherine's story would have been evoked by this woman's armorial? Winstead observes that, 'while writers of late medieval conduct books agreed that women should be gracious, humble, obedient, and soft-spoken, virgin martyrs tended to be abrasive, defiant, shrewish, and sharp-tongued'.[31] How can these women have been used to promote a positive image? The saints' 'unfeminine' behaviour appears to have been forgiven because they used their shrewishness to the defence of God. And within this can be detected a clarity of thought and soundness of mind that are usually associated in medieval texts not with women but with men. The saints' female status makes them vulnerable; they are after all the inferior sex. But their abilities lift them above the role of mere females to the higher status usually reserved for men. In this it would seem that a fourteenth-century female wishing to aspire to the levels of these paradigms was setting herself a task too far. A saint may be able to reach levels not normally associated with women, but could a mere secular female do the same?

There are many elements of St Katherine's tale that would have inspired females and provided, if not a role model as such, then certainly aspects of character and personality that could be used to promote their own status. Katherine Swynford was not the only woman associated with the English royal family who displayed a devotion to St Katherine: 'Her popularity with those of the highest status can be accounted for, in part, by her role as a particularly powerful intercessor. In addition, as a queen, and the daughter of a king, she shares that status, and would, therefore, have been seen as an appropriate saint by a royal devotee.'[32] Indeed, although all virgin martyrs are of noble status, only St Katherine is described explicitly as a sovereign queen.[33] The adoption of the Katherine wheels, then, and the affiliation with this saint, were clearly a representation of Katherine's desire to create for herself an image of royalty and respectability. The link as intercessor is important here also. Saints were, after all, intercessors. Crudely put, devotees prayed to the saints for help; if the saints looked on one kindly, then they would intercede with God on one's behalf. Likewise, noble women were a channel of intercession and patronage in the earthly world. If someone was out of favour with the ruling lord, then an appropriate approach to the lady might prove successful. In this respect, the link between saints and noble females is clear. It has already been noted that Katherine's role as patron was limited. Katherine of Alexandria's noble status and her explicit royal link will have provided one reason why Katherine wished to affiliate herself to this particular saint. On her marriage to Gaunt she had to lift herself from the marginal role of mistress to that of first lady of England. She needed to appear royal and respectable, and the badge of St Katherine will have helped her to promote this image.

Katherine's association with the Hospital of St Katherine by the Tower of London is also revealing here. The hospital was under royal control and, more importantly, was associated specifically with royal women. From Eleanor of Provence onwards the hospital was patronised by the Queens of England. Lewis has argued that through this patronage 'a connection to St Katherine came to be an intrinsic part of the conception and practice of English queenship for the rest of the middle ages'.[34] This in itself may have proved of importance for Katherine's devotion. As first lady of England after her marriage to Gaunt, and as second lady after Richard II's marriage to the very young Isabella, it is highly probable that Katherine was involved in the role of patron of the hospital. Her family was certainly connected to the institution. It was here that John Beaufort wrote his will: 'In the year following our Lord's incarnation in the English Church, 1409, on 16 March, at the hospital of Saint Katherine by the tower of London.'[35] It is probable that the eldest Beaufort shared his mother's devotion. A Book of Hours commissioned for himself and his wife, Margaret, contains an exquisite illumination of St Katherine kneeling before her wheel.[36] More significant than this is the fact that John of Gaunt set up a chantry at the Hospital.[37] Unfortunately the details are not known, but it would seem more than probable that Katherine was to be one of the benefactors.

Another aspect of the saint that may have appealed directly to Katherine is that of her educated status. All the virgin martyrs had the ability to answer their oppressors fluently, and this ability was accredited to them through the grace of God. However, the majority of the middle English lives of St Katherine describe her as learned through her own study.[38] As an educator herself in her previous role as governess and as educated herself, as shown through her involvement in book networks, Katherine may have been attracted by this aspect of her name saint. She was not only royal, as she herself had now become, but was also of similar intellectual status.

The appeal may of course have lain purely in the saint's role as intercessor. Katherine's piety has already been demonstrated, yet her life had been lived in a way that did not accord with the standard Christian values. Katherine may just have been appealing to her name saint to help her achieve the goal of a place in heaven. Katherine was the member of at least two religious fraternities that had dedications to St Katherine. As Duchess of Lancaster, she was admitted to the Coventry Guild of the Holy Trinity, St Mary, St John the Baptist and St Katherine.[39] As a member of the fraternity of Lincoln Cathedral, Katherine received the spiritual benefits of the thirty or forty masses celebrated on behalf of the brothers and sisters in the cathedral, and mass was said for the fraternity at the altar of St Katherine.[40]

However, it seems unlikely that, if this had been the case, Katherine would have adopted the saint's emblem as her own. If her concern was merely with prayer and intercession, the traditional devotion, then surely she would have had images of St Katherine on her altars and in her chapels but would not have specifically displayed these images as her own through the use of livery badges and armorial. Her choice of armorial suggests that a clearer link with the saint was manifest in Katherine's mind, and she undoubtedly wanted this link to be manifest in the minds of others. She certainly strongly promoted the use of the Katherine wheel as a personal badge. Both Gaunt and Katherine made considerable gifts to Lincoln Cathedral after their marriage. These gifts were adorned with the insignia of the couple. A falcon holding a fetterlock in his beak was one of Gaunt's badges, and he donated to the cathedral, out of 'a certain devotion' to the Church, cloths decorated with these emblems. Other decorations included his collar of esses.[41] Katherine's gifts to the cathedral were:

Item a chesable of Rede bawdkyn w^t orfreys of gold w^t leopardes powdered w^t blake treyfolyes and ij tunacles and iij albes of the same suete w^t all the apparell of the gyft of the duchese of lancast.

Item xx fayre copes of the same suete every of then having iij wheils of sylver in the hoodes of the gift of same duches of lancast.

Item a chesuble of Rede velvett w^t Kateryn wheils of gold w^t ij tunacles & iij albes w^t all the apparell of the same suete of the gyft of the duches of lancastr.

Item v coopes of Rede velvett w^t Kateryn wheils of gold of the wyche iij hath orfreis of blak cloth of gold and other ij hath orfreys w^t Images Kateryn wheils and sterres.

Item other iiij coopes of Rede sateñ fygurys w^t Kateryn wheilles of gold w^t orfreys havyng Images staffes & Kateryn wheilles.

Item two clothes of redd velvett brodered wth Katherine wheeles of gould of divers lengths and divers breadths, wth a frontlett of ye same worke perteyning to one of ye clothes.[42]

Here Katherine is clearly using the Katherine wheel as her badge of identity in the same way that Gaunt used his esses. When the cloths were used or displayed, the imagery of the wheel would not only evoke the saint but would remind all that the Duchess of Lancaster was the benefactor from whom these gifts came. Using the wheel as her badge, Katherine was associating herself with the saint in a manner that demonstrates more than piety – it demonstrates a clear desire to be seen in the same positive light in which the saint was seen, royal, respectable and educated. Indeed, the very giving of cloth was an association in itself. The courtesy text *The Book of the Knight of the Tower* states that, 'As of seynt Elyabeth, of seynt Katheryn and of seynt Agathe and other mo, that gaue their gownes to the poure folke for the loue of god And soo ought to doo euery good woman.'[43] Furthermore, a medieval altar panel in Bruges has St Katherine depicted in a gown embroidered with wheels, and it was gowns such as this that Katherine was giving to the cathedral.[44]

Beyond the issue of how others would view her is the issue of how Katherine viewed herself. To take on the emblem of Katherine of Alexandria in this way indicates, I believe, a great deal of what Katherine thought of herself. To promote herself as royal and respectable suggests that this is what Katherine believed herself to be. Indeed, if her bearing and character were as I have laid out in previous chapters, refined and noble in behaviour, accomplished in many arts, then to see herself as capable of carrying out her new royal role would not have been ambitious. The link with St Katherine may also have been self-affirming. Lewis states that the saint provides a supreme example of faith and fortitude. It may be that in moments of personal doubt, in the face of gossip from others at court, particularly from females born into noble status, the adoption of the wheel reminded Katherine that she was worthy of her new role and provided her with the personal strength to ignore the slanders.

It is clear elsewhere that Katherine viewed herself as capable of the role of duchess and that, after her marriage to Gaunt, she wished not to be remembered for her marginal role as mistress but for her respectable role as royal wife. She was clearly anxious that her reputation throughout perpetuity had no association with Swynford or her role as mistress. Her tomb is an interesting testament to this: 'the burial of the noblewomen may be viewed as her last public appearance and one which she often appeared eager to make the most of and prepare for carefully.'[45] As Jones and Underwood state, 'death in the later middle ages was a voyage from one world into another for which careful preparations had to be made'.[46] The increasing awareness in the fourteenth century of the concept of purgatory clearly had influence here. People were aware that they needed intercessors to help them through purgatory, and the decoration of tombs with religious images and the setting-up of chantries so mass would be performed for them after death, were all part of this awareness. Death to medieval people was a larger concern in life than it is to the modern mind. Preparations for death were a display of piety: 'The belief in the efficacy of prayers was deep-rooted, and it was held that the soul's time in purgatory could be shortened as a result of prayers said on earth.'[47]

Women were involved in preparations for death, for themselves and for members of their families. For example, wills provide evidence that women were explicit in their instructions for what decoration their tombs were to have, not just in terms of piety but also as to family connections displayed in the form of seals and armorials on the tomb.[48] Reputation was equally important in death as in life, and it would seem that women as well as men were concerned with their associations throughout perpetuity. Previous discussion of Thomas Chaucer's tomb and the arms he chose to display provides a male example of this creation of bonds, no doubt driven by ambition, in death.

Although people undoubtedly wished to have their own influence on their own tomb, as evidenced through wills and chantry instructions, sometimes families had more influence than the deceased: 'A long time could elapse before an image was erected. In some cases its appearance had more to do with ancestry and claims of ancient possession of a manor than to the desire to honour the deceased. Matters of prestige were involved; the necessity of doing what was fitting and proper.'[49] For example, Sir Thomas Stathum of Morley, Derbyshire, who died in the fifteenth century, was explicit in his will of how he wished his tomb to be, yet the extant monument is different in a number of ways.[50]

On the whole effigies and brasses were stylistically similar. Female effigies were not in any sense intended to be individual portraits; 'the stock physical features of the idealised portrait are often apparent.'[51] Furthermore, the tombs of women are often more uniform in design than those of men:

Women are normally shown, whether alone or besides their husbands, as if they were standing still, looking youthful and slender, their feet often resting on an image of a cherished pet dog. They are represented with eyes open, either engrossed in prayer with their hands folded, or holding a heart, a heraldic shield or a cloak strap. For most of the period there is little variation in fashion, clothes tending to be all-enveloping and voluminously draped, but towards the end of the fourteenth century a shift in attitude is heralded by the tomb of Edward III's queen, Philippa of Hainault, at Westminster Abbey, showing her, presumably as she chose to be represented, as a middle-aged and portly figure in a fashionably close-fitting dress.[52]

Brasses, as well as effigies, had many common features – any desire to see true representations of facial characteristics in medieval monuments must be frustrated. The standard conventions of female beauty – youth, high forehead, long neck, narrow waist and long arms – are all that are represented. The fourteenth century did see a change in the nature of brasses, though:

Having become widely established, brasses increasingly reflected the religious and social sentiments of the time. They become more picturesque, by incorporating representations of favourite saints, especially the iconography of the Virgin Mary and the Trinity . . . Brasses also become more family-minded, by referring to the lineage of the deceased in an inscription, by showing married couples . . . and eventually by showing children.

Originally brasses were memorials for highly placed ecclesiastical patrons, but by the late fourteenth century the brass was principally the monument of the middle ranks of society, the new gentry classes.[53]

Wylie described Katherine as being buried with 'monumental magnificence'.[54] This is an interesting choice of description. John H. Harvey, in the Lincoln Minster pamphlet about Katherine's tomb, provides the fullest detail of the monument and its probable origins. His opening statement is 'On the south side of the presbytery of Lincoln Cathedral, and in the western arch of the two bays forming the sanctuary, stand two medieval tombs beneath a stone canopy.'[55] This is a much more stark description than that of Wylie, but I believe it is the more accurate for its starkness. Compared to other tombs of the same period, Katherine's monument is noticeably less magnificent than the norm. Indeed, particularly with regard to the actual tomb and brass, it could be described as very plain and simple. The monument has several unusual features, and Harvey describes in detail the surrounding structure and the general architecture of the tomb. The monument that stands today is not that of the medieval period (the brasses and other images were destroyed in 1644), but descriptions of the tomb are extant that were made prior to this date of destruction. I think it is notable that in these the description is not that the tomb was magnificent but rather that it is 'curious'.[56] A planned restoration of the monument in the nineteenth century came to nought. Harvey believes this was due to comments that the proposed design was too elaborate, as the belief was that the original was 'plain'.[57]

There are a number of features that are noteworthy. In particular, why was there a brass and not a marble or stone effigy? Given the normal extravagance of royal and noble tombs in the same period and Binski's conclusion that brasses were the domain of the gentry and merchant ranks, this seems odd. The brass itself was very simple. Katherine was depicted recumbent, her head on a pillow and her hands together in prayer. She wore the veil of a widow on her head and a simple robe and cloak. Available pictures of the brasses are not clear enough to allow conclusions as to the presence of jewellery or other additional ornamentation. Katherine lay under a single canopy above which were two coats of arms, her own and those of Gaunt. A simple epitaph ran around the outside of the brass, and there was no other detailing. Along the sides of the tomb chest are indents for shields within garters; the detail of which shields were represented here are not known. It would appear that Katherine's tomb and that of her daughter Joan were enclosed. John Leland in *c.* 1540 described the two tombs as being in a chapel, suggesting an enclosed space. Presumably the enclosure was made of iron grills, accounting for the name by which Katherine's chapel was known, 'le Irons'.[58]

In contrast to Katherine's simple tomb are those of Gaunt and of their eldest son, John Beaufort. Gaunt was buried, as requested in his will, at St Paul's, alongside his first wife, Blanche of Lancaster. His monument is everything one would expect from such a high-ranking and influential member of late medieval society. Likewise that of John Beaufort. John's widow Margaret assured him a magnificent tomb of Purbeck marble with alabaster effigy in St Michael's Chapel in Canterbury Cathedral. The tomb was built on such a scale that the Norman apsidal chapel was taken down and rebuilt on a more extended scale to allow for the planned design of the monument.[59]

Again the loss of Katherine's testament means the loss of information, on this occasion with regard to who chose the position and detailing of her monument. Presumably her will would have included details of her own wishes on this matter. No document concerned with the making of the tomb is extant, again compounding the lack of knowledge. It would seem certain that it was Katherine's choice to be buried at Lincoln. She had several attachments to the town, choosing to live there on various occasions in her life. She was also attached to the cathedral through her admittance to the Fraternity of the Cathedral and through her giving of gifts. It is probable that this link was due to her devotion to and association with St Katherine. Devotion to saints centred around pilgrimage to and worship at a shrine of the saint, the favoured one being where the body actually lay. St Katherine's body, or what was believed to be her body, was entombed in a chapel on the top of Mount Sinai. Obviously pilgrimage to this site was out of the reach of most English devotees. The answer was to have alternative shrines. For St Katherine these shrines tended to be chapels on the top of hills, mimicking that of Mount Sinai – for example, at Abbotsbury in Dorset. Here, other relics of the saint could be venerated. It is possible that Lincoln Cathedral may have offered such an experience to Katherine devotees. The cathedral is, after all, on the top of a hill, and among the cathedral's relics was a finger of St Katherine, contained in a long pearled case.[60] Presumably this relic was held at the altar of St Katherine in the splendid thirteenth-century Angel Choir. The Angel Choir was where Katherine's monument was placed.

Of course, Katherine was not in the position of being entombed next to her husband. Gaunt had already made his decision that he would lie with Blanche, the woman who had brought him the lands that led to his wealth and power. The monument was designed and made before Gaunt's own death. There was no space for an additional spouse. However, Gaunt did wish to make provision for Katherine in death. A royal licence for the foundation of a chantry of two chaplains in Lincoln Cathedral was granted to Gaunt on 17 September 1398 for the good estate of himself and Katherine.[61] However, it would appear that this was never established, possibly in the confusion surrounding the confiscation of the Lancastrian estates on Gaunt's death. Katherine's daughter Joan felt it necessary in 1437 to found a perpetual chantry for her mother, suggesting that one was not already in place:

Licence for Joan, countess of Westmorland, and her heirs, to found a perpetual chantry of two chaplains to celebrate divine service daily at the altar before which her mother Katherine, late duchess of Lancaster, is buried, in the cathedral church of Lincoln, for the good estate of the king and of Henry, cardinal of England, and of the said countess while alive, and for their souls after death, and for the souls of Henry IV, Henry V, John, late duke of Lancaster, and the said Katherine, late his wife, Ralph, late earl of Westmorland, sometime the husband of the said countess, and for the souls of the ancestors and benefactors of the said earl and countess and of all the faithful departed; the said chantry to be called the Chantry of Katherine late duchess of Lancaster, in the cathedral church of Lincoln.[62]

The celebration of divine service in Katherine's chantry happened daily at 7 a.m. and continued into the sixteenth century, with its presence recorded in the cathedral timetables of 1506–7 and 1531.[63]

The actual date of the building of Katherine's monument is unknown. It is possible that the building of the monument as a chantry chapel started at the time of this grant. However, as Katherine's son Henry was Bishop of Lincoln at the time of her death, it would seem likely that he would have ensured the construction of a worthy monument, and it seems most probable that the tomb and monument were constructed around 1404–5.[64] Harvey has argued that:

> The form taken by the monument and its enclosure within iron grilles probably did reflect the known intention to found a chantry. . . . It is worth noting that Richard Fleming, Bishop of Lincoln 1420–1431, was buried in the tomb said to have been made before his death, yet his chantry was not founded until the period when his nephew Robert Fleming was dean (1452–1483).[65]

It is therefore most likely that Henry and Joan Beaufort were carrying out the wishes of their mother in the construction of the monument and foundation of a chantry, following instructions, certainly for the monument at least, from Katherine's will.[66] Any reason for the delay on the part of the chantry can only be conjecture, but the decision to right the situation in 1437 was probably made out of Joan's preparations for her own death. Indeed, in her will she requests to be buried 'in the same altar where the body of lady Katherine, Duchess of Lancaster, my mother is buried'.[67] However, Harvey speculates that this was an afterthought, the original tomb and canopy of Katherine suggesting that the design was meant for a single tomb only. The additions of Joan's tomb, now placed head to toe with her mother's, was originally placed to the side of Katherine's tomb and extended beyond the constraints of the stonework.[68] This again suggests that Katherine was the influence behind the design to the monument. She would not have made allowance for additional tombs in her chantry, as she would not have believed that there was anyone to be buried with her. Her husbands were dead and placed elsewhere, and she presumably believed that her daughter would be buried with her husband, as indeed Ralph Neville had intended, given the effigies on his tomb at Staindrop.

It is interesting to speculate as to the nature of the altar in this chantry. Draper states that 'chantries could be endowed at existing altars, but new altars were founded and furnished for this purpose wherever space could be found in the church, even up against a pier'.[69] The wording of Joan's request for a chantry does not make it clear whether the altar existed before Katherine's monument or not. Clearly an altar was in place, as the request states for mass to be said at the altar at which Katherine was buried, but whether this was new with the monument is not known. The wording perhaps suggests this to be the more favourable option. Surely if the altar was in existence prior to Katherine's monument, it would have had a name that would have have been referred to subsequently by Joan. Indeed, the styling chosen by Joan in the name of the chantry is notable and will be discussed in more detail below.

Katherine's devotion would suggest that in her will she requested that the altar in her chantry be dedicated to St Katherine. Images of the saint were probably on display here. Indeed, it is interesting to speculate that the gifts given to the cathedral by Katherine, embroidered with the emblem of the saint, were intended to be used in her own chantry. Beyond the link with St Katherine, the simpleness of the tomb is revealing. Again it indicates the discretion apparent in Katherine's character. She could have chosen an elaborate tomb and placed this at Westminster or St Paul's, yet she went for a discreet, almost private display. She certainly could not be accused of being tasteless or lewd or obsessed with finery on account of her monument. There is no sense of pride or conceit. Although we can only guess at the heraldry displayed on the side of her tomb, those included in her brass are known, described by Dugdale as:

> Arms, in pale
> (1) France and England, quarterly; a label of 3 points ermine,
> (2) Gules, three Catherine wheels or.[70]

These arms reflect solely Katherine and Gaunt. There is no reference to Katherine's past, no mention of Swynford or Roet. This is echoed in her epitaph:

Here lies dame Katherine, Duchess of Lancaster, third wife of the very noble and very gracious prince John Duke of Lancaster, son of the very noble king Edward III. The which Katherine died the tenth day of May the year of our grace 1403. On which our Lord have mercy. Amen.

She is simply Dame Katherine, Duchess of Lancaster, wife of the very noble and very gracious prince John, Duke of Lancaster. She did not include elaborate descriptions of herself; the adjectives were reserved for her husband alone. And John's presence in her epitaph is almost one of status confirmation only; she was duchess because she was married to the duke.

This sense of emphasising her status of duchess to the exclusion of any other status she held is apparent again in the documents of her daughter. The licence granting the right for celebrating mass at Katherine's tomb would have been written by a scribe to a standard format. However, within it, it is notable that Katherine's only description is as the wife of John, Duke of Lancaster. Further, the name of the chantry, which will have been given to the scribe by Joan, presumably from details in Katherine's will, was to be, simply, the Chantry of Katherine, late Duchess of Lancaster. In her own will, Joan refers to Katherine twice, once as 'the lady Katherine, Duchess of Lancaster, my mother', and the second time as 'the illustrious lady and my mother Lady Katherine, Duchess of Lancaster'.[71] Connections to the ducal house of Lancaster were obviously important to Joan – in her own epitaph she is described as the daughter of the Duke of Lancaster:

> Filia Lancastri ducis inclyta sponsa Johannis,
>   Westmorland primi subiacet hic Comitis.
> Desine scriba suas virtutes promere, nulla
>   vox valeat merita vix reboare sua.
> Stirpe, decore, fide, tum fama, spe, prece, prole,
>   actibus et vita polluit ymmo sua.
> Nacio tota dolet pro morte, Deus tulit ipsam
>   in Bricii festo C quater M. quater x.

153

Here lies the daughter of John, duke of Lancaster, and glorious spouse of the first Lord Westmorland. Author, cease the list of her virtues – there scarcely exists a voice capable of extolling her merits. Great she was in her lineage, beauty, faith, fame, promise, piety and offspring, greater still in her actions and life. The entire nation grieves her death. God took her on St Brice's Day, 1440.[72]

Henry Beaufort also mentions his parents in his will: 'and because those who have in special memory masses for their souls John Duke of Lancaster and Katherine his wife and my parents . . .'.[73] Again, Katherine is granted respectability; no mention of a Roet or Swynford background is made. In all these documents and descriptions she is merely Duchess of Lancaster.

I believe that this was Katherine's own terminology for herself and one she would have used in her will. It certainly does not seem that she referred to herself as Swynford, regardless of her Lincolnshire landholdings. Obviously she wished to limit her reputation to that of noble status and respectable wife. This is further evidenced in the documentation surrounding the inheritance problems of Thomas Swynford. I believe that in these documents it is likely that Katherine was referred to in the same terminology as that of her testament, as they regarded the passage of inheritance that would have followed the inquisition into her death. Obviously, the scribe would have had influence here, but in both the entry in the Patent Rolls and in Henry IV's accompanying letter she is termed Katherine de Roet, late Duchess of Lancaster.[74] Roet is no doubt included because the inheritance originated from the Roet family. But nowhere is she Katherine Swynford, lady of Kettlethorpe. Given that the dispute was due to a doubt that Thomas was born in lawful matrimony, it seems odd that 'Swynford' was not included. The royal letters merely state that Thomas was legitimate, not who his father was nor Katherine's link to the Swynfords.

Interestingly, in the letter of John and Katherine to the Pope regarding the ratification of their marriage, Katherine is styled Catherine de Swynforde. But would Katherine have had a choice in how she was named here, or any influence over the content of this document at all? It seems unlikely. The petition to which this was a response was presumably prepared by a scribe with the briefest of instructions as to its contents. It seems clear that Katherine's own choice was to style herself Duchess of Lancaster, and it is as certain as it is possible to be without recourse to her actual will that Katherine did not include Swynford in her final document. This image of respectable duchess is apparent in the proceedings surrounding her marriage. In the petition, Gaunt and Katherine emphasised that Katherine was unmarried at the time of their adultery. In addition to this is the issue of the Beauforts as mantle-children.

After the marriage of the couple came the legitimation ceremony in parliament of the Beaufort children. The Beauforts clearly took on the role of mantle-children here. Mantle-children were so called as they were covered with a mantle or care-cloth at their parents' wedding and the four Beaufort children were placed under the care-cloth along with their parents. However, the Beauforts were not strictly speaking mantle-children. This designation was usually saved for children who were born out of wedlock to two single parents who subsequently married, not for the offspring of an adulterous relationship.[75] It would appear that the couple were attempting to dissolve the stain of adultery, promoting their children as born out of wedlock but not as a result of adultery. It is as if the new Duchess of Lancaster believed that God now blessed her unity with Gaunt and therefore her past role as mistress was absolved. Here, also, a link to St Katherine can be made. The saint was known as a marriage broker and a help to wives. Perhaps Katherine believed that her prayers to the saint had been answered and Katherine of Alexandria had interceded on her behalf in ensuring the marriage took place and her children were therefore accepted into society.

But to whom was Katherine promoting this respectable image? God was all-seeing, and, although she may have been granted divine forgiveness for her sin, He would still have remembered it. Katherine was anxious to emphasise her image as duchess for earthly perpetuity. The concern for reputation was paramount.

Criseyde's recurring question was 'What will they think?' Perhaps here there is a link between Katherine and Chaucer's heroine. The lack of Katherine's testament means that much of what we know about her is based on conjecture. But it would seem clear that Katherine was concerned with issues of identity and reputation, was anxious to promote a respectable construction of herself. The link here to St Katherine, manifest through her armorial and the use of the Katherine wheel and her badge, enforces this view. The association in the medieval mind with St Katherine as royal, respectable, educated and noble would have been transferred to Katherine through her choice of livery. Katherine was deeply devoted to the saint, but this use of her emblem in the construction of identity was surely beyond that of piety alone. Katherine wished to carve a respectable reputation for herself, and the saint provided a model with which she could do this.

CHAPTER 6

Saintly Appropriations

I started the previous chapter by asking to what extent a medieval woman could have agency over her own public identity and over the construction and promotion of this identity. Katherine Swynford clearly provides a positive answer to this question. Moreover, her example suggests that not only could a female have and maintain control over her own image but that the models and associations she used could be female as well. Katherine's armorial clearly shows that she purposely appropriated the symbol of St Katherine for her own use. Kolve discusses the language of sign in the fourteenth century, stating that there were three levels to this:

> There is first of all a vocabulary of *attribute*, which allows the ready identification of certain historical or pseudo-historical persons: the crown and the harp that indicates King David, for example, or St Catherine with her wheel, or St Lawrence with the gridiron of his martyrdom. Such objects mean themselves literally, but their significance derives from a history or legend which must be learned. There is also a vocabulary of *symbol*, in which things mean other than themselves: the Holy Ghost is not a dove, but a dove can stand for the Holy Ghost, in painting or in literature. And finally, there are complex *allegorical figures*, generally abstract ideas expressed in human form, often accompanied by other conventional symbols: Fortune as a woman blindfolded, beautiful on one side, ugly on the other, turning a wheel in the midst of the sea; or Avarice as an old man wearing torn clothes sitting at a counting table with money.[1]

Clearly Katherine's emblem would have been recognised as the symbol of St Katherine. The wheel represented St Katherine's holiness, her ability to withstand torture; but, more than this, it stood for her whole story and emphasised her whole character. The appropriation of this symbol shifted the desirable traits of the saint's character to Katherine's public persona, or so Katherine hoped. Which connections were made between the two women may not always have been the ones that Katherine desired, but surely her audience would have made connections between Katherine and the saint? The story of the saint was extremely well known to the population of late medieval England. Importantly, Katherine consciously chose this emblem as her own, understanding fully its representation in art as the emblem of a female saint, a virgin martyr. She would have understood that people would make connections between her and the saint based on this emblem – it must therefore be beyond dispute that she deliberately based the construction of her public persona on that of St Katherine. Her agency in this is manifest, her model clearly that of another female.

Moreover, Katherine was not alone in doing this. There is evidence that other women used saints to construct and promote identity. The saints they chose and the ways they did this manifest themselves differently, but it would appear that medieval women had female role models who provided them with help, support, self-affirmation and examples of behaviour.

Of course, shared gender need not be the only reason why these women made connections with the saints. But this aspect of shared femininity does seem to have been of importance. Katherine L. French's study of women's bequests to the church reveals much here. Her investigation of the wills of two dioceses demonstrates that women were more likely than men to leave domestic items to the church. Where women did leave items such as dresses, tablecloths, handkerchiefs and so on, they were often explicit in how they should be used: 'in the process they left their aesthetic and spiritual imprint on their parish.'[2] Men, on the other hand, seemed more willing for the churchwardens to make these decisions for themselves. The most favoured request by women was that their goods should be used to adorn the saints. Agnes Petygrew asked for her wedding ring to be given to the image of St Mary 'at the pillar'; Agnes Awmbler gave a kerchief to 'the image of Our Lady within the quore'; more significantly, Sybil Pochon left 'her best silk robe' to St Katherine on the understanding that on special occasions such as her saint's day the image would be dressed in it.[3] The link between females seems explicit here: 'The saints received items that had physically marked the donor as a woman. The items were intended to adorn these female saints in similar ways: kerchiefs on the head and decorative girdles around a robe or skirt.'[4] Household items such as sheets and tablecloths became altar clothes; in donating these, the women were providing not only for their own households but the household of God.

This seems at odds with the teaching of the Church. The Virgin Mary was held as an exemplar of perfect femininity, beyond that which the vast majority of women could expect to reach. But the hagiography of the virgin martyrs portrays them in many ways as the opposite of what a good medieval wife should be – shrewish, stubborn, wilful, a bad role model when viewed against the women portrayed in the courtesy texts of the time. Why then did these women connect with them on such a basic feminine level:

How, one wonders, did the assertive, often destructive heroines of Middle English hagiography speak to the experience of medieval men and women? To be sure, many women probably found the examples of feminine mastery in virgin martyr legends rather attractive. Yet there is little evidence that the male authors of virgin martyr legends were writing specifically for women or that they anticipated a predominantly female audience. Indeed, if they were tailoring their narratives to women, it is hard to see why they would exaggerate behaviour that they would surely not want their readers to emulate. On the other hand, it is certainly not obvious how the self-confident heroines who best all the men they meet could have appealed either to the clerics who composed saints' lives or to the men who must have constituted a substantial segment of their audience.[5]

But these women who gave clothes and domestic items were following examples that were not only set by the saints but also told to them through courtesy texts. *The Knight of la Tour Landry* encouraged the use of female saints as role models. Inevitably, this included the perfect Virgin Mary, an example of humility and courtesy. But the knight also specifically ordered his daughters to follow the examples of the virgin martyrs as well, stating that they provided examples of proper behaviour.[6] In this, then, were women following the orders of a man, rather than the examples of the saints, in copying these models of behaviour? But the stories of the saints would have been well known, the behaviour they displayed understood more than that described in the courtesy texts. The less desirable traits of the saints would have been as familiar to medieval women as those expounded in texts as examples of good feminine behaviour. And, moreover, although the hagiographies were written by men, female influence in the pictorial depictions of the stories was possible:

> Images of the saints surely influenced the ways in which people understood the legends they read or heard, just as written text must in turn have shaped viewers' interpretations of the images. Because thirteenth and fourteenth century lay people played an active role both in producing and in commissioning religious images, the visual arts provide especially useful evidence of lay 'readings' of saints' legends.[7]

The production and commission of these images would not have been the sole domain of men; women too would have orchestrated the design of images for wall paintings or manuscript decoration.

This again provides evidence of a connection based on shared gender. The authors of the hagiographies may have felt able to ascribe the saints with roles and attributes that were not really deemed suitable for women, because they were not writing about average women. The saints were special, on another level, above mere mortals, so their 'unfeminine' behaviour could be forgiven. But, increasingly, in the depictions produced by the laity, the saints were represented as mere women, wearing contemporary clothes, pictured in contemporary surroundings, undertaking contemporary roles. This did not happen only with the virgin martyrs but with all female saints. It would seem that the laity wanted their saints to be not just holy figures but real, everyday people.

As early as 1300 women were associated with the teaching of reading. A growing image in the thirteenth and fourteenth centuries was that of St Anne teaching the Virgin Mary to read:

> There are two ways of interpreting such scenes. One is that they were symbolic. Mary's reading may be meant to emphasise her role in conceiving and giving birth to the word of God, hence the liking of artists to place texts on her book which speak of praise to God. Equally, her act of reading may have been meant to be real. The scene of Mary and Anne appears in art just as we hear in literature that 'women teacheth child on book', at a time when artists were portraying Mary and Jesus in lifelike houses and landscapes. These portrayals tended to imagine the holy family living in the style of wealthy people of the latter middle ages, and it would have been natural to attribute Mary with the kind of education current among such people. In turn, the scene may have affirmed such education, encouraging mothers to teach their children to read.[8]

Therefore, the images depicted real medieval issues and confirmed these issues – Anne was shown teaching Mary because in late medieval society women taught children and through the power of these images more women felt able to teach children. The image and the reality were self-supporting. Other aspects of St Anne's life were adopted, the saint setting the precedent for certain behaviours and therefore affirming that these behaviours were acceptable. Indeed, Anne can be seen to have 'represented the cult of the family'.[9] She was a 'constructed' saint, for the actual details of Mary's family were unknown. By the late Middle Ages, however, Anne's entire life story was 'known', including, famously, her remarriage. This was one of the reasons for Anne's popularity. The widow's choice was normally of a chaste life within a convent – Anne's marriages to three different men, bearing a child to each before vowing herself to this chaste life, provided women with an alternative choice. She represented the value of motherhood to married women and was also the patron of widows.

Virgin martyrs, too, despite their status being very different from that of wives, could provide assurances. St Margaret was seen as the patron of childbirth and St Katherine as a marriage broker. Indeed, St Katherine, after her mystical marriage to Christ, is depicted in the role of household manager.[10] It was not only wives who could find self-affirmation in female saints. Agnes Sorel, mistress of the French king Charles VII in the 1440s, had a devotion to St Mary Magdalene.[11]

Of course, different readings of saints' lives were possible. The saints could mean different things to different people: 'Virgin martyrs were presented as models to women but that does not mean that they internalised her example in uncomplicated and unresponsive ways.'[12] One medieval woman who clearly appropriated the female virgin saints as role models was Margery Kempe. This was not merely in terms of echoing those behaviours that perhaps were seen as most appropriate, but in adopting all behaviours, most certainly in a responsive way. In this she becomes an extreme example of medieval women appropriating and reflecting saintly attributes, but a discussion on how saints were adopted as role models cannot be complete without her inclusion.

Margery Kempe (born *c.* 1373) lived in East Anglia, in the town of King's Lynn. She was a wife, a mother to fourteen children, and a businesswomen. Her father had been mayor of Lynn – presumably this was where she received the capital and the contacts to set up her businesses, first in brewing then in milling. Both were unsuccessful. We know of her life through her book, the single extant manuscript of which was at Mount Grace Priory in Yorkshire in the fifteenth century, where the story of Margery's life seems to have found favour. It is clear from her book that she saw herself as extremely pious, to the extent that she believed herself capable of sainthood. Moreover, it is manifest that she believed she was capable of this through her deliberate attempts to echo the lives of the female saints so well known to medieval people. The book depicts her life story, seemingly dictated by Margery to a scribe. However, the authorship and the truth of the content of the book are under debate.

Lynn Staley, for example, argues that *The Book of Margery Kempe* is a work of fiction featuring a radical, exceptional figure fighting against the restrictions of her society.[13] Staley clearly distinguishes between the author and the textual subject:

Implicitly . . . Kempe's achievement is undervalued precisely because, before we even begin to talk about that achievement, we define the *Book* in terms of its author's gender and so circumscribe our response to it by assuming an absolute equation between the book's author and its subject.[14]

Because Margery is a woman, Staley believes that readers will not credit her with the role of conscious author, and therefore Staley chooses to read the *Book* as a biography not an autobiography, 'Kempe' prescribing the life of 'Margery'. Staley chooses to limit the role of the two scribes in Margery's text, stating that 'I would like to say that the scribe never existed' and believing that the scribes are a fictional device used by Kempe to 'authorise' the text through a male voice.[15] For Staley, any reading of the text should highlight the skill of the female author, the ability of Kempe to write the tale of an extraordinary woman.

But the *Book* is undoubtedly an autobiography. The subject and the author are the same. This is not to deny Margery the role of textual authority because of her female status but rather to acknowledge that the subject she constructed, or desired to construct, in the text was her own identity. Also, to acknowledge the existence of a scribal authority is not to limit the influence of Margery over the textual structure. Rather, it leads to the question of Margery's intent and motivation in writing and portraying her own identity. The influences and relationship between Margery and her second scribe echo hagiographical techniques, and this in itself provides information on how Margery desired to be perceived. The scribe is only able to believe in Margery, and therefore able to write the text, after reading the lives and works of other female mystics and saints. From this point he believes in Margery's holiness, and adopts the role of disciple. His intent for the text then becomes the same as Margery's; he too wishes to advance her saintly identity.

Timea Szell states that it is possible to argue that Margery Kempe's construction of herself reflects many of the psychological and spiritual concerns of the lives of women saints, and represents a hagiographical tradition. However, Szell continues that, ultimately, Margery does not fit any of the recognised categories of saints' lives, and that Margery 'proudly and stubbornly cultivates her identity as marginal outsider'.[16] Clarissa Atkinson argues that the 'received categories of social and religious history do not easily accommodate Margery Kempe',[17] reflecting Szell's concerns of how to 'categorise' Margery. But does Margery have to fit a refined category? It is a mistake to pigeonhole her within the constraints of modern understanding, or of modern influences such as feminism or Marxism. Surely one should read the *Book* to discover Margery's own intents and the motivations surrounding her portrayal, not to fit modern preconceived ideas or formats to the *Book*? Margery herself tells us that she is familiar with the lives of female saints, and throughout the *Book* her identity can be seen to be influenced and empowered by the precedents set by these figures. It is this influence and empowerment that necessitate the use of the third person in the text, as Margery could not have easily narrated a saint's life in the first person, the difficulty of which she acknowledges, stating that the *Book* was 'written to show the homely intimacy and goodness of our merciful Lord Christ Jesus, and not to commend this creature'.[18] The *Book* represents the sanctity of Margery, which is ultimately the work of Christ; therefore the subject of the *Book*, the channel of Christ's work, has to be discussed as a separate entity from that of the author.

The influences of female saints on Margery have been acknowledged by many, but Margery's reasons for accepting these influences have been glossed over. It would seem that, because Margery never achieved official, recognised sainthood, then her desire to be seen and recognised as a saint takes second place to a portrayal of her as a radical, anxious, marginal, hysterical, exceptional, essentially unorthodox figure battling against the conventional restrictions of her society. But it is within the context of these saintly influences that Margery would have seen herself. The medieval culture, in which Margery resided and wrote, was profoundly mimetic. Ideals and archetypes were blatantly 'copied' by individuals who saw this as a means of attaining similar levels of achievement of those they were copying. Margery was familiar with the lives of the saints and believed that, if she lived a similar life, she too would demonstrate her holiness and would achieve sainthood.

This placing of Margery firmly in the context of medieval culture and society indicates the empowerment an individual could gain from the lives and precedents of female saints. Therefore, Margery is clearly the author of the text; she is the creator of a subject influenced by other writing and the genre of saintly literature, and the *Book* is not a literal autobiography. But the subject created is Margery and Margery's sanctity, a sanctity that, while not recognised through history, was not a fiction to Margery but ordained in her by God, as her text makes clear:

Those who believe that God loves you shall be blessed without end.[19]

Daughter, I shall make the whole world wonder at you, and many men and women shall speak of me for love of you, and *honour me in you*.[20]

As Fanous states, the subject of the *Book* is not 'a projection of her fictive narrative person, in a Chaucerian or Langlandian way' but 'so widespread is the mimetic topos in medieval literature that to ignore its use is to show a marked antipathy towards one of the most fundamental of medieval impulses'.[21] Margery was a deliberate, conscious author, but the text is edited to emphasise the message she wanted to portray, and this message firmly links her self to female saints and the precedents they provided for the role she desired and believed she was ordained to hold. Therefore, Margery's female status is empowered, as Staley would desire, through an acknowledgement of the authorial abilities and skill of Margery, but these abilities are firmly interlinked with the chosen portrayal of identity, an identity influenced by the precedents available to the author in the form of female sanctity. Establishing the links between Margery and these saints will therefore unwrap Margery's editorial decisions, and consequently will provide a picture of Margery's identity as she wished it to be seen.

Margery states that the purpose of the *Book* is to provide 'great solace and comfort' for 'sinful wretches'.[22] This is a clear hint at an intercessory role; through reading and understanding the grace Christ provided in Margery, the reader will gain comfort. Margery is to be a helper and a healer – a traditional saintly function. Margery anticipates her veneration and aid as intercessor elsewhere in the *Book*.

> Lord, I ask for mercy and preservation from everlasting damnation for me and for all the world.[23]

> Daughter, there is no man so sinful alive on earth that, if he will give up his sin and do as you advise, then such grace as you promise him I will confirm for love of you.[24]

> Daughter . . . in this church and in this place I will be worshipped in you.[25]

She also establishes herself as a patron, a protector of travellers. Through her trials of sea travel and her accounts of bad weather and conditions against her that through the grace of God she survives, Margery links herself to a role of protection and provider of aid.

Afterwards, as this creature was in contemplation, our Lord warned her in her mind that she should not sail in that ship, and He assigned her another ship, a galley, that she should sail in. Then she told this to some of the company, and they told it to others of their party, and then they dared not sail in the ship which they had arranged.[26]

Margery also provides traditional saintly functions through the establishment of miracle stories. For example, she survives the church stone falling on her, although the weight and height from which it fell should have warranted serious injury.[27]

Therefore Margery establishes her saintly credentials as intercessor, protector and worker of miracles. But she specifically connects herself to the female saints Mary Magdalene, Bridget of Sweden, and the most popular virgin martyrs for the late medieval period, Katherine of Alexandria and Margaret of Antioch. Mary Magdalene and St Bridget offer instant and obvious comparisons, namely in their sexual status. They too had renounced the pleasures of the flesh to become chaste followers of Christ. As Carolyn Coulson states, 'the Magdalene serves as the perfect model for the reader who cannot achieve the unattainable, singular perfection of the Virgin Mary. At the most fundamental level, Mary Magdalene rèpresents the quintessential forgiven sinner saved by the love and mercy of Christ.'[28] Susan Eberly suggests that the dating of the commencement of the *Book* 'on the next day after Mary Magdalene' should alert us to the importance of this saint to Margery.[29] While the use of dating in the *Book* is scarce and therefore the inclusion of dates potentially significant, this seems a strange detail to choose to link Margery and the Magdalene. The *Book* offers much more emphatic links than this. In the visions Margery experiences around her meditations of the Crucifixion she takes over the role of the Magdalene, present at a scene with Christ and the Virgin Mary, where the Virgin pleads with Christ to stay with them.[30] In *The Meditations on the Life of Christ* Mary Magdalene also pleads with Christ; in the *Book* Margery becomes the pleader, and Mary Magdalene is not present.[31]

Margery therefore places herself firmly in the female community surrounding Christ, utilising the example and role of the Magdalene to authorise her own relationship with Christ. Margery also adopts the role of St Bridget in a similar way: 'specific examples imitated from St Bridget, such as the bowl of water thrown over her head, confirm that Bridget's life served as a direct model.'[32] Both women were delivered from the perils of childbirth, and called to become brides of Christ, undertaking extensive pilgrimages:

> Kempe not only replicates Bridget's book and pilgrimages with her own; she also takes pains to visit Brigittine houses, the Hospice in Rome near the English college where Bridget wrote so much of her *Revelations* and other books and where she died, perhaps the Norwegian Brigittine convent of Munkaliv, almost certainly the Brigittine convent of Manenbrunn at Gdansk, and also English Brigittine Syon and Carthusian Sheen.[33]

Bridget became a model as bookwriter, pilgrim and non-virgin saint and therefore provided Margery with the precedent for her achievements. As with the Magdalene, Margery 'lived' the Brigittine experience; both persuaded husbands to adopt a chaste marriage, both were reduced to begging in the city of Rome, both combated Paul's dictate against preaching.[34] More importantly, Christ himself links the two women. 'For in truth I tell you, just as I spoke to St Bridget, just so I speak to you, daughter, and I tell you truly that every word that is written in Bridget's book is true, and through you shall be recognised as truth indeed.'[35] And when witnessing mass: 'Therefore thank God that you have seen it. My daughter Bridget never saw me in this way.'[36]

Here reference to St Bridget is clearly authorising Margery's holiness. Margery's words and works will spread the word of Bridget and establish the veracity of her work, and Margery's holiness is compared to Bridget's and found to be superior. Using Bridget as an example and paradigm in the text benefits the status of Margery, who is living the life of Bridget, and gains assurance from God that Margery is on a par with the saint in His eyes.

While the Magdalene and St Bridget appear as obvious models for the assurance and confirmation of Margery's status and identity, the virgin martyrs SS Katherine and Margaret initially appear to be awkward paradigms for a creature who previously led such a worldly lustful life. But the influence of Katherine and Margaret was integral in medieval society; Margery's own parish church in King's Lynn was dedicated to St Margaret, Mary Magdalene and all the Virgins. They were clearly important figures in Christ's female community and therefore needed as advocates for Margery. Moreover, despite their virgin status, they were linked to female identities with which Margery was familiar. Margaret, as the patron saint of childbirth, provided a link for Margery with the suffering she endured during her sexual life; and St Katherine would have helped Margery to overcome the anxieties she felt surrounding her lack of virginity.[37] Katherine's conversion of the Empress that appears in her *Vita*, and the saint's reassurance that married women could be included in the community of Christ's brides, was clearly an important message for Margery, emphasising the worth and value of a mental desire and conviction of virginity over and above the physical state.[38] This distinction was recognised and understood by Margery, who perceived herself to be a maiden in her soul. Wives also feature strongly in the text as helping Margery. In Leicester, when the Steward sends to the jailer for her, the jailer's wife would not let her go.[39] And in York, the goodwife of the house where Margery was held gave her wine to drink without the knowledge of her husband.[40]

Therefore, although virgins in both the mental and the physical sense, the martyr saints held practical appeal for Margery. The symbolic renouncing of a previous life or a status in society, implicit in Margery's text, is also present in the tales of the virgins: 'before the virgin martyr takes up her vocation she must first renounce the world, its honours, privileges, and pleasures, her heritage, social position and above all, her sexuality.'[41] In this context another character in the *Book* links Margery and St Katherine. The Mayor of Leicester asks Margery 'from which part of the country she came, and whose daughter she was',[42] which echoes the first encounter of

St Katherine with Maxentius.[43] The Mayor himself appears to make this connection, stating after Margery's response: 'St Katherine told of what kindred she came, and yet you are not alike, for you are a false strumpet, a false Lollard, and a false deceiver of the people and therefore I shall have you in prison.'[44] This was a deliberate attempt by Margery to link her story to that of the female saints: 'for by drawing an equation between Margery's kindred and Katherine's the Mayor effectively contextualises Margery's trial in the tradition of the virgin martyr's ordeal.'[45]

Here lies the major role of the virgin martyrs in the *Book*. Many have noted the hostility directed towards Margery, the threat to her chaste status, and the trials and persecution she underwent as a suspected Lollard or heretical figure, and many have interpreted this as a representation of Margery's unorthodox nature, and radical hysterical behaviour. But, as Fanous argues, if the *Book* is analysed too closely for fact, then 'we endow the text with a historicity which its author would not have recognised and ignore the dualism characteristic of any saint's life: ethos and praxis, or ethical and historical truth'.[46] The issue that should arise is not the factual truth surrounding the events of the *Book* but the motivation. The travels in England and the people encountered by Margery in the hostile situation of a trial or questioning are all in one way or another notable for their anti-heretical activity: 'her flight directly to these places and the prominence accorded to the subsequent trials point to their outcome, which is surely a vindication of her orthodoxy. Having passed through the courts of the harshest and most active heretical repressors, her credentials were impeccable.'[47] This quest for orthodoxy provided proof of her sanctity, both in terms of establishing her beliefs firmly within the context of the Church, and through placing herself in a trial situation reminiscent of the trials of the virgin martyrs, themselves emulations of the trial of Christ.

Laurie Finke has argued that 'the trials in hagiographies of early Christian martyrs are quite different from the examinations for heresy represented in Kempe's narrative. The saints in these narratives need not prove the orthodoxy of their Christian beliefs; rather the trial serves as a forum for their proclamation of a faith that is never in question.'[48] However, this is to limit the situation of the martyrs. Undoubtedly the detail of their faith was not questioned, but the trials were based on the faith they held, the pagan judges of their trials against the morals of their faith. Indeed, the connections between the trials of Margery and SS Katherine and Margaret are clear. As Lewis states, as Katherine 'faced the 50 philosophers, so too Margery is publicly examined on several occasions by groups of learned clerics. Like St Katherine, Margery always gets the better of them.'[49] As St Katherine converted the fifty philosophers to the Christian faith, so the examiners of Margery have to concede to her orthodoxy and beliefs. For example, in Leicester: 'The Mayor, who was her deadly enemy, said, "Truly, she does not mean with her heart what she says with her mouth." And the clerics said to him, "Sir, she answers us very well."'[50] Unable to find fault with the orthodoxy of her beliefs, the Mayor then has to resort to name calling and the use of 'indecent words', presenting Margery 'in the tradition of the embattling saint who outwits her inquisitor'.[51]

Moreover, Margery manifestly attempts to associate herself with the martyrdom of these saints. Inevitably the virgin martyrs suffered torture and death. Margery is never tortured, but she makes the threat implicit. In Canterbury the people cried, 'You shall be burnt you false lollard,' 'take her and burn her,' and in York the Archbishop's household 'swore many a horrible oath that she should be burned'.[52] The lack of any real threat to Margery emphasises the placing of this tension in the text, tying her into the tradition of the suffering virgin, and the suffering of injustice, cruel words and punishment.[53] As Margaret and Katherine during torture elicit sympathy from their observers, so Margery in Beverley moves the female audience with edifying stories so that the women wept and said, 'alas, woman, why should you be burned?'[54]

Along with these threats, real or otherwise, Margery imagines her torture and death, reassured by Christ that such physical suffering was not necessary. 'I thank you, daughter, that you would be willing to suffer death for my love, for as often as you think so, you shall have the same reward in heaven as if you had suffered that same death.'[55] Margery is aware of the need to associate herself with the torture trope of the martyrs, and is also aware that this was hardly likely to occur. For Margery, the torture would be mental, her suffering the abuse and hostility she received. The emphasis in the text on the antagonism and enmity she suffered highlights Margery's intent to make obvious her martyrdom. Christ again confirms this message for the audience of the text. 'Daughter, it is more pleasing to me that you suffer scorn and humiliation, shame and rebukes, wrongs and distress, than if your head were struck off three times a day every day for seven years.'[56] As Henrietta Leyser argues: 'Bitter as the accounts of those who try to silence her are, it would be as well not to imagine her as a marginal figure or a social outcast. Rather, allowance must be made for Margery's need to experience persecution as a form of martyrdom.'[57]

Margery places dispute and suffering at the forefront of her text to attach herself undeniably to the genre of the virgin martyrs, seeking an implicit connection in the mind of the reader between her life and those of SS Katherine and Margaret: 'the extent of Margery's martyrdom can be measured by the number of times she reports being told to shut up.'[58] The very acts of hostility that critics have interpreted as indicative of Margery's radical or marginal status were intended by the author to embrace her in the wholly orthodox and socially acceptable lives of the virgin martyrs. For Margery the animosity she receives is a tool to authorise and underpin her sanctity. The information we have of this hostility is edited and chosen by Margery as an essential element of her identity construct, a self-representation of her desired sanctity.

Linking hostility to a sexual threat also echoes hagiographical tradition. Margery has to battle to gain and keep her chastity. The very act of achieving her chastity becomes a trade-off between the worldly material life of her past and the Christian ideal she wishes to follow. On the road to Bridlington Margery gains her chastity from John, her husband, by paying his debts. She exchanges money, a symbol of her past status as a proud businesswoman, for her symbol of holiness, her chastity.[59] The various threats she then overcomes against her new virginal state are highly reminiscent of the sexual threats of the pagan emperors against the Christian virgins. There is no pagan king to force Margery to abandon her faith through sexual attack, so the Steward of Leicester adopts this role. Unable to outwit Margery with words, the Steward resorts to physical attack. She is saved through telling him 'how she had her speech and conversing from the Holy Ghost and not from her own knowledge'.[60] The constancy and veracity of her faith both protect her from attack and necessitate attack.

As Staley argues, Margery's textual achievements should be acknowledged. Margery was a conscious author, editing her text to bring to the forefront the issues she desired to be associated with. But the work is an autobiography, Margery discussing her self and constructing her identity in a way that a medieval audience would have implicitly linked to the lives of female saints. The *Book* may not fit squarely into a set hagiographical category of virgin martyr or reformed sinner, but clear connections exist that demonstrate Margery's awareness of the format of saintly literature. The *Book* represents Margery's sanctity as she has prescribed it, through the acknowledgement, influence, authorisation and assimilation of the hagiographical texts that Margery herself tells us she was familiar with. In a context and society of mimetic culture the importance of literary identification with an archetypal pattern was firmly established.

The problem for the modern reader is that 'St Margery' is not a figure embraced by the 500 years between the writing of and the discovery of the text. But the text was clearly intended to be read with Margery's saintly manifestation established. Margery believed that her sanctity was ordained by God, and imparts her saintly credentials throughout the *Book* as intercessor, protector, and miracle-worker. Her authorisation was the powerful status of female saints in medieval life. She may not fit a neat modern category, but that is explained by the varying models she adopted, and the varying influences of the sexual and the virgin. The precedents of the Magdalene and the more contemporary St Bridget were necessary to authorise Margery's renouncement of past lusts, and the recognisable trial and martyrdom suffered by the virgin saints and echoed by Margery were necessary to embed her status of female sanctity. The formats of the hagiographical tradition echo throughout Margery's text as a device to encompass the acts and events of Margery's life in the lives of female saints. The *Book* may not fit some modern commentators' ideals and interpretations of what constitutes 'official' hagiography, and, indeed, the failing of Margery's saintly ambitions leads to the uniqueness of the text. Moreover, we do not know whether Margery undertook the actual events in her *Book*; there is no other evidence but her text. But the author clearly sought identification with the female community that surrounded Christ, and Margery believed that she would take her place here as ordained by Christ. Margery sought and confirmed her orthodox status in terms of her beliefs through her trials and questionings, and the adoption of hagiographical structures that are evident throughout the *Book* confirms the orthodoxy of Margery's literary style.

Of course, it was not just women who looked to the saints to provide affirmation of identity. Evidence shows that men too appropriated the images and emblems of the saints for their own purposes, the most well-known case in the fourteenth century being Richard II. Richard was devoted to Edward the Confessor. Edward was king of England from 1042 to 1066, but most of his life prior to accession had been spent in Normandy. His early years as king saw a number of notable magnates exiled, which led to later political problems for Edward when these exiles returned. His reign was also troubled with issues of succession – although Edward had married in 1045, by 1050 it was clear that no offspring were forthcoming. Indeed, Edward does not seem to have married happily. He was in his 40s before he married and, when his wife's father, Godwin, was exiled, his wife was despatched to a convent. However, Godwin returned and Edith was reinstated as Edward's wife.

The Life of King Edward was written after his death, but, states the author, at the request of Edith, so it must have been composed prior to 1075, the date of Edith's death.[61] The *Life* was written in two parts, one covering Edward's political life, the other his spiritual, personal life. Elements of the work reflect that of hagiography. In the first part of the book appears the assertion that a monk of Glastonbury had a vision predicting Edward's holiness as St Peter marked him out for a chaste life. The second part emphasises again his chastity and attributes him with the ability to perform miraculous cures. The cult of Edward probably started in his own court before his demise: 'the idea of a holy king was fashionable in the eleventh century. The power to cure illness, an adjunct of sainthood, had become in France an adjunct of kingship.'[62] Edward was canonised in 1161, by the authority of the Pope and not merely by the existence of a cult, and in 1163 he was translated to a new shrine within the abbey of Westminster.

The cult of Edward was clearly important to the early Plantagenet kings, in particular Henry III.[63] Henry was the patron of Westminster Abbey, and rebuilt the church from 1245 at massive cost, the equivalent of two years' royal revenue. Edward the Confessor himself had undertaken the construction of the original Romanesque abbey that Henry rebuilt, and also established the palace of Westminster as a major royal residence: 'In the twelfth and thirteenth century cult literature of St Edward, it is striking that all the important events of his reign are presented as having occurred either within the king's household at the palace or in the abbey at Westminster.'[64] Together with his shrine at the Abbey, Henry obviously saw the palace as an important manifestation of the saint. This devotion explains his interest in rebuilding Westminster on such a scale, but it is unclear why Edward's cult suddenly came to prominence under this king. Binski argues that it was possibly a counterattack on the cult of St Thomas Beckett, the rise of a royal saint over that of a rebellious magnate. However, 'Henry III attended St Thomas's translation at Canterbury in 1220, gave relics of his vestment, comb, and blood to Westminster Abbey, and regularly honoured the saint's memory, as did his son to an even greater degree'.[65] Binski continues that the emergence of St Edward was more likely due to the idea of the construction of the monarchy and the growth of the sense of nation with Westminster at the heart, stating that, while Henry III's request to be buried at Westminster was probably in part an act of piety, it was also 'an acknowledgement of the political centralisation of the kingdom, a centralisation which was simultaneously acquiring a mythology in the life and character of St Edward'.[66]

The fourteenth century saw a dip in the popularity of Edward's cult. However, it re-emerged under the reign of Richard II. From what has been discovered about Henry III and the growth of the cult of Edward, it would appear that Edward was closely associated with the sense of royal authority and power: in this context a link between Richard and Edward would seem manifest, one king using the cult of another to uphold monarchical strength. This would seem particularly true given Richard's known thoughts on the absolute power of kingship granted by God. Richard was clearly devoted to Edward, even impaling his arms with those of the saint, an act usually reserved for man and wife. And Edward was one of the saints who appeared with Richard in his supplication to the Virgin Mary on the Wilton Diptych.

But it would appear that Richard's appropriation of the images of St Edward in this way was beyond that of shared kingship. Lewis has argued that Richard's devotion to Edward was a way of enforcing not just his kingly authority but his masculine status. As well as kingship, Richard and Edward shared the status of childlessness.[67] These two issues do not sit well together; part of the role of king is to produce an heir. Neither Richard nor Edward seemed particularly anxious to achieve this. It has already been stated that Edward married late in life and sent his wife off to a convent at the first opportunity. Richard was married twice, first to Anne of Bohemia, traditionally seen as a love match, and then again to the extremely young Isabella of France, only 7 years of age at the time of the wedding. It seems odd that, after a childless first marriage, Richard would marry a bride who could not produce heirs for several years at least. Politically, the marriage was necessary to promote links with France and to secure peace, but dynastically it was disastrous. It was after this second marriage in 1397 that Richard probably adopted the impaled arms, although he first used them in the period between the death of Anne and his remarriage. The arms of Richard and Edward together appeared on silver vessels, on his banner and on his signet seals.[68]

Edward's sanctity was based on his lack of children. The myth grew that this was due to Edward and Edith's chastity and Edward's virginity was lauded. Obviously, in the thirteenth and fourteenth centuries, virginity was seen as the ideal state, leaving the body pure, as intended by God. However, in reality this was a status associated with women. Masculinity called for more physical prowess in the securing of dynasty and power. Clerics were, of course, both male and virgin, but they were seen as above the level of the laity, closer to God and removed from the rest of society through their ability to perform the miracle of the holy mass. In secular society maleness and virginity were not ideal partners. Lewis argues that this is where Richard's appropriation of the image of Edward the Confessor is most significant: 'by representing himself as heroically chaste Richard could demonstrate that he was a real man, even without fathering children or having sex with wife or mistresses.'[69] Whatever Richard's actual sexual status, whether virgin, impotent, or married to a barren wife, his adoption of the emblems of Edward led to an association of holy chastity, and affirmation that it was possible to be a successful king but be childless: 'for the surviving partner of a childless, royal marriage, reconstructing that marriage as one of deliberate sexual abstinence could be a means of self-validation, not to say self-preservation.'[70]

Here, as seen with Katherine Swynford and Margery Kempe, the issue of shared gender is significant. Richard and Edward were both male and both kings. If Edward had not been of the same royal status, then the appropriation of his image would not have carried the same meaning. In this, gender is secondary to role. However, Richard's appropriation of the emblem of a virgin queen would not have conveyed the same message. As already mentioned, virginity in women was seen in a very different light from that of men. The saints, for Richard II, Katherine Swynford, Margery Kempe and the women mentioned as leaving gifts to the church, were clearly gendered role models.

But this did not have to be the case. Evidence shows that cross-gender devotions were present. The clearest example of this is with the worship of the Virgin Mary, her growth in importance and popularity in the fourteenth century happening in all elements of society, both male and female. The Wilton Diptych demonstrates that Richard had a Marian devotion; her role of intercessor is clear in this iconography. John of Gaunt also appears to have been a Marian devotee. She is mentioned in his will on numerous occasions to the exclusion of any other saint bar the twelve apostles. John Beaufort appears to have shared his mother's devotion to St Katherine. He died at the hospital of St Katherine by the Tower of London, and owned a book of hours with an exquisite depiction of the saint with her wheel.

Men also gave gifts of household items and personal clothing to the Church. Gaunt bequeathed to the Church of the Annunciation of our Lady of the Newarke in Leicester his red garment of velvet embroidered with gold suns.[71] However, as French found, there was a difference in the manner in which men and women bequeathed these items. Women specifically stated how they should be used, and these uses were gender based – ornamentation for female saints, or coverings for altars. It would appear that gender played an important role in the way devotions manifested themselves. Cross-gender devotions were possible and happened frequently. But it would seem that the actual appropriation of a saint's image – the manifestation of the individual with part of the saint's life, the adoption of the saint's emblem as a personal badge, the self-affirmation that was a possible part of devotion – was based on shared gender and the shared understanding of role that this led to.

Clearly, medieval society viewed the saints as significant figures, not just in the traditional sense of holy figures to pray to for intercession, but as models of certain lifestyles or characteristics that could be appropriated for an individual's own use. Women in particular connected with the virgin martyrs, viewing them as intrinsically female as well as holy, as can be seen in the instructions given for the use of bequests and gifts to local churches. But there is evidence that men also saw the saints as human beings who could help them in their process of self-affirmation. Within this context Katherine's use of the spiked wheel as her armorial and livery badge seems a natural step for a woman of previously dubious position who wished to emphasise her newly confirmed royal status, her respectability and her nobility of character, traits that were central to the story of St Katherine. The evidence is plain: Katherine Swynford had agency over how her character was presented and used a female role model to help her create an image that matched her new status as Duchess of Lancaster.

Epilogue

So, as we reach the end of this book, who was Katherine Swynford? Clearly, the role she has been assigned throughout history as the mother or lover of others is correct. She was the mistress of John of Gaunt, and she was the mother of numerous important people. However, she clearly was also much more than this. She was educated, intelligent, pious, no doubt beautiful and, moreover, politically discreet. She was also an accomplished diplomat, maintaining relationships with both Richard II and Henry IV in politically turbulent times. She was involved within extensive female networks of book ownership and literary patronage, clearly well read and accomplished.

Katherine also manifestly had a sense of her place, if not in history, then within her own society. Her choice of armorial associates her with the legend of St Katherine and the attributes of this saint. Moreover, this was a conscious decision by Katherine, an adoption of this saint's 'worthiness' as her own. For me, this is the most interesting aspect of Katherine Swynford, and leads to a whole host of questions about women in medieval society. Katherine provides the example that medieval women were conscious, intelligent beings who could control their own image and portray themselves in a way they wished, influenced by other women, and who were not stereotyped, downtrodden, oppressed figures controlled by men. History is full of the achievements of white men, with other categories of society marginalised. Perhaps one of the achievements of these white men is the amount of male authority that permeates beliefs about how societies in the past were structured. Katherine Swynford offers a contrast to this, a look at women through their own eyes, with this overriding sense of male control removed. The Church, in the form of Walsingham and

Knighton, tried to dismiss Katherine as Eve, and in part succeeded as the writings of these monks were read in literal ways by many historians and scholars. But Katherine herself, through her own decisions, wanted to portray herself in a different way, and this self-portrayal deserves to be acknowledged. She is an interesting woman, and her example suggests that there are many others like her who were able to feel in control of some aspects of their lives, without the influence of men but within the influence of women. Perhaps the most ironic part is that the women who provided the role models were female saints such as St Katherine and Mary Magdalene, whose stories themselves were suppressed by male authority, their importance within a masculine Church limited to the ways in which men wrote about them. Katherine Swynford clearly shows that they failed, and that women could claim these saints as their own.

Notes

Introduction

1. Anya Seton, *Katherine* (London, 1956), p. 20.
2. Anthony Goodman, *Katherine Swynford* (Lincoln, 1999), p. 7.
3. Seton, *Katherine*, p. 35.
4. Derek Pearsall, *The Life of Geoffrey Chaucer* (Oxford, 1994), p. 7.
5. Nancy F. Partner, 'No Sex, No Gender', *Speculum*, 68/2 (1993), 423.

Chapter One

1. Anthony Goodman, *Katherine Swynford* (Lincoln, 1999), p. 7; Albert Stanburrough Cook, 'Chaucerian Papers I', *Connecticut Academy of Arts and Sciences*, 23 (1919), 57–8; Margaret Galway, 'Walter Roet and Philippa Chaucer', *Notes and Queries* (1954), 48.
2. Cook, 'Chaucerian Papers', p. 57; *Œuvres de Froissart*, vol. 15: *1392–1396*, ed. Kervyn de Lettenhove (Osnabrück, 1967), p. 399.
3. Cook, 'Chaucerian Papers', p. 60; *Œuvres de Froissart*, ed. Lettenhove, vol. 23, p. 38.
4. *Œuvres de Froissart*, ed. Lettenhove, vol. 15, pp. 215–16. English translation in Edith Rickert, *Chaucer's World* (New York and London, 1964), p. 307.
5. Margaret Galway, 'Philippa Pan; Philippa Chaucer', *Modern Language Review*, 35 (1960), 485; John M. Manly, *Some New Light on Chaucer* (Gloucester, Mass., 1959), pp. 50–1; *Cartulaire des Comtes de Hainaut*, vol. 1, ed. Léopold Devillers (Brussels, 1881), pp. 764, 766.
6. Cook, 'Chaucerian Papers', p. 59.
7. *Cartulaire*, p. 766.
8. John Weaver, *Ancient Funerall Monuments* (Amsterdam, 1979), p. 661. My translation of the original Latin.

9. Galway, 'Walter Roet', p. 49; Manly, *New Light on Chaucer*, pp. 51–2; *Cartulaire*, pp. 321–2.

10. Girls often entered the monastic life at the age of 13 or so. See, e.g., Eileen Power, *Medieval English Nunneries* (Cambridge, 1922), pp. 25, 26.

11. *Chartes du Chapite de Sainte-Waudru de Mons*, ed. Léopold Devillers, vol. 2 (Brussels, 1903), pp. 478, 515. My translation from the original French.

12. *Register of Edward, The Black Prince*, pt 4 (London, 1933), pp. 114, 128, 162. See also Galway, 'Walter Roet', p. 48.

13. Galway, 'Philippa Pan', p. 481.

14. Manly, *New Light on Chaucer*, pp. 57–61.

15. Haldeen Braddy, 'Chaucer's Philippa, daughter of Panneto', *Modern Language Notes* (1949), 343.

16. Galway, 'Philippa Pan', pp. 481–2, 487.

17. *Chaucer Life-Records*, ed. Martin M. Crow and Clair C. Olson (Oxford, 1966), pp. 65, 67, 85, 88, 91; Margaret Galway, 'Geoffrey Chaucer, JP and MP', *Modern Language Review*, 36 (1941), 2.

18. T. Speght, *The Works of our Ancient, Learned and Excellent Poet Jeffrey Chaucer* (London, 1687). Although Speght referred to Philippa on the progenie page as 'the daughter of Payne Roet', his work contains a second genealogy table within an unpaginated biographical section on Chaucer. It is in this table that he states that Philippa was 'altera filiarum'.

19. *Œuvres de Froissart*, ed. Lettenhove, vol. 15, p. 238.

20. George Williams, *A New View of Chaucer* (Durham, NC, 1965), p. 45.

21. Anne Crawford (ed.), *Letters of the Queens of England 1100–1547* (Stroud, 1994), pp. 92–100.

22. Goodman, *Katherine*, p. 10.

23. *Calendar of Inquisitions Post Mortem Edward III*, vol. 2, entry 197. From this entry the birth of Hugh can be dated to 1340 at the latest. Cole believes Hugh's date of birth to be 1333. R.E.G. Cole, 'The Manor and Rectory of Kettlethorpe', *Architectural Societies Reports*, 31, report 66 (1911), 51.

24. Graham Platts, *Land and People in Medieval Lincolnshire* (Lincoln, 1985), pp. 144, 153, 220; *Calendar of Patent Rolls Edward III 1364–1367*, p. 136; Cole, 'Manor and Rectory of Kettlethorpe', p. 41.

25. J.W.F. Hill, *Medieval Lincoln* (Cambridge, 1965), pp. 312–13.

26. Cole, 'Manor and Rectory of Kettlethorpe', pp. 51–2.

27. *Ibid.*, pp. 58–9.

28. Goodman, Katherine, p. 11; Chris Given-Wilson and Alice Curteis, *The Royal Bastards of Medieval England* (London, 1984), p. 148; Sydney Armitage-Smith, *John of Gaunt: King of Castile and Leon, Duke of Aquitaine and Lancaster, Earl of Derby, Lincoln and Leicester, Seneschal of England* (Westminster, 1904), p. 461; Joel T. Rosenthal, *Nobles and the Noble Life 1295–1500* (London, 1976), p. 174.

29. Galway, 'Philippa Pan', p. 482.

30. Marie Louise Bruce, *The Usurper King, Henry of Bolingbroke 1366–99* (London, 1998), p. 10.

31. Lewis Bostock Radford, *Henry Beaufort, Bishop, Chancellor, Cardinal* (London, 1908), p. 1; Keith Dockray, in *Biographical Dictionary of British Women*, ed. Anne Crawford *et al.* (London, 1983), pp. 385–6.

32. The inquisition into Hugh's death was held in Lincoln on 24 June 1372 and states that he died 'on the Thursday after St Martin in the last winter' (Cole, 'Manor and Rectory of Kettlethorpe', p. 54).

33. Armitage-Smith, *John of Gaunt*, p. 463. Goodman also comments that 'The first grant made on 15 May 1372 was a life annuity of 50 marks, which more than doubled the annuities which Katherine received for her past service to Blanche' (*Katherine*, p. 11).

34. Anthony Goodman, *John of Gaunt: The Exercise of Princely Power in Fourteenth Century Europe* (Harlow, 1992), pp. 47–8. The papal response is documented in Rosenthal, *Noble and the Noble Life*, p. 174.

35. P.E. Russell, *The English Intervention in Spain and Portugal in the Time of Edward III and Richard II* (Oxford, 1955), p. 179; Goodman, *John of Gaunt*, pp. 50–1. The relationship between Katherine and Constance will be addressed in Chapter Four.

36. *JGR 1372–6*. See, e.g., entries 1289, 1356 and 1357.

37. *Records of the Borough of Leicester*, vol. 2, ed. Mary Bateson (London, 1901), p. 155.

38. *JGR 1379–83*, entries 108–15; *Knighton's Chronicle 1337–1396*, ed. G.H. Martin (Oxford, 1995), p. 237; *The Anonimalle Chronicle 1333–1381*, ed. V.H. Galbraith (Manchester, 1970), pp. 153–4; *Thomas Walsingham's Chronicon Angliae*, ed. Edward Maunder Thompson (London, 1965), p. 328.

39. Goodman, *Katherine*, p. 12; *JGR 1379–83*, p. 183, entry 558. My translation from the original French.

40. *JGR 1379–83*, p. 307, entry 989; p. 366, entry 1157.

41. The enclosing of parkland was just one of many improvements Katherine made to the Kettlethorpe manor. See Cole, 'Manor and

Rectory of Kettlethorpe', pp. 42, 55–6. *CPR 1381–5*, p. 317, entry 20 October 1383; Goodman, *Katherine*, p. 15.

42. J.H. Wylie, *History of England under Henry the Fourth*, vol. 3 (London, 1896), p. 258; Jennifer Ward, *Women of the English Nobility and Gentry 1066–1500* (Manchester, 1995), p. 63; Goodman, *Katherine*, pp. 14–15.

43. G.F. Beltz, *Memorials of the Order of the Garter* (London, 1841), p. 250; G.E. Cokayne, *The Complete Peerage*, vol. 1 (Gloucester, 1982), p. 534.

44. *CPR 1381–5*, p. 501, entry 17 August 1384.

45. Goodman, *Katherine*, p. 25.

46. J.H. Wylie, *History of England under Henry the Fourth*, vol. 4 (London, 1898), pp. 162, 165; Rosenthal, *Nobles and the Noble Life*, p. 153.

47. D. Pearsall, *The Life of Geoffrey Chaucer* (Oxford, 1994), p. 27; Given-Wilson and Curteis, *Royal Bastards*, pp. 149–50; Russell, *English Intervention*, p. 525. Constance was buried in the Church of the Annunciation of Our Lady of Newarke in Leicester. Leland described her tomb: '[She] lieth before the high altar in a tomb of marble with an image of brass (like a queen) on it.' The church was destroyed in the late sixteenth century. C.J. Billson, *Medieval Leicester* (Leicester, 1920), p. 81.

48. James H. Ramsay, *Genesis of Lancaster*, vol. 2 (Oxford, 1913), p. 308; Goodman. *Katherine*, p. 15.

49. *The Register of the Guild of the Holy Trinity, St Mary, St John the Baptist and St Katherine of Coventry*, vol. 1, ed. Mary Dormer Harris (London, 1935), p. 49.

50. *CPR 1396–99*, p. 412.

51. Christopher Wordsworth, 'Inventories of Plate, Vestments, etc., Belonging to the Cathedral Church of the Blessed Mary of Lincoln', *Archaeologia*, 2nd ser. 53 (1892), 23–5, 62, 71. These gifts, and in particular the significance of the insignia, will be discussed in detail in Chapter Five.

52. Hill, *Medieval Lincoln* (Cambridge 1965), p. 167.

53. Francis Blomefield, *An Essay towards a Topographical History of the County of Norfolk*, vol. 3 (London, 1769), p. 549.

54. Walter Rye, 'John of Gaunt and Katherine Swynford', *Times Literary Supplement*, 17 April 1924, p. 240.

55. *Excerpta Historica or, Illustrations of English History*, ed. Samuel

Bentley (London, 1833), p. 154; Given-Wilson and Curteis, *Royal Bastards*, p. 150.

56. *CPR 1396–9*, pp. 516, 555; *DNB*, vol. lv, p. 243; *CCR 1401–5*, p. 218; Crawford, *Letters of the Queens of England*, p. 111; Wylie, History of England, vol. 4, p. 186; Robert Somerville, *History of the Duchy of Lancaster*, vol. I: *1265–1603* (London, 1953), pp. 135n., 156–7 and n.

57. John H. Harvey, *Catherine Swynford's Chantry* (Lincoln Minster Pamphlets, 2nd ser. no. 6), p. 19; Robert Sanderson, *Lincoln Cathedral: An Exact Copy of all the Ancient Monumental Inscriptions Collected by Robert Sanderson and Compared with and Corrected by Sir W. Dugdale's MS Survey* (London and Lincoln, 1851), pp. 11–12.

58. *JGR 1372–6*, entry 181.

59. Rosenthal, *Nobles and the Noble Life*, p. 174.

60. Galway, 'Philippa Pan', p. 482.

61. Goodman, *Katherine*, p. 24.

62. *CPR 1370–4*, p. 202.

63. Simon Walker, *The Lancastrian Affinity 1361–1399* (Oxford, 1990), pp. 82, 217, 282; C.D. Ross, 'The Yorkshire Baronage 1399–1433' (unpublished D.Phil. thesis), fo. 202.

64. *Excerpta Historica*, p. 157.

65. *CPR 1391–6*, p. 266.

66. *Derby Accounts*, ed. Lucy Toulmin Smith (London, 1894), pp. 38, 100, 121, 128, 133, 138, 301–2.

67. *The Chronicle of Adam Usk 1377–1421*, ed. Chris Given-Wilson (Oxford, 1997), pp. 89–91.

68. *Ibid.*; Beltz, *Memorials of the Garter*, p. 236.

69. *CPR 1399–1401*, pp. 42, 295; Chris Given-Wilson, *The Royal Household and the King's Affinity* (New Haven and London, 1986), p. 195.

70. *DNB*, vol. 55, p. 244; Somerville, *Duchy of Lancaster*, p. 528.

71. Cole, 'Manor and Rectory of Kettlethorpe', p. 60. The request for the letters to be in Latin and not French could, however, have been a matter of political posturing.

72. *Excerpta Historica*, p. 157; *CPR 1408–13*, pp. 323–4.

73. *Excerpta Historica*, p. 158.

74. http://familytreemaker.genealogy.com/users/s/t/e/Thomas-E-Stevenson/FILE/0003page.html?Welcome=1040309424, accessed

19 December 2002. Information on this website was taken from A. Campling, *The History of the Family of Drury* (London, 1937).

75. J. Elder, 'A Study of the Beauforts and their Estates' (unpublished Ph.D. thesis, Bryn Mawr, 1964), fo. 211.

76. *DNB*, vol. 55, p. 244.

77. *Chaucer Life Records* (Oxford, 1966), p. 67.

78. These have been collated in the invaluable *Chaucer Life Records*. The biographical information on Chaucer that I have included here is, unless otherwise cited, from *The Riverside Chaucer*, ed. Larry D. Benson (Oxford, 1988).

79. Derek Brewer, *An Introduction to Chaucer* (London, 1984), pp. 2–3.

80. Power, *Medieval English Nunneries*, p. 19.

81. Williams, *New View*, pp. 46–8.

82. Edith Rickert, 'Elizabeth Chausir, a Nun at Barking', *Times Literary Supplement*, 18 May 1933, p. 348; William Page and J. Horace Round (eds), *The Victoria History of the County of Essex*, vol. 2 (London, 1907), pp. 118–19.

83. Russell Krauss, 'Chaucerian Problems: Especially the Petherton Forestship and the Question of Thomas Chaucer', in Russell Krauss, *Three Chaucer Studies* (Oxford, 1932), p. 169.

84. Photographs of the tomb are included in Pearsall, *Geoffrey Chaucer*, pp. 280–1.

85. *Ibid.*, p. 279.

86. A full list of the arms can be found in Krauss, 'Chaucerian Problems', pp. 49–50.

87. *Ibid.*, p. 37.

88. Joseph Arthur Dodd, *A Historical Guide to Ewelme Church* (London, 1916), pp. 1, 7, 8.

89. *CPR 1396–9*, pp. 490, 494; *CCR 1402–5*, pp. 11, 46; Pearsall, *Geoffrey Chaucer*, pp. 124, 494, 498–9, 539, 544.

90. See, e.g., Armitage-Smith, *John of Gaunt*, p. 389.

91. Cook, 'Chaucerian Papers', pp. 44–55.

92. I believe that John and Joan were named for their father, and that Henry and Thomas were named after the Lancastrian heritage of Blanche's family.

93. Armitage-Smith, *John of Gaunt*, p. 199; Given-Wilson and Curteis, *Royal Bastards*, pp. 148–9. See also Goodman, *Katherine*, p. 12, for an explanation as to the origins of the Beaufort name.

94. G.L. Harris, *Cardinal Beaufort* (Oxford, 1988), p. 2. See Elder, 'A Study of the Beauforts', for a detailed appraisal of the Beauforts' offices, lands, wealth and households.

95. Harris, *Cardinal Beaufort*, pp. 1–3.

96. *The Chronicles of Froissart*, vol. 2, ed. Thomas Johnes (London, 1852), pp. 434–46.

97. Radford, *Henry Beaufort*, p. 1.

98. Harris, *Cardinal Beaufort*, p. 2.

99. K.B. McFarlane, *The Nobility of Later Medieval England* (Oxford, 1973), p. 134.

100. Harris, *Cardinal Beaufort*, p. 3.

101. *CPR 1391–6*, p. 196.

102. *CPR 1388–92*, p. 409; Harris, *Cardinal Beaufort*, p. 2.

103. Given-Wilson and Curteis, *Royal Bastards*, p. 49.

104. G.E. Cockayne, *The Complete Peerage*, 2nd edn, vol. 12 (London, 1953), pp. 40–1.

105. Harris, *Cardinal Beaufort*, pp. 4–5; *CPR 1396–9*, pp. 289, 334; Ross, 'Yorkshire Baronage', fos 26–7.

106. Michael K. Jones and Malcolm G. Underwood, *The King's Mother: Lady Margaret Beaufort, Countess of Richmond and Derby* (Cambridge, 1995), p. 21.

107. Harris, *Cardinal Beaufort*, p. 10.

108. Jones and Underwood, *The King's Mother*, p. 22; A.L. Brown, 'The Reign of Henry IV', in S.B. Chrimes, C.D. Ross and R.A. Griffiths (eds), *Fifteenth Century England 1399–1509* (Manchester, 1974), p. 6.

109. Harris, *Cardinal Beaufort*, pp. 10–11; Cockayne, *Complete Peerage*, vol. 12, p. 42.

110. *CPR 1401–5*, p. 34.

111. *Ibid.*, p. 298; *CPR 1402–5*, pp. 342–3.

112. Cockayne, *Complete Peerage*, vol. 12, pp. 42–3; Ross, 'Yorkshire Baronage', fo. 29.

113. C.E. Woodruff and W. Danks, *Memorials of Canterbury Cathedral* (London, 1912), p. 201; Cockayne, *Complete Peerage*, vol. 12, p. 44.

114. *CPR 1396–9*, pp. 171, 414.

115. Harris, *Cardinal Beaufort*, p. 16.

116. *DNB*, vol. 4, p. 50; *CCR 1402–5*, p. 415.

117. Ross, 'Yorkshire Baronage', fo. 47.

118. R.B. Dobson, *Durham Priory 1400–1450* (Cambridge, 1973), p. 28.

119. *William Worcestre Itineraries*, ed. John H. Harvey (Oxford, 1969), pp. 355–7.

120. *DNB*, vol. 4, p. 50.

121. P. Strong and F. Strong, 'The Last Will and Codicils of Henry V', *English Historical Review*, 96 (1981), 84–5.

122. K.B. McFarlane, *Lancastrian Kings and Lollard Knights* (Oxford, 1972), pp. 106–7.

123. Goodman, *Katherine*, p. 22.

124. *CPR 1391–6*, p. 529; Cockayne, *Complete Peerage*, vol. 12, p. 39n.; Goodman, *Katherine*, p. 22; Harris, *Cardinal Beaufort*, p. 6.

125. Ross, 'Yorkshire Baronage', fo. 38. Joan left 300 marks in her will to her daughter Mary, and Elizabeth married John Lord Greystoke on 28 October 1409 with a dowry of 440 marks. *Ibid.*, fos 38n., 48; *Historiæ Dunelmensis Scriptores Tres*, ed. James Raine (London, 1834), p. cclix.

126. Cockayne, *Complete Peerage*, vol. 12, p. 39n; Goodman, *Katherine*, p. 23.

127. Ross, 'Yorkshire Baronage', fo. 35.

128. Goodman, *Katherine*, p. 23.

129. S.B. Chrimes, *Lancastrians, Yorkists and Henry VII* (London, 1966), p. 87; Jennifer Ward, *English Noblewomen in the Later Middle Ages* (London, 1992), p. 27; Ross, 'Yorkshire Baronage', fos 28–9.

130. M.H. Keen, *England in the Later Middle Ages* (London, 1997), pp. 436, 464.

131. Ross, 'Yorkshire Baronage', fos 39–40. Katharine Stafford is an error for Margaret.

132. *Ibid.*, fos 40–5.

133. Dobson, *Durham Priory*, pp. 187–90.

134. J.R. Lander, 'Marriage and Politics in the Fifteenth Century: The Nevilles and the Wydevilles', *Bulletin of the Institute of Historical Research*, 36 (1963), 120.

135. Ross, 'Yorkshire Baronage', fo. 2.

136. *CPR 1436–41*, p. 137.

137. Goodman, *Katherine*, p. 23; Francis Peck, *Desiderata Curiosa* (London, 1779), p. 301; *Historiae Dunelmensis Scriptores*, p. cclviii. In Joan's will the request to be buried with her mother is clear: 'In primis, do et lego animam meam Deo omnipotenti, et beatæ Mariæ virgini, et omnibus Sanctis, corpusque meum ad sepeliendum in ecclesiæ Cathedrali Lincolniensi, ad idem altare ubi corpus dominæ Katerinæ Ducissæ Lancastriæ, matris meæ, sepelitur . . .'. Katherine is

later described as 'illustrissimæ dominæ et matris meæ dominæ
Katerinæ Ducissæ Lancastriæ . . .'.

138. *Three Books of Polydore Vergil's English History Comprising the Reigns of Henry VI, Edward IV and Richard III*, ed. Henry Ellis (London, 1844), pp. 73–4.
139. Harris, *Cardinal Beaufort*, p. v.
140. Cook, 'Chaucerian Papers', p. 49.
141. *CPR 1396–9*, p. 46; Harris, *Cardinal Beaufort*, pp. 7–8; *Œuvres de Froissart*, ed. Lettenhove, vol. 15, pp. 238–9; Cook, 'Chaucerian Papers', pp. 49, 51; Radford, *Henry Beaufort*, p. 1.
142. Harris, *Cardinal Beaufort*, p. 9.
143. *Ibid.*, p. 18.
144. *DNB*, vol. 4, pp. 42–3.
145. Lander, 'Marriage and Politics', p. 130.
146. Ross, 'Yorkshire Baronage', fos 113–14.
147. *Ibid.*, fo. 114.
148. *Ibid.*, fo. 41; Given-Wilson and Curteis, *Royal Bastards*, p. 151.
149. Given-Wilson and Curteis, *Royal Bastards*, p. 151. Walsingham suggested that Henry was nominated for the papal throne at the Council of Constance. Ross, 'Yorkshire Baronage', fo. 36n.
150. *Chronicles of London*, ed. C.L. Kingsford (Stroud, 1977), p. 95.
151. Antonia Gransden, *Historical Writing in England*, vol. 2: *c. 1307 to the Early Sixteenth Century* (London, 1998), pp. 199–200.
152. *DNB*, vol. 4, p. 47.
153. Given-Wilson and Curteis, *Royal Bastards*, pp. 151–2.
154. Radford, *Henry Beaufort*, p. 3.
155. *Excerpta Historica*, p. 154.
156. *Ibid.*
157. *DNB*, vol. 4, p. 41.

Chapter Two

1. *An English Chronicle of the Reigns of Richard II, Henry IV, Henry V and Henry VI Written before the Year 1471*, ed. J.S. Davies (London, 1856), p. 114.
2. Alice Perrers was mistress to Edward III.
3. *The Brut or The Chronicles of England*, ed. Friedrich W.D. Brie, pt 2 (EETS; London, 1908), pp. 329–30, 334.
4. *Ibid.*, p. 595.

5. *Three Fifteenth Century Chronicles*, ed. James Gairdner (London, 1965), p. 24.

6. *The Chronicle of John Hardyng*, ed. Henry Ellis (London, 1812), pp. 290–1, 339; Sydney Armitage-Smith, *John of Gaunt: King of Castile and Leon, Duke of Aquitaine and Lancaster, Earl of Derby, Lincoln and Leicester, Seneschal of England* (Westminster, 1904), p. 362; Antonia Gransden, *Historical Writing in England*, vol. 2: *c. 1307 to the Early Sixteenth Century* (London, 1998), pp. 276–9.

7. Anthony Goodman, *John of Gaunt: The Exercise of Princely Power in Fourteenth Century Europe* (Harlow, 1992), p. 15.

8. *John Capgrave's Abbreuiacion of Cronicles*, ed. Peter J. Lucas (EETS; Oxford, 1983), p. 205; Gransden, *Historical Writing*, vol. 2, pp. 389–90.

9. *Capgrave's Abbreuiacion*, p. 205.

10. J. Elder, 'A Study of the Beauforts and their Estates' (unpublished Ph.D. thesis, Bryn Mawr, 1964), fo. 22.

11. *English Historical Documents*, vol. 4: *1327–1485*, ed. D.C. Douglas and A.R. Myers (London, 1969), p. 343.

12. *The Paston Letters*, vol. 2, ed. John Fenn, re-ed. L. Archer-Hind (London, 1924), p. 237n.

13. Margaret Aston, 'Richard II and the Wars of the Roses', in F.R.H. du Boulay and C.M. Barron (eds), *The Reign of Richard II* (London, 1971), p. 283.

14. J.D. Mackie, *The Earlier Tudors 1485–1588* (Oxford, 1992), p. 46.

15. *Ibid.*, p. 60.

16. John Weaver, *Ancient Funerall Monuments* (Amsterdam, 1979), p. 365.

17. Ex qua numerosam suscepit prolem, uncle genus ex matre duxit Henricus Septimus Rex Anglie prudentissimus.

18. R.A. Griffiths and Roger S. Thomas, *The Making of the Tudor Dynasty* (Gloucester, 1985), pp. 192–3.

19. *The Anglica Historia of Polydore Vergil 1485–1537*, ed. Denys Hay (London, 1950), pp. xxviii, xxix; Gransden, *Historical Writing*, vol. 2, pp. 427–40.

20. Cited in Gransden, *Historical Writing*, vol. 2, p. 274.

21. Cited in *Ibid.*, vol. 2, p. 316.

22. *Polydore Vergil's English History*, ed. Henry Ellis (London, 1846), p. 124.

23. Cited in Gransden, *Historical Writing*, vol. 2, pp. 246–7, 469.

24. *Ibid.*, vol. 2, p. 231.

25. Robert Fabyan, *The New Chronicles of England and France, in Two Parts*, ed. Henry Ellis (London, 1811), p. 533.

26. The writings of the fourteenth-century chroniclers will be discussed in detail in the following chapter.

27. *The English Works of John Fisher*, ed. John E.B. Mayor (EETS; London, 1876), pp. 290–1.

28. Edward Hall, *Hall's Chronicle*, ed. Henry Ellis (London, 1809), pp. 2, 26.

29. *Ibid.*, p. 130.

30. John Hayward, *The Life and Raigne of King Henrie IIII*, ed. John J. Manning (London, 1991), pp. 68–9, 204.

31. Goodman, *John of Gaunt*, p. 19.

32. *Ibid.*

33. Cited in Chris Given-Wilson and Alice Curteis, *The Royal Bastards of Medieval England* (London, 1984), p. 41.

34. Weaver, *Ancient Funerall Monuments*, p. 661.

35. Giovanni Francesco Biondi, *A History of the Civil Wars of England between the Two Houses of Lancaster and York*, trans. Henry, Earl of Monmouth (London, 1641), vol. 1, p. 51.

36. T. Speght, *The Works of our Ancient, Learned and Excellent Poet Jeffrey Chaucer* (London, 1687), preface.

37. Richard Baker, *A Chronicle of the Kings of England from the Time of the Romans Government unto the Death of King James I* (London, 1696), p. 236.

38. M. Rapin de Thoyras, *The History of England*, trans. John Kelly (London, 1732), pp. 524, 754.

39. *Ibid.*, pp. 507–8.

40. *Excerpta Historica or, Illustrations of English History*, ed. Samuel Bentley (London, 1833), p. 152.

41. J.H. Wylie, *History of England under Henry the Fourth*, vol. 3 (London, 1896), p. 260.

42. William Godwin, *The Life of Geoffrey Chaucer* (London, 1804), vol. 2, pp. 198–9, 380; vol. 4, p. 104.

43. Lewis Bostock Radford, *Henry Beaufort, Bishop, Chancellor, Cardinal* (London, 1908), pp. 1–2.

44. Armitage-Smith, *John of Gaunt*, p. 392.

45. James H. Ramsay, *Genesis of Lancaster*, vol. 2 (Oxford 1913), p. 47n.

46. *Ibid.*, p. 47.

47. Philip Lindsay, *King Henry V: A Chronicle* (London, 1934), p. 17.

48. R.E.G. Cole, 'The Manor and Rectory of Kettlethorpe', *Architectural Societies Reports*, 31, report 66 (1911), 41–86.

49. Alison Weir, *Lancaster and York: The Wars of the Roses* (London, 1995), pp. 27–8. Anya Seton's novel has: 'The Bishop of Lincoln had not failed to point this out in a sermon, with reference to Adam and Lilith, and a long diatribe about shameless, scheming magdalenes. This sermon was preached at Katherine during the first hullabaloo after her return' (*Katherine* (London, 1956), p. 532).

50. Seton, *Katherine*, p. 7.

51. Marchette Chute, *Geoffrey Chaucer of England* (London, 1951), pp. 47, 85.

52. See, e.g., Margaret Galway, 'Geoffrey Chaucer, JP and MP', *Modern Language Review*, 36 (1941), 1–36; 'Chaucer's Hopeless Love', *Modern Language Notes*, 60 (1945), 431–8; 'The Troilus Frontispiece', *Modern Language Review*, 44 (1949), 161–77; 'Walter Roet and Philippa Chaucer', *Notes and Queries* (1954), 48–9; 'Philippa Pan; Philippa Chaucer', *Modern Language Review*, 55 (1960), 481–7; John M. Manly, *Some New Light on Chaucer* (Gloucester, Mass., 1959); George Williams, 'The Troilus and Criseyde Frontispiece Again', *Modern Language Review*, 57 (1962), 173–8; *A New View of Chaucer* (Durham, NC, 1965).

53. Williams, *New View*, pp. 16–17.

54. K.B. McFarlane, *Lancastrian Kings and Lollard Knights* (Oxford, 1972), p. 15.

55. S.B. Chrimes, *Lancastrians, Yorkists and Henry VII* (London, 1966), pp. 8–9.

56. Joel T. Rosenthal, *Nobles and the Noble Life 1295–1500* (London, 1976), p. 34.

57. Given-Wilson and Curteis, *Royal Bastards*, pp. 10–11, 148–50.

58. Goodman, *John of Gaunt*, pp. 50, 156, 362; Anthony Goodman, *Katherine Swynford* (Lincoln, 1999), pp. 8–20.

59. Anil de Silva-Vigier, *This Moste Highe Prince, John of Gaunt* (Edinburgh, 1992), p. 153.

60. *Ibid.*, p. 155.

61. *Ibid.*

Chapter Three

1. *Thomas Walsingham's Chronicon Angliae*, ed. Edward Maunde Thompson (London, 1965), p. 196. My translation. There has been much debate over the authorship of this text. For the purposes of this

analysis I concur with Galbraith's view that the chronicle was the record of one writer. V.H. Galbraith, 'Thomas Walsingham and the Saint Alban's Chronicle, 1272–1422', *English Historical Review*, 47 (1932), 29.

2. *The St Albans Chronicle: The Chronica Maiora of Thomas Walsingham 1376–1394*, ed. John Taylor and Wendy R. Childs, trans. Leslie Watkiss (Oxford, 2002), pp. xvii–xxi, xxxiii.

3. *Ibid.*, p. 13.

4. *Ibid.*

5. A. Goodman, *John of Gaunt: The Exercise of Princely Power in Fourteenth Century Europe* (Harlow, 1992), p. 260.

6. *The St Albans Chronicle*, p. 9.

7. *Ibid.*, p. 39.

8. *Ibid.*, p. 61.

9. Goodman, *John of Gaunt*, pp. 260–1.

10. Antonia Gransden, *Historical Writing in England*, vol. 2: *c. 1307 to the Early Sixteenth Century* (London, 1998), pp. 138–9.

11. *Ibid.*, vol. 2, p. 129.

12. *Ibid.*, vol. 2, pp. 133–5. Kim M. Philips, *Medieval Maidens: Young Women and Gender in England, 1270–1540* (Manchester, 2003), p. 155.

13. Gransden, *Historical Writing*, vol. 2, pp. 146–7.

14. Christiane Klapisch-Zuber, 'Including Women', in Christiane Klapisch-Zuber, *A History of Women: Silences of the Middle Ages* (Cambridge, Mass., 1994), pp. 7–8.

15. Derek Brewer, 'Gothic Chaucer', in Derek. Brewer (ed.), *Writers and their Background: Geoffrey Chaucer* (London, 1974), p. 17.

16. Marbod of Rennes (*c.* 1035–1123), *The Femme Fatale*.

17. *Malleus Maleficarum* (1486).

18. Elisabeth van Houts, 'Women in Medieval History and Literature', *Journal of Medieval History*, 20/3 (1994), 282.

19. D.W. Robertson, *A Preface to Chaucer: Studies in Medieval Perspectives* (Princeton, 1963), p. 227.

20. Nigel Saul, *Richard II* (New Haven and London, 1997), p. 35. Saul states that Gaunt's delay was due to the logistical problem of a shortage in his fleet.

21. Goodman, *John of Gaunt*, p. 362.

22. Chris Given-Wilson and Alice Curteis, *The Royal Bastards of Medieval England* (London, 1984), p. 40.

23. *The St Albans Chronicle*, p. 567.

24. *JGR 1379–83*, p. 366, entry 1157, 14 February 1382.

25. *Knighton's Chronicle 1337–1396*, ed. G.H. Martin (Oxford, 1995), p. 237; *The Anonimalle Chronicle 1333–1381*, ed. V.H. Galbraith (Manchester, 1970), pp. 153–4.

26. See Chapter One for further information on these connections.

27. *The St Albans Chronicle*, p. 891.

28. *Ibid.*, p. 947.

29. Gransden, *Historical Writing*, vol. 2, p. 178.

30. *Ibid.*, vol. 2, p. 159.

31. *Knighton's Chronicle*, p. 233.

32. *Ibid.*, p. 237.

33. *Ibid.*, p. 235.

34. Goodman, *John of Gaunt*, contains these and numerous other references to the relationship between Gaunt, Wyclif and the Lollards.

35 Gransden, *Historical Writing*, vol. 2, p. 170.

36. *Knighton's Chronicle*, p. 313.

37. *Ibid.*, p. 251.

38. May McKisack, *The Fourteenth Century 1307–1399* (Oxford, 1997), p. 393. Gransden, *Historical Writing*, vol. 2, p. 138.

39. *The St Albans Chronicle*, p. 75.

40. . . . et fletibus ac singultu facere videbatur poenitentiae dignos fructus.

41 . . . conversus ad religionem . . .

42. *The St Albans Chronicle*, p. 13.

43. Sydney Armitage-Smith, *John of Gaunt: King of Castile and Leon, Duke of Aquitaine and Lancaster, Earl of Derby, Lincoln and Leicester, Seneschal of England* (Westminster, 1904), p. 409.

44. Cited in Gransden, *Historical Writing*, vol. 2, p. 131.

45. *The Anonimalle Chronicle*, p. 153. Translation in Anthony Goodman, *Katherine* (Lincoln, 1999), p. 14.

46. *Ibid.*, p. 154. My translation.

47. Goodman, *Katherine*, p. 14.

48. *The Anonimalle Chronicle*, p. xxiii.

49. *Ibid.*, p. xxxiv.

50. Goodman, *Katherine*, p. 17.

51. Chris Given-Wilson, *The Royal Household and the King's Affinity* (New Haven and London, 1986), p. 147.

52. F. George Kay, *Lady of the Sun: The Life and Times of Alice Perrers* (London, 1966), p. 7.

53. *The St Albans Chronicle*, p. 43.
54. *Ibid.*, p. 45.
55. *Ibid.*, p. 47.
56. *Ibid.*, p. 57.
57. James Bothwell, 'The Management of Position: Alice Perrers, Edward III and the Creation of a Landed Estates, 1362–1377', *Journal of Medieval History*, 24 (1998), 31.
58. *Ibid.*, p. 46.
59. *The Anonimalle Chronicle*, pp. 87–8.
60. *The Westminster Chronicle*, ed. L.C. Hector and Barbara F. Harvey (Oxford, 1982); *The Chronicle of Adam Usk 1377–1421*, ed. Chris Given-Wilson (Oxford, 1997).
61. *Adam Usk*, p. 63.
62. *Westminster Chronicle*, p. 193.
63. Gransden, *Historical Writing*, vol. 2, pp. 166, 176–7.
64. *Westminster Chronicle*. For positive portrayals see pp. 67, 407–9; for negative portrayals see pp. 37, 68–70, 519.
65. *Ibid.*, pp. 188–90.
66. *The St Albans Chronicle*, p. 823.
67. *Ibid.*
68. *Historica Vitae et Regni Ricardi Secundi*, ed. George B. Stow Jr (Pennsylvania, 1997), p. 135. My translation.
69. *The St Albans Chronicle*, pp. xxviii, lxvi.
70. Galbraith, 'Thomas Walsingham', p. 25.
71. *Thomas Walsingham's Chronicon Angliae*, pp. xix–xxiii.
72. *The St Albans Chronicle*, p. 221.
73. *Ibid.*, p. 229.
74. Gransden, *Historical Writing*, vol. 2, p. 152.
75. *Ibid.*, vol. 2, pp. 89, 174.
76. *The Chronicles of Froissart*, vol. 2, ed. Thomas Johnes (London, 1852), pp. 599–600.
77. *Ibid.*, p. 600.
78. *Ibid.*
79. Philips, *Medieval Maidens*, p. 156.
80. *Ibid.*
81. *Ibid.*, p. 601; *Œuvres de Froissart*, vol. 15: *1392–1396*, ed. Kervyn de Lettenhove (Osnabrück, 1967), p. 240.
82. Given-Wilson and Curteis, *Royal Bastards*, p. 149.
83. Goodman, *Katherine*, p. 19.

84. Geoffrey Chaucer, *The Canterbury Tales*, trans. Nevill Coghill (London, 2003), p. 234.

85. *The Riverside Chaucer*, ed. Larry D. Benson (Oxford, 1987), p. 903.

86. Charles A. Owen Jr, 'Relationship between *The Physician's Tale* and *The Parson's Tale*', *Modern Language Notes*, 72 (1956), 85.

87. Nicholas Orme, *From Childhood to Chivalry* (London, 1984), p. 27 (emphasis added).

88. Owen, 'Relationship', p. 85.

89. *Riverside Chaucer*, p. 901.

90. *The Canterbury Tales*, ll. 121–90.

91. Lynn Staley, 'Chaucer and the Postures of Sanctity', in David Aers and Lynn Staley, *The Powers of the Holy* (Pennsylvania, 1996), 180–1.

92. Emerson Brown Jr, 'What is Chaucer doing with the Physician and his Tale?' *Philological Quarterly*, 60 (1981), 134.

93. Goodman, *Katherine*, p. 19; *Riverside Chaucer*, p. 929.

94. Edith Rickert, *Chaucer's World* (New York and London, 1964), p. 325.

95. Aage Brusendorff, *The Chaucer Tradition* (Oxford, 1967), pp. 22–3.

96. George Williams, 'The Troilus and Criseyde Frontispiece Again', *Modern Language Review*, 57 (1962), 173. All future references to Williams's view of the frontispiece are from this article.

97. Margaret Galway, 'The Troilus Frontispiece', *Modern Language Review*, 44 (1949), 161. All future references to Galway's view of the frontispiece are from this article.

98. *Riverside Chaucer*, pp. 1020–1.

99. George Williams, *A New View of Chaucer* (Durham, NC, 1965), pp. 17, 19, 73.

100. *Ibid.*, p. 74.

101. *Ibid.*, pp. 176–95; quotations from p. 66.

102. *Ibid.*, pp. 67–9.

103. *Ibid.*, pp. 56–65.

104. *Ibid.*, p. 58.

105. G.T. Shepherd, 'Troilus and Criseyde', in D.S. Brewer (ed.), *Chaucer and Chaucerians: Critical Studies in Middle English Literature* (London, 1966), p. 79.

106. We know of four children but there is, of course, the possibility that Katherine had others that died at birth or in infancy.

107. Anil de Silva-Vigier, *This Moste Highe Prince, John of Gaunt* (Edinburgh, 1992), p. 154.

108. L.D. Benson, 'Chaucer: A Select Bibliography', in Derek Brewer (ed.), *Writers and their Background: Geoffrey Chaucer* (London, 1974), p. 361.
109. Williams, *New View*, p. 69.
110. *Ibid.*, p. 79 (emphasis added).
111. *Ibid.*, p. 80.
112. *Ibid.*, pp. 45, 58.
113. Robertson, *A Preface to Chaucer*, p. 482.
114. *Ibid.*, p. 499.
115. *Ibid.*

Chapter Four

1. *The Chronicles of Froissart*, vol. 2, ed. Thomas Johnes (London, 1852), p. 601.
2. Anthony Goodman, *Katherine Swynford* (Lincoln, 1999), p. 10.
3. George Williams, *A New View of Chaucer* (Durham, NC, 1965), p. 45.
4. Anne Crawford (ed.), *Letters of the Queens of England 1100–1547* (Stroud, 1994), pp. 92–100.
5. M. Galway, 'Philippa Pan; Philippa Chaucer', *Modern Language Review*, 55 (1960), 482.
6. *Ibid.*, p. 481.
7. *Œuvres de Froissart*, vol. 15: *1392–1396*, ed. Kervyn de Lettenhove (Osnabrück, 1967), p. 238.
8. Goodman, *Katherine*, p. 10.
9. Nicholas Orme, *Education and Society in Medieval and Renaissance England* (London, 1989), p. 164.
10. Katherine did not join the Fraternity when her sister and her children underwent the initiation ceremony in 1386 with Henry of Derby. *Chaucer Life Records*, ed. Martin M. Crow and Clair C. Olson (Oxford, 1966), p. 91. This indicates that Katherine was already a member by 1386.
11. Christopher Wordsworth, *Notes on Medieval Services in England* (London, 1898), p. 170. The significance of St Katherine to Katherine will be discussed fully in Chapter Five.
12. Goodman, *Katherine*, p. 24.
13. *Knighton's Chronicle 1337–1396*, ed. G.H. Martin (Oxford, 1995). See, e.g., pp. 239, 241.

14. *John of Gaunt's Register 1379–1383*, ed. E.C. Lodge and Robert Somerville (London, 1937), p. xxii.

15. Sharon D. Michalore, 'The Education of Aristocratic Women in Fifteenth Century England', in Sharon D. Michalore and A. Compton Reeves (eds), *Estrangement, Enterprise and Education in Fifteenth Century England* (Stroud, 1998), p. 123.

16. Anne Crawford (ed.), *Letters of Medieval Women* (Stroud, 2002), pp. 228–9.

17. Nicholas Orme, *From Childhood to Chivalry* (London, 1984), p. 29.

18. The following information on the education of noble women was obtained from Nicholas Orme's excellent study *Education and Society in Medieval and Renaissance England* (London, 1989), pp. 162–75.

19. Goodman, *Katherine*, p. 18.

20. For further information on the practice of mass and private devotion, see, e.g., Eamon Duffy, *The Stripping of the Altars* (New Haven and London, 1992), particularly pp. 91–130; *The Book of Margery Kempe*, ed. B.A. Windeatt (London, 1985).

21. R.E.G. Cole, 'The Manor and Rectory of Kettlethorpe', *Architectural Societies Reports*, 31, report 66 (1911), 55.

22. Nicholas Orme, 'The Education of the Courtier', in V.J. Scattergood and J.W. Sherbourne (eds), *English Court Culture in the Later Middle Ages* (London, 1983), p. 63.

23. Alexandra Barrett, *Women's Writing in Middle English* (London, 1999), p. 3.

24. Anthony Goodman, *John of Gaunt: The Exercise of Princely Power in Fourteenth Century Europe* (Harlow, 1992), p. 38.

25. Susan H. Cavanaugh, 'A Study of Books Privately Owned in England 1300–1450' (Ph.D. thesis, University of Pennsylvania, 1980), fos 474–6.

26. *Ibid.*, fo. 279; Richard F. Green, 'King Richard II's Books Revisited', *The Library*, 5th ser., 31 (1976), 238–9. A particular favourite of Richard's appears to have been the 'Roman de la Rose'.

27. Mary Erler, *Women, Reading and Piety in Late Medieval England* (Cambridge, 2002), p. 3; Cavanaugh, 'A Study of Books Owned', fo. 9.

28. Cavanaugh, 'A Study of Books Owned', fos 725–31.

29. *Ibid.*, fos 154–5.

30. *Ibid.*, fo. 211.

31. Nigel J. Morgan and Lucy Freeman Sandler, 'Manuscript Illumination of the Thirteenth and Fourteenth Centuries', in Jonathan Alexander and Paul Binski (eds), *Age of Chivalry* (London, 1987), p. 155.

32. *Ibid.*, pp. 108–9, 110–12; Karen K. Jambeck, 'Patterns of Women's Literary Patronage: England, 1200–ca. 1475', in June Hall McCash (ed.), *The Cultural Patronage of Medieval Women* (Athens, Ga., and London, 1996), pp. 236–7.
33. Cavanaugh, 'A Study of Books Owned'. fos 408–11.
34. Nicholas Orme, 'Education of the Courtier', in K.B. McFarlane (ed.), *The Nobility of Later Medieval England* (Oxford, 1973), p. 43.
35. Mary Anne Everett Wood (ed.), *Letters of Royal and Illustrious Ladies of Great Britain*, vol. 1 (London, 1846), p. 90.
36. Sydney Armitage-Smith, *John of Gaunt: King of Castile and Leon, Duke of Aquitaine and Lancaster, Earl of Derby, Lincoln and Leicester, Seneschal of England* (Westminster, 1904), p. 415; J.H. Wylie, *History of England under Henry the Fourth*, vol. 2 (London, 1894), p. 332.
37. Jambeck, 'Patterns of Patronage', pp. 235–6.
38. Wylie, *History of England*, vol. 2, p. 333.
39. Jennifer Ward, *English Noblewomen in the Later Middle Ages* (London, 1992), p. 160.
40. Francis Sandford, *A Genealogical History of the Kings of England* (London, 1677), p. 252.
41. www.ampthillhistory.co.uk, accessed 5 May 2001.
42. Jambeck, 'Patterns of Patronage', p. 235.
43. *Ibid.*
44. *Ibid.*
45. Carol M. Meale, '". . . alle the bokes that I have of latyn, englisch, and frensch": Lay Women and their Books in Late Medieval England', in Carol M. Meale (ed.), *Women and Literature in Britain 1150–1500* (Cambridge, 1996), p. 145; *The Book of Margery Kempe*, p. 173.
46. Meale, 'Lay Women and their Books', p. 142.
47. *Hoccleve's Works*, vol. 1: *The Minor Poems*, ed. Frederick J. Furnivall (EETS; Oxford, 1892), p. 242; Jambeck, 'Patterns of Patronage', p. 242.
48. Meale, 'Lay Women and their Books', pp. 140–1; John Nichols (ed.), *Royal Wills* (London, 1780), p. 254; Jambeck, 'Patterns of Patronage', p. 239.
49. Crawford, *Letters of Medieval Women*, p. 59.
50. R.D. Dobson, *Durham Priory 1400–1450* (Cambridge, 1973), p. 187.
51. *Ibid.*
52. *Historiae Dunelmensis Scriptores Tres*, ed. James Raine (London, 1834), p. cclviii. This is the only record I have so far found that provides evidence of the books owned by Katherine herself.

53. Meale, 'Lay Women and their Books', p. 145.
54. Jambeck, 'Patterns of Patronage', p. 240; Michalore, 'The Education of Women', p. 127.
55. Jambeck, 'Patterns of Patronage', pp. 240–3.
56. Erler, *Women, Reading and Piety*, p. 25.
57. Nicholas Orme, *Medieval Children* (New Haven and London, 2003), p. 243.
58. Cavanaugh, 'A Study of Books Owned', fo. 18.
59. Barrett, *Women's Writing*, p. 5.
60. Cole, 'Manor and Rectory of Kettlethorpe', p. 60.
61. Cavanaugh, 'A Study of Books Owned', fo. 179.
62. Jambeck, 'Patterns of Patronage', pp. 243–4.
63. *Ibid.*, p. 244.
64. Cavanaugh, 'A Study of Books Owned', fos 81–3.
65. See, e.g., *CPR 1388–1392*, p. 409, entry 17 April 1391, 'Grant to the king's kinsman Henry de Beaufort . . .'.
66. *Excerpta Historica or, Illustrations of English History*, ed. Samuel Bentley (London, 1833), pp. 153–4.
67. Chris Given-Wilson and Alice Curteis, *The Royal Bastards of Medieval England* (London, 1984), p. 49.
68. *Ibid.*, p. 57.
69. Joel T. Rosenthal, *Nobles and the Noble Life 1295–1500* (London, 1976), p. 153.
70. For gifts to the Beauforts, see *CPR 1391–6*, pp. 15, 63; *CPR 1396–9*, pp. 171, 205, 211, 410, 414, 532. These are references to just some of the gifts received by the Beauforts.
71. *CPR 1391–6*, p. 266, entry 12 May 1393.
72. *Excerpta Historica*, p. 157.
73. *CPR 1402–5*, p. 473, entry 17 October 1404.
74. See, e.g., *CFR 1399–1405*, pp. 85, 250, 316; *CFR 1405–13*, pp. 24, 45, 71, 116, 185.
75. *CPR 1401–5*, p. 34, entry 26 November 1401.
76. Given-Wilson and Curteis, *Royal Bastards*, p. 51.
77. Anil de Silva-Vigier, *This Moste Highe Prince . . . John of Gaunt 1340–1399* (Edinburgh, 1992), p. 148.
78. Given-Wilson and Curteis, *Royal Bastards*, p. 54; Crawford, *Letters of Medieval Women*, p. 56.
79. Chris Given-Wilson, *The Royal Household and the King's Affinity* (New Haven and London, 1986), p. 195.

80. *The Chronicle of Adam Usk 1377–1421*, ed. Chris Given-Wilson (Oxford, 1997), pp. 89–91.

81. G.F. Beltz, *Memorials of the Order of the Garter* (London, 1841), p. 236: 'Cuidam valtetto Thome Swynford militis venienti de castro de Pountfreyt versus Lond. ad certificand. cons°. R. de c^rtis materiis com` odu- d?i Reg. Concernentibus In denar. Sibi lib^rat pro vad. Et exp. Suis et locatione unius equi causa festinaco`is viaii pd`ci – xxvi s. viii d.'

82. Cole, 'Manor and Rectory of Kettlethorpe', p. 60; *Derby Accounts*, ed. Lucy Toulmin Smith (London, 1894), pp. 38, 100, 121, 128, 133, 138, 301–2.

83. *CPR 1408–13*, pp. 323–4, entry 5 October 1411.

84. *Excerpta Historica*, p. 157.

85. Cited in Judy Perry, 'Katherine Roet's Swynfords: A Re-Examination of Interfamily Relationships and Descent, Part 2', *Foundations*, 1/3 (2004), 166.

86. *CPR 1381–5*, pp. 501, 504, entries August and September 1384; J.W.F. Hill, *Medieval Lincoln* (Cambridge, 1965), p. 259.

87. *CPR 1381–5*, p. 503, entry 20 September 1384. Accusation of robbery made by Roger Langford.

88. Cole, 'Manor and Rectory of Kettlethorpe', p. 55.

89. James H. Ramsay, *Genesis of Lancaster*, vol. 2 (Oxford, 1913), p. 308.

90. *CPR 1396–9*, p. 516, entry 9 March 1399; *CFR 1391–9*, p. 303, entry 1 May 1399; *CCR 1396–9*, p. 476, entry 23 May 1399.

91. *CPR 1399–1401*, pp. 58, 218, 408, entries 9 November 1399, 25 January 1401, 12 April 1403.

92. Henry also referred to his mother-in-law Joan de Bohun as 'his beloved mother', but this only emphasises the familial nature of his relationship with Katherine. Jennifer Ward, *Women of the English Nobility and Gentry 1066–1500* (Manchester, 1995), p. 153.

93. *The Chronicles of Froissart*, vol. 2, ed. Johnes, p. 600.

94. Nigel Saul, *Richard II* (New Haven and London, 1997), p. 183; Anthony Steel, *Richard II* (Cambridge, 1941), p. 112.

95. Joanna Chamberlayne, 'Joan of Kent's Tale: Adultery and Rape in the Age of Chivalry', *Medieval Life*, 5 (1996), 9.

96. James Bothwell, 'The Management of Position: Alice Perrers, Edward III and the Creation of a Landed Estates, 1362–1377', *Journal of Medieval History*, 24 (1998), 48.

97. Chamberlayne, 'Joan of Kent', p. 7.

98. Carolyn P. Collette, 'Joan of Kent and Noble Women's Roles in Chaucer's World', *Chaucer Review*, 33/4 (1999), 351.

99. Given-Wilson and Curteis, *Royal Bastards*, p. 9.

100. *JGR 1379–83*, p. 183, entry 558; *JGR 1372–6*, p. 19, entries 1356, 1357.

101. Goodman, *Katherine*, p. 12.

102. *JGR 1372–6*, pp. 60–1, entry 718. The phrase 'nostre tres chere et tres amee fille Katerine' suggests this to be the case.

103. *CPR 1396–9*, p. 412, entry 17 September 1398.

104. *Excerpta Historica*, p. 154.

105. Janet Coleman, *English Literature in History 1350–1400: Medieval Readers and Writers* (London, 1981), p. 18.

106. Armitage-Smith, *John of Gaunt*, p. 357.

107. Goodman, *John of Gaunt*, p. 362.

108. P.E. Russell, *The English Intervention in Spain and Portugal in the Time of Edward III and Richard II* (Oxford, 1955), p. 179.

109. G.E. Cokayne, *The Complete Peerage*, vol. 1 (Gloucester, 1982).

110. Derek Pearsall, *The Life of Geoffrey Chaucer* (Oxford, 1994), p. 271; Given-Wilson and Curteis, *Royal Bastards*, pp. 149–50; Russell, *English Intervention*, p. 525.

111. Gaunt and Constance married in September 1371, but lived separately from the November of that year and for most of 1372. Gaunt and Katherine's relationship appears to have started in the spring of 1372. Goodman, *John of Gaunt*, pp. 48, 50–1.

Chapter Five

1. Many thanks must go to Nicholas Bennett of Lincoln Cathedral for his assistance in attempting to track down Katherine's testament.

2. Katherine J. Lewis, *The Cult of St Katherine of Alexandria in Late Medieval England* (Woodbridge, 2000), pp. 63, 66. Lewis has also speculated as to the significance of St Katherine to Katherine Swynford within the context of the saint's status as a model of respectable femininity.

3. Anthony Goodman, *John of Gaunt: The Exercise of Princely Power in Fourteenth Century Europe* (Harlow, 1992), p. 217; Ann Payne, 'Medieval Heraldry', in Jonathan Alexander and Paul Binski (eds), *Age of Chivalry* (London, 1987), p. 59.

4. Felicity Heal, 'Reciprocity and Exchange in the Late Medieval Household', in B.A. Hanawalt and D. Wallace (eds), *Bodies and*

Discipline: Intersections of Literature and History in Fifteenth Century England (Minneapolis, 1996), pp. 184–5.

5. *Ibid.*

6. George Williams, *A New View of Chaucer* (Durham, NC, 1965), p. 72; John Cherry, 'Jewellery', in Alexander and Binski (eds), *Age of Chivalry*, p. 178.

7. Williams, *New View*, p. 72.

8. Jeffrey Denton, 'Image and History', in Alexander and Binski (eds), *Age of Chivalry*, 24.

9. Arthur P. Purey-Cust, *The Collar of SS: A History and Conjecture* (Leeds, 1910), pp. 14–15.

10. *Ibid.*, pp. 17–18.

11. Doris Fletcher, 'The Lancastrian Collar of Esses: Its Origins and Transformations down the Centuries', in James L. Gillespie (ed.), *The Age of Richard II* (Stroud and New York, 1997), 191. Fletcher also records in a footnote that Richard had his cook make jumbles in the form of an S.

12. Purey-Cust, *Collar of SS*, p. 19. Both Purey-Cust and Fletcher list the details of several tombs that display the collar of esses.

13. Fletcher, 'The Lancastrian Collar', p. 192.

14. *Ibid.*, pp. 193–4.

15. *Ibid.*, pp. 196–7.

16. *Ibid.*, p. 199.

17. Payne, 'Heraldry', p. 55.

18. *Ibid.*, pp. 58–9.

19. Veronica Sekules, 'Women and Art in England in the Thirteenth and Fourteenth Centuries', in Alexander and Binski (eds), *Age of Chivalry*, 44.

20. *Excerpta Historica or, Illustrations of English History*, ed. Samuel Bentley (London, 1833), p. 155; Chris Given-Wilson and Alice Curteis, *The Royal Bastards of Medieval England* (London, 1984), p. 50.

21. Robert Sanderson, *Lincoln Cathedral: An Exact Copy of all the Ancient Monumental Inscriptions Collected by Robert Sanderson and Compared with and Corrected by Sir W. Dugdale's MS Survey* (London and Lincoln, 1851), p. 12. Many thanks must go to Dr Nicholas Bennett of Lincoln Cathedral for his kind assistance in establishing Holles's description and illustration of Katherine's arms.

22. Photographs of both Thomas Chaucer's tomb and the 'Progenie' page are in Derek Pearsall, *The Life of Geoffrey Chaucer* (Oxford, 1994), pp. 280–1.

23. John Nichols (ed.), *Royal Wills* (London, 1780), p. 259.

24. Joseph Hunter, 'The Seal of Chaucer: Copy of the Deed to which it is Appended . . .', *Archaeologia*, 34 (1852), 42.
25. Sanderson, *Lincoln Cathedral*, p. 12.
26. Peter Coss, *The Lady in Medieval England 1000–1500* (Stroud, 1998), p. 45.
27. Karen A. Winstead, *Virgin Martyrs: Legends of Sainthood in Late Medieval England* (Ithaca, NY, and London, 1997), p. 3.
28. *Ibid.*, p. 12.
29. *Ibid.*, p. 89.
30. Lewis, *St Katherine*, p. 69.
31. Winstead, *Virgin Martyrs*, p. 98.
32. Lewis, *St Katherine*, p. 63.
33. Katherine J. Lewis, 'Model Girls? Virgin Martyrs and the Training of Young Women in Late Medieval England', in Katherine J. Lewis, N.J. Menuge and K.M. Philips (eds), *Young Medieval Women* (New York, 1999), p. 33.
34. Lewis, *St Katherine*, pp. 56, 66.
35. Nichols (ed.), *Royal Wills*, p. 208. My translation.
36. Anthony Goodman, *Katherine Swynford* (Lincoln, 1999), p. 21.
37. Catherine Jamison, *The History of the Royal Hospital of St Katherine by the Tower of London* (Oxford, 1952), pp. 38–9.
38. Lewis, 'Model Girls', p. 35.
39. *The Register of the Guild of the Holy Trinity, St Mary, St John the Baptist and St Katherine of Coventry*, vol. 1, ed. Mary Dormer Harris (London, 1935), p. 49.
40. *Chaucer Life Records*, ed. Martin M. Crow and Clair C. Olson (Oxford, 1966), p. 92; Christopher Wordsworth, *Notes on Medieval Services in England* (London, 1898), p. 170.
41. Christopher Wordsworth, 'Inventories of Plate, Vestments, etc., Belonging to the Cathedral Church of the Blessed Mary of Lincoln', *Archaeologia*, 2nd ser. 53 (1892), pp. 23, 25; J.F. Wickenden, '"Joyalx" of John of Gaunt, Bequeathed to the Cathedral Church of Lincoln', *Archaeological Journal*, 32 (1875), 318–19.
42. Wordsworth, 'Inventories of Plate', pp. 23, 62.
43. *The Book of the Knight of the Tower*, trans. William Caxton, ed. M.Y. Offord (EETS; London, 1971), p. 76.
44. Winstead, *Virgin Martyrs*, p. 1.
45. Jennifer Ward, *English Noblewomen in the Later Middle Ages* (London, 1992), p. 161.

46. Michael K. Jones and Malcolm G. Underwood, *The King's Mother: Lady Margaret Beaufort, Countess of Richmond and Derby* (Cambridge, 1995), p. 232.
47. Ward, *English Noblewomen*, p. 149.
48. Coss, *The Lady in Medieval England*, p. 47.
49 *Ibid.*, p. 105.
50. *Ibid.*
51. *Ibid.*, pp. 74, 78.
52. Sekules, 'Women and Art', p. 45. The dog in medieval art was a symbol of faithfulness.
53. Paul Binski, 'Monumental Brasses', in Alexander and Binski (eds), *Age of Chivalry*, p. 172.
54. J.H. Wylie, *History of England under Henry the Fourth*, vol. 3 (London, 1896), p. 259.
55. John H. Harvey, *Catherine Swynford's Chantry* (Lincoln Minister Pamphlets, 2nd ser. no. 6), p. 1.
56. *Ibid.*, pp. 1, 19.
57. *Ibid.*, pp. 22–3.
58. *Ibid.*, p. 9.
59. C.E. Woodruff and W. Danks, *Memorials of Canterbury Cathedral* (London, 1912), p. 201.
60. Wordsworth, 'Inventories of Plate', p. 14.
61. Harvey, *Catherine Swynford's Chantry*, p. 11.
62. *CPR 1436–41*, p. 137, entry 28 November 1437.
63. Wordsworth, *Notes on Medieval Services*, pp. 194, 217.
64. Harvey, *Catherine Swynford's Chantry*, pp. 14–15.
65. *Ibid.*, p. 15.
66. Katherine may not have left instructions for a chantry because of her belief that Gaunt's request was operable. It is probable, however, that she made reference to it in her will.
67. *Historiae Dunelmensis Scriptores Tres*, ed. James Raine (London, 1834), p. cclviii. My translation of the original Latin.
68. Harvey, *Catherine Swynford's Chantry*, p. 9.
69. Peter Draper, 'Architecture and Liturgy', in Alexander and Binski (eds), *Age of Chivalry*, p. 89.
70. Sanderson, *Lincoln Cathedral*, p. 12.
71. *Historiae Dunelmensis*, p. cclviii. My translation of the original Latin.
72. Harvey, *Catherine Swynford's Chantry*, pp. 19–20.
73. Nichols (ed.), *Royal Wills*, p. 322.

74. *CPR 1408–13*, pp. 323–4, entry 5 October 1411; *Excerpta Historica*, p. 157.
75. Given-Wilson and Curteis, *Royal Bastards*, p. 49.

Chapter Six

1. V.A. Kolve, 'Chaucer and the Visual Arts', in Derek Brewer (ed.), *Writers and their Background: Geoffrey Chaucer* (London, 1974), pp. 310–11.
2. Katherine L. French, ' "I leave my best gown as a vestment": Women's Spiritual Interests in the Late Medieval Parish', *Magistra*, 4/1 (1998), 58.
3. *Ibid.*, pp. 70–1.
4. *Ibid.*, p. 71.
5. Karen A. Winstead, *Virgin Martyrs: Legends of Sainthood in Late Medieval England* (Ithaca, NY, and London, 1997), p. 100.
6. *Ibid.*, p. 117.
7. *Ibid.*, p. 86.
8. Nicholas Orme, *Medieval Children* (New Haven and London, 2003), pp. 244–5.
9. Kathleen Ashley and Pamela Sheingorn, *Interpreting Cultural Symbols: Saint Anne in Late Medieval Society* (Athens, Ga., and London, 1990), p. 2.
10. Katherine J. Lewis, 'Model Girls? Virgin Martyrs and the Training of Young Women in Late Medieval England', in Katherine J. Lewis, N.J. Menuge and K.M. Philips (eds), *Young Medieval Women* (New York, 1999), p. 35.
11. M.G.A. Vale, *Charles VII* (London, 1974), p. 92.
12. Lewis, 'Model Girls', p. 26.
13. Lynn Staley, *Margery Kempe's Dissenting Fictions* (Pennsylvania, 1994), pp. 35–41, 171.
14. *Ibid.*, p. 3.
15. *Ibid.*, p. 36.
16. Timea K. Szell, 'From Woe to Weal and Weal to Woe: Notes on the Structure of *The Book of Margery Kempe*', in Sandra J. McEntire (ed.), *Margery Kempe: A Book of Essays* (New York and London, 1992), pp. 83–5.
17. Clarissa W. Atkinson, *Mystic and Pilgrim: The Book and the World of Margery Kempe* (Ithaca, NY, and London, 1983), p. 13.

18. *The Book of Margery Kempe*, ed. B.A. Windeatt (London, 1985), p. 90.
19. *Ibid.*, p. 88.
20. *Ibid.*, p. 109 (emphasis added).
21. S.B. Fanous, 'Biblical and Hagiographical Imitatio in The Book of Margery Kempe' (D.Phil. thesis, Oxford 1997), fos 3–4.
22. *The Book of Margery Kempe*, p. 33.
23. *Ibid.*, p. 55.
24. *Ibid.*, p. 57.
25. *Ibid.*, p. 195.
26. *Ibid.*, pp. 102–3.
27. *Ibid.*, pp. 56–7.
28. Carolyn Coulson, *Mysticism, Meditation and Identification in The Book of Margery Kempe* www.luc.edu/publications/medieval/vol12/coulson.html, accessed 22 November 2000.
29. Susan Eberly, 'Margery Kempe, St Mary Magdalene, and Patterns of Contemplation', *Downside Review* (1989), 213.
30. Coulson, *Mysticism, Meditation*; *The Book of Margery Kempe*, p. 229.
31. Coulson, *Mysticism, Meditation*.
32. Fanous, 'Biblical and Hagiographical Imitatio', fo. 179.
33. Julia Bolton Holloway, 'Bride, Margery, Julian and Alice: Bridget of Sweden's Textual Community in Medieval England', in Sandra J. McEntire (ed.), *Margery Kempe: A Book of Essays* (New York and London, 1992), p. 203.
34. *Ibid.*, p. 214.
35. *The Book of Margery Kempe*, p. 83.
36. *Ibid.*
37. Katherine J. Lewis, *The Cult of St Katherine of Alexandria in Late Medieval England* (Woodbridge, 2000), p. 244.
38. *Ibid.*, pp. 242–6.
39. *The Book of Margery Kempe*, p. 150.
40. *Ibid.*, p. 169.
41. Fanous, 'Biblical and Hagiographical Imitatio', fo. 255.
42. *The Book of Margery Kempe*, p. 149.
43. Lewis, *St Katherine*, pp. 251–2.
44. *The Book of Margery Kempe*, p. 149.
45. Fanous, 'Biblical and Hagiographical Imitatio', fo. 261.

46. *Ibid.*, fo. 200.
47. *Ibid.*
48. Laurie A. Finke, *Women's Writing in English* (London and New York, 1999), p. 215.
49. Lewis, *St Katherine*, p. 249.
50. *The Book of Margery Kempe*, p. 153.
51. Fanous, 'Biblical and Hagiographical Imitatio', fos 268–9.
52. *The Book of Margery Kempe*, pp. 64, 162.
53. Fanous, 'Biblical and Hagiographical Imitatio', fo. 272.
54. *Ibid.*
55. *The Book of Margery Kempe*, p. 65.
56. *Ibid.*, p. 170.
57. Henrietta Leyser, *Medieval Women: A Social History of Women in England 450–1500* (London, 1997), p. 28.
58. Elizabeth Alvilda Petroff (ed.), *Medieval Women's Visionary Literature* (Oxford and New York, 1986), p. 302.
59. *The Book of Margery Kempe*, p. 60.
60. *Ibid.*, p. 151.
61. The following information on *The Life of St Edward* is from Antonia Grandsen, *Historical Writing in England c. 550 to c. 1307* (London and New York, 1998), pp. 60–6.
62. *Ibid.*, p. 42.
63. The following information is derived from Paul Binski, *Westminster Abbey and the Plantagenets: Kingship and the Representation of Power 1200–1400* (New Haven and London, 1995).
64. *Ibid.*, p. 5.
65. *Ibid.*, p. 4.
66. *Ibid.*, p. 5.
67. K.J. Lewis, 'Becoming a Virgin King: Richard II and Edward the Confessor', in S.J.E. Riches and Sarah Salih (eds), *Gender and Holiness: Men, Women and Saints in Late Medieval Europe* (London and New York, 2002), pp. 86–100.
68. *Ibid.*, p. 93.
69. *Ibid.*
70. *Ibid.*, p. 94.
71. C.J. Billson, *Medieval Leicester* (Leicester, 1920), p. 80.

Bibliography

Primary Texts

The Anonimalle Chronicle 1333–1381, ed. V.H. Galbraith (Manchester, 1970)

The Book of the Knight of the Tower, trans. William Caxton, ed. M.Y. Offord (EETS; London, 1971)

The Brut or The Chronicles of England, ed. Friedrich W.D. Brie, pt 2 (EETS; London, 1908)

Calendar of Close Rolls

Calendar of Fine Rolls

Calendar of Inquisitions Post Mortem

Calendar of Patent Rolls

John Capgrave's Abbreuiacion of Cronicles, ed. Peter J. Lucas (EETS; Oxford, 1983)

Cartulaire des Comtes de Hainaut, vol. 1, ed. Léopold Devillers (Brussels, 1881)

Chartes du Chapite de Sainte-Waudru de Mons, ed. Léopold Devillers, vol. 2 (Brussels, 1903)

Chaucer, Geoffrey, *The Riverside Chaucer*, ed. Larry D. Benson (Oxford, 1987)

—— *The Canterbury Tales*, trans. Nevill Coghill (London, 2003)

—— *Chaucer Life Records*, ed. Martin M. Crow and Clair C. Olson (Oxford, 1966)

Chronicles of London, ed. C.L. Kingsford (Stroud, 1977)

Derby Accounts, ed. Lucy Toulmin Smith (London, 1894)

An English Chronicle of the Reigns of Richard II, Henry IV, Henry V and Henry VI Written before the year 1471, ed. J.S. Davies (London, 1856)

English Historical Documents, vol. 4: *1327–1485*, ed. D.C. Douglas and A.R. Myers (London, 1969)

211

Excerpta Historica or, Illustrations of English History, ed. Samuel Bentley (London, 1833)

Fabyan, Robert, *The New Chronicles of England and France, in Two Parts*, ed. Henry Ellis (London, 1811)

Fisher, John, *The English Works of John Fisher*, ed. John E. B. Mayor (EETS; London, 1876)

Froissart, *The Chronicles of Froissart*, vol. 2, ed. Thomas Johnes (London, 1852)

—— *Œuvres de Froissart*, vol. 15, *1392–1396*, ed. K. de Lettenhove (Osnabrück, 1967)

Hall, Edward, *Hall's Chronicle*, ed. Henry Ellis (London, 1809)

Hardyng, John, *The Chronicle of John Hardyng*, ed. Henry Ellis (London, 1812)

Hayward, John, *The Life and Raigne of King Henrie IIII*, ed. John J. Manning (London, 1991)

Historiæ Dunelmensis Scriptores Tres, ed. James Raine (London, 1834)

Historica Vitae et Regni Ricardi Secundi, ed. George B. Stow Jr (Pennsylvania, 1997)

Hoccleve's Works, vol. 1, *The Minor Poems*, ed. Frederick J. Furnivall (EETS; Oxford, 1892)

John of Gaunt's Register 1372–1376, ed. Sydney Armitage-Smith (London, 1911)

John of Gaunt's Register 1379–1383, ed. E.C. Lodge and Robert Somerville (London, 1937)

Kempe, Margery, *The Book of Margery Kempe*, ed. B.A. Windeatt (London, 1985)

Knighton's Chronicle 1337–1396, ed. G.H. Martin (Oxford, 1995)

The Paston Letters, vol. 2, ed. John Fenn, re-ed. L. Archer-Hind (London, 1924)

Records of the Borough of Leicester, vol. 2, ed. Mary Bateson (London, 1901)

Register of Edward, The Black Prince, pt 4 (London, 1933)

The Register of the Guild of the Holy Trinity, St Mary, St John the Baptist and St Katherine of Coventry, vol. 1, ed. Mary Dormer Harris (London, 1935)

Three Fifteenth Century Chronicles, ed. James Gairdner (London, 1965)

Usk, Adam, *The Chronicle of Adam Usk 1377–1421*, ed. Chris Given-Wilson (Oxford, 1997)

Vergil, Polydore, *Three Books of Polydore Vergil's English History comprising the reigns of Henry VI, Edward IV, and Richard III*, ed. Henry Ellis (London, 1844)

Bibliography

—— *Polydore Vergil's English History*, ed. Henry Ellis (London, 1846)

—— *The Anglica Historia of Polydore Vergil 1485–1537*, ed. Denys Hay (London, 1950)

Thomas Walsingham's Chronicon Angliae, ed. Edward Maunde Thompson (London, 1965)

The St Albans Chronicle: The Chronica Maiora of Thomas Walsingham 1376–1394, ed. John Taylor and Wendy R. Childs, trans. Leslie Watkiss (Oxford, 2002)

The Westminster Chronicle, ed. L.C. Hector and Barbara F. Harvey (Oxford, 1982)

William Worcestre Itineraries, ed. John H. Harvey (Oxford, 1969)

Secondary Texts

Alexander, Jonathan, and Binski, Paul (eds), *Age of Chivalry* (London, 1987)

Armitage-Smith, Sydney, *John of Gaunt: King of Castile and Leon, Duke of Aquitaine and Lancaster, Earl of Derby, Lincoln and Leicester, Seneschal of England* (Westminster, 1904)

Ashley, Kathleen, and Sheingorn, Pamela, *Interpreting Cultural Symbols: Saint Anne in Late Medieval Society* (Athens, Ga., and London, 1990)

Aston, Margaret, 'Richard II and the Wars of the Roses', in F.R.H. Du Boulay and C.M. Barron (eds), *The Reign of Richard II* (London, 1971), pp. 280–318

Atkinson, Clarissa W., *Mystic and Pilgrim: The Book and the World of Margery Kempe* (Ithaca, NY, and London, 1983)

Baker, Richard, *A Chronicle of the Kings of England from the Time of the Romans Government unto the Death of King James I* (London, 1696)

Barrett, Alexandra, *Women's Writing in Middle English* (London, 1999)

Beltz, G.F., *Memorials of the Order of the Garter* (London, 1841)

Bennett, Judith M., 'Medievalism and Feminism', *Speculum*, 68/2 (1993), 309–31

Benson, L.D., 'Chaucer: A Select Bibliography', in D. Brewer (ed.), *Writers and their Background: Geoffrey Chaucer* (London, 1974), pp. 352–72

Billson, C.J., *Medieval Leicester* (Leicester, 1920)

Binski, Paul, *Westminster Abbey and the Plantagenets: Kingship and the Representation of Power 1200–1400* (New Haven and London, 1995)

Biographical Dictionary of British Women, ed. Anne Crawford *et al.* (London, 1983)

Biondi, Giovanni Francesco, *A History of the Civil Wars of England between the Two Houses of Lancaster and York*, trans. Henry, Earl of Monmouth (London, 1641)

Blomefield, Francis, *An Essay towards a Topographical History of the County of Norfolk*, vol. 3 (London, 1769)

Bolton Holloway, Julia, 'Bride, Margery, Julian and Alice: Bridget of Sweden's Textual Community in Medieval England', in Sandra J. McEntire (ed.), *Margery Kempe: A Book of Essays* (New York and London, 1992), pp. 203–21

Bothwell, James, 'The Management of Position: Alice Perrers, Edward III and the Creation of a Landed Estates, 1362–1377', *Journal of Medieval History*, 24 (1998), 31–51

Braddy, Haldeen, 'Chaucer's Philippa, Daughter of Panneto', *Modern Language Notes* (1949), 342–3

Brewer, Derek, 'Gothic Chaucer', in D. Brewer (ed.), *Writers and their Background: Geoffrey Chaucer* (London, 1974), pp. 1–32
—— *An Introduction to Chaucer* (London, 1984)

Brown, A.L., 'The Reign of Henry IV', in S.B. Chrimes, C.D. Ross and R.A. Griffiths (eds), *Fifteenth Century England 1399–1509* (Manchester, 1974), pp. 1–28

Brown, Emerson, Jr, 'What is Chaucer doing with the Physician and his Tale?', *Philological Quarterly*, 60 (1981), 129–49

Bruce, Marie Louise, *The Usurper King: Henry of Bolingbroke 1366–99* (London, 1998)

Brusendorff, Aage, *The Chaucer Tradition* (Oxford, 1967)

Cavanaugh, Susan H., 'A Study of Books Privately Owned in England 1300–1450' (Ph.D. thesis, University of Pennsylvania, 1980)

Chamberlayne, Joanna, 'Joan of Kent's Tale: Adultery and Rape in the Age of Chivalry', *Medieval Life*, 5 (1996), 7–9

Chrimes, S.B., *Lancastrians, Yorkists and Henry VII* (London, 1966)

Chute, Marchette, *Geoffrey Chaucer of England* (London, 1951)

Cokayne, G.E., *The Complete Peerage*, vol. 1 (Gloucester, 1982)
—— *The Complete Peerage*, 2nd edn., vol. 12 (London, 1953)

Cole, R.E.G., 'The Manor and Rectory of Kettlethorpe', *Architectural Societies Reports*, 31, report 66 (1911), 41–86

Coleman, Janet, *English Literature in History 1350–1400: Medieval Readers and Writers* (London, 1981)

Collette, Carolyn P., 'Joan of Kent and Noble Women's Roles in Chaucer's World', *Chaucer Review*, 33/4 (1999), 350–62

214

Cook, Albert Stanburrough, 'Chaucerian Papers I', *Connecticut Academy of Arts and Sciences*, 23 (1919), 1–63

Coss, Peter, *The Lady in Medieval England 1000–1500* (Stroud, 1998)

Coulson, Carolyn, *Mysticism, Meditation and Identification in The Book of Margery Kempe*, www.luc.edu/publications/medieval/vol12/coulson.html, accessed 22 November 2000

Crawford, Anne (ed.), *Letters of the Queens of England 1100–1547* (Stroud, 1994)

—— (ed.), *Letters of Medieval Women* (Stroud, 2002)

Dobson, R.B., *Durham Priory 1400–1450* (Cambridge, 1973)

Dodd, Joseph Arthur, *A Historical Guide to Ewelme Church* (London, 1916)

Duffy, Eamon, *The Stripping of the Altars* (New Haven and London, 1992)

Eberly, Susan, 'Margery Kempe, St Mary Magdalene, and Patterns of Contemplation', *Downside Review* (1989), 209–23

Elder, J., 'A Study of the Beauforts and their Estates' (unpublished Ph.D. thesis, Bryn Mawr, 1964)

Erler, Mary, *Women, Reading and Piety in Late Medieval England* (Cambridge, 2002)

Fanous, S.B., 'Biblical and Hagiographical Imitatio in The Book of Margery Kempe' (D.Phil. thesis, Oxford, 1997)

Finke, Laurie A., *Women's Writing in English* (London and New York, 1999)

Fletcher, Doris, 'The Lancastrian Collar of Esses: Its Origins and Transformations down the Centuries', in James L. Gillespie (ed.), *The Age of Richard II* (Stroud and New York, 1997), pp. 191–204

French, Katherine L., ' "I leave my best gown as a vestment": Women's Spiritual Interests in the Late Medieval Parish', *Magistra*, 4/1 (1998), 57–77

Galbraith, V.H., 'Thomas Walsingham and the Saint Alban's Chronicle, 1272–1422', *English Historical Review*, 47 (1932), 12–29

Galway, Margaret, 'Geoffrey Chaucer, JP and MP', *Modern Language Review*, 36 (1941), 1–36

—— 'Chaucer's Hopeless Love', *Modern Language Notes*, 60 (1945), 431–8

—— 'The Troilus Frontispiece', *Modern Language Review*, 44 (1949), 161–77

—— 'Walter Roet and Philippa Chaucer', *Notes and Queries* (1954), 48–9

Galway, Margaret, 'Philippa Pan; Philippa Chaucer', *Modern Language Review*, 55 (1960), 481–7

Given-Wilson, Chris, *The Royal Household and the King's Affinity* (New Haven and London, 1986)

—— and Curteis, Alice, *The Royal Bastards of Medieval England* (London, 1984)

Godwin, William, *The Life of Geoffrey Chaucer* (London, 1804)

Goldberg, P.J.P., *Women in England c. 1275–1525* (Manchester, 1995)

Goodman, Anthony, *John of Gaunt: The Exercise of Princely Power in Fourteenth Century Europe* (Harlow, 1992)

—— *Katherine Swynford* (Lincoln, 1999)

Gransden, Antonia, *Historical Writing in England c. 550 to c. 1307* (London and New York, 1998)

—— *Historical Writing in England*, vol. 2: *c. 1307 to the Early Sixteenth Century* (London, 1998)

Green, Richard F., 'King Richard II's Books Revisited', *The Library*, 5th ser. 31 (1976), 235–9

Griffiths, R.A., and Thomas, Roger S., *The Making of the Tudor Dynasty* (Gloucester, 1985)

Harris, G.L., *Cardinal Beaufort* (Oxford, 1988)

Harvey, John H., *Catherine Swynford's Chantry* (Lincoln Minster Pamphlets, 2nd ser. no. 6)

Heal, Felicity, 'Reciprocity and Exchange in the Late Medieval Household', in B.A. Hanawalt and D. Wallace (eds), *Bodies and Discipline: Intersections of Literature and History in Fifteenth Century England* (Minneapolis, 1996), pp. 179–98

Hicks, Michael, *Who's Who in Late Medieval England* (London, 1991)

Hill, J.W.F., *Medieval Lincoln* (Cambridge, 1965)

Hunter, Joseph, 'The Seal of Chaucer: Copy of the Deed to which it is appended . . .', *Archaeologia*, 34 (1852), 42–5

Jambeck, Karen K., 'Patterns of Women's Literary Patronage: England, 1200–ca. 1475', in June Hall McCash (ed.), *The Cultural Patronage of Medieval Women* (Athens, Ga., London, 1996), 228–65

Jamison, Catherine, *The History of the Royal Hospital of St Katherine by the Tower of London* (Oxford, 1952)

Jones, Michael K., and Underwood, Malcolm G., *The King's Mother: Lady Margaret Beaufort, Countess of Richmond and Derby* (Cambridge, 1995)

Kay, F. George, *Lady of the Sun: The Life and Times of Alice Perrers* (London, 1966)

Keen, M.H., *England in the Later Middle Ages* (London, 1997)

Klapisch-Zuber, Christiane, 'Including Women', in Christiane Klapisch-Zuber (ed.), *A History of Women: Silences of the Middle Ages* (Cambridge, Mass., 1994), pp. 1–14

Kolve, V.A., 'Chaucer and the Visual Arts', in Derek Brewer (ed.), *Writers and their Background: Geoffrey Chaucer* (London, 1974), 290–320

Krauss, Russell, *Three Chaucer Studies* (Oxford, 1932)

Lander, J.R., 'Marriage and Politics in the Fifteenth Century: The Nevilles and the Wydevilles', *Bulletin of the Institute of Historical Research*, 36 (1963), 119–52

Lee, Sidney (ed.), *Dictionary of National Biography*, vol. 55 (London, 1898)

Lewis, Katherine J., 'Model Girls? Virgin Martyrs and the Training of Young Women in Late Medieval England', in Katherine J. Lewis, N.J. Menuge and K.M. Philips (eds), *Young Medieval Women* (New York, 1999), pp. 25–46

—— *The Cult of St Katherine of Alexandria in Late Medieval England* (Woodbridge, 2000)

—— 'Becoming a Virgin King: Richard II and Edward the Confessor', in S.J.E. Riches and Sarah Salih (eds), *Gender and Holiness: Men, Women and Saints in Late Medieval Europe* (London and New York, 2002), pp. 86–100

Leyser, Henrietta, *Medieval Women: A Social History of Women in England 450–1500* (London, 1997)

Lindsay, Philip, *King Henry V: A Chronicle* (London, 1934)

McFarlane, K.B., *Lancastrian Kings and Lollard Knights* (Oxford, 1972)

—— (ed.), *The Nobility of Later Medieval England* (Oxford, 1973)

Mackie, J.D., *The Earlier Tudors 1485–1588* (Oxford, 1992)

Manly, John M., *Some New Light on Chaucer* (Gloucester, Mass., 1959)

Martin, Priscilla, *Chaucer's Women: Nuns, Wives and Amazons* (London, 1990)

McKisack, May, *The Fourteenth Century 1307–1399* (Oxford, 1997)

Meale, Carol M., '". . . alle the bokes that I have of latyn, englisch, and frensch": Lay Women and their Books in Late Medieval England', in Carol M. Meale (ed.), *Women and Literature in Britain 1150–1500* (Cambridge, 1996), pp. 128–58

Michalore, Sharon D., 'The Education of Aristocratic Women in Fifteenth Century England', in Sharon D. Michalore and A. Compton Reeve (eds), *Estrangement, Enterprise and Education in Fifteenth Century England* (Stroud, 1998), pp. 117–39

Nichols, John (ed.), *Royal Wills* (London, 1780)

Orme, Nicholas, *Education and Society in Medieval and Renaissance England* (London, 1989)

—— 'The Education of the Courtier', in V.J. Scattergood and J.W. Sherbourne (eds), *English Court Culture in the Later Middle Ages* (London, 1983), pp. 63–85

—— *From Childhood to Chivalry* (London, 1984)

—— *Medieval Children* (New Haven and London, 2003)

Owen, Charles A., Jr, 'Relationship between The Physician's Tale and The Parson's Tale', *Modern Language Notes*, 72 (1956), 84–7

Page, William, and Round, J. Horace (eds), *The Victoria History of the County of Essex*, vol. 2 (London, 1907)

Partner, Nancy F., 'No Sex, No Gender', *Speculum*, 68/2 (1993), 419–43

Pearsall, Derek, *The Life of Geoffrey Chaucer* (Oxford, 1994)

Peck, Francis, *Desiderata Curiosa* (London, 1779)

Perry, Judy, 'Katherine Roet's Swynfords: A Re-Examination of Interfamily Relationships and Descent, Part 2', *Foundations*, 1/3 (2004),164–74

Petroff, Elizabeth Alvilda (ed.), *Medieval Women's Visionary Literature* (Oxford and New York, 1986)

Philips, Kim M., *Medieval Maidens: Young Women and Gender in England, 1270–1540* (Manchester, 2003)

Platts, Graham, *Land and People in Medieval Lincolnshire* (Lincoln, 1985)

Power, Eileen, *Medieval English Nunneries* (Cambridge, 1922)

Purey-Cust, Arthur P., *The Collar of SS: A History and Conjecture* (Leeds, 1910)

Radford, Lewis Bostock, *Henry Beaufort, Bishop, Chancellor, Cardinal* (London, 1908)

Ramsay, James H., *Genesis of Lancaster*, vol. 2 (Oxford, 1913)

Rapin de Thoyras, M., *The History of England*, trans. John Kelly (London, 1732)

Rickert, Edith, 'Elizabeth Chausir, a nun at Barking', *Times Literary Supplement*, 18 May 1933, p. 348

—— *Chaucer's World* (New York and London, 1964)

Robertson, D.W., *A Preface to Chaucer: Studies in Medieval Perspectives* (Princeton, 1963)

Rosenthal, Joel T., *Nobles and the Noble Life 1295–1500* (London, 1976)

Ross, C.D., 'The Yorkshire Baronage 1399–1433' (unpublished D.Phil. thesis).

Russell, P.E., *The English Intervention in Spain and Portugal in the Time of Edward III and Richard II* (Oxford, 1955)

Bibliography

Rye, Walter, 'John of Gaunt and Katherine Swynford', *Times Literary Supplement*, 17 April 1924, p. 240

Sanderson, Robert, *Lincoln Cathedral: An Exact Copy of all the Ancient Monumental Inscriptions Collected by Robert Sanderson and Compared with and Corrected by Sir W. Dugdale's MS Survey* (London and Lincoln, 1851)

Sandford, Francis, *A Genealogical History of the Kings of England* (London, 1677)

Saul, Nigel, *Richard II* (New Haven and London, 1997)

Seton, Anya, *Katherine* (London, 1956)

Shepherd, G.T., 'Troilus and Criseyde', in D.S. Brewer (ed.), *Chaucer and Chaucerians: Critical Studies in Middle English Literature* (London, 1966), pp. 65–87

Silva-Vigier, Anil de, *This Moste Highe Prince, John of Gaunt* (Edinburgh, 1992)

Somerville, Robert, *History of the Duchy of Lancaster*, vol. I: *1265–1603* (London, 1953)

Speght, T., *The Works of our Ancient, Learned and Excellent Poet Jeffrey Chaucer* (London, 1687)

Staley, Lynn, *Margery Kempe's Dissenting Fictions* (Pennsylvania, 1994)

—— 'Chaucer and the Postures of Sanctity', in David Aers and Lynn Staley, *The Powers of the Holy* (Pennsylvania, 1996), pp. 179–259

Steel, Anthony, *Richard II* (Cambridge, 1941)

Strong, P., and Strong, F., 'The Last Will and Codicils of Henry V', *English Historical Review*, 96 (1981), 79–102

Szell, Timea K., '"From Woe to Weal and Weal to Woe": Notes on the Structure of *The Book of Margery Kempe*', in Sandra J McEntire (ed.), *Margery Kempe: A Book of Essays* (New York and London, 1992), pp. 73–91

Vale, M.G.A., *Charles VII* (London, 1974)

van Houts, Elisabeth, 'Women in Medieval History and Literature', *Journal of Medieval History*, 20/3 (1994), 277–92

Walker, Simon, *The Lancastrian Affinity 1361–1399* (Oxford, 1990)

Ward, Jennifer, *English Noblewomen in the Later Middle Ages* (London, 1992)

—— *Women of the English Nobility and Gentry 1066–1500* (Manchester, 1995)

Weaver, John, *Ancient Funerall Monuments* (Amsterdam, 1979)

Weir, Alison, *Lancaster and York: The Wars of the Roses* (London, 1995)

Bibliography

Wickenden, J.F., '"Joyalx" of John of Gaunt, Bequeathed to the Cathedral Church of Lincoln', *Archaeological Journal*, 32 (1875), 317–25

Williams, George, 'The Troilus and Criseyde Frontispiece Again', *Modern Language Review*, 57 (1962), 173–8

—— *A New View of Chaucer* (Durham, NC, 1965)

Winstead, Karen A., *Virgin Martyrs: Legends of Sainthood in Late Medieval England* (Ithaca, NY, and London, 1997)

Wood, Mary Anne Everett (ed.), *Letters of Royal and Illustrious Ladies of Great Britain*, vol. 1 (London, 1846)

Woodruff, C.E., and Danks, W., *Memorials of Canterbury Cathedral* (London, 1912)

Wordsworth, Christopher, 'Inventories of Plate, Vestments, etc., Belonging to the Cathedral Church of the Blessed Mary of Lincoln', *Archaeologia*, 2nd ser. 53 (1892), 1–82

—— *Notes on Medieval Services in England* (London, 1898)

Wylie, J.H., *History of England under Henry the Fourth*, vol. 2 (London, 1894)

—— *History of England under Henry the Fourth*, vol. 3 (London, 1896)

—— *History of England under Henry the Fourth*, vol. 4 (London, 1898)

Internet Sites

www.ampthillhistory.co.uk, accessed 5 May 2001

www.kettlethorpe.com, accessed 22 October 2000

http://familytreemaker.genealogy.com/users/s/t/e/Thomas-E-Stevenson/FILE/0003page.html?Welcome=1040309424, accessed 19 December 2002

Index

Index